This volume of meditations is dedicated to the
memories of **Peter Greer** and **Christine Robinson**
and to the Reverend **Robert Thompson** in
gratitude for their years of service in support of the
Meditation Program in Phillips Church.

— A BOOK OF —
MEDITATIONS

VOLUME IV
2008-2016

READINGS FROM
PHILLIPS EXETER ACADEMY

EDITED BY

Mercy Carbonell

Todd Hearon

Matt Miller

Eimer Page

PHILLIPS **EXETER** ACADEMY

Exeter, New Hampshire
2017

COVER PHOTO
"The Kendra Stearns O'Donnell Window"
by Cheryl Senter

TABLE OF CONTENTS

ACKNOWLEDGMENTS

The editors are indebted to the following:

Donna Archambault, Kathy Pottle and the staff of Information Technology Services, for converting hard-copy versions of some of these meditations to electronic files; Academy Librarian **Gail Scanlon**, Academy Archivist **Peter Nelson** and **Tom Wharton** for their aid in assembling this volume; **Linda Safford** for her years of dedicated service and help with Wednesday-morning meditation and for her caretaking of the texts and recordings of the meditations; the Communications Department for their assistance with the printing and design of this volume; and **Ethan Shapiro**, dean of faculty, for his sponsorship of this publishing project. We are especially grateful to **Cheryl Senter** for the use of *The Kendra Stearns O'Donnell Window* photograph and to **Diego Melendez** for the design of the book's cover and layout.

Beyond these specific debts in the preparation of the physical volume, we would like to thank the community members who have given, and attended, Wednesday meditation in Phillips Church and thus directly helped to keep the practice alive.

PREFACE

This volume takes up where Volume III left off, bringing together 36 of the approximately 280 meditations delivered in Phillips Church from 2008 to the winter of 2016. In the fall and winter of each year, the speakers are generally adult members of the community; the spring season is reserved exclusively for members of the senior class. In 2011, owing to the establishment of the Shannon Nissa Bailey Powers '97 Memorial Fund, these senior meditations began to be collected into print each spring. For this reason, the editors have included senior meditations up to 2011 in the present volume; seniors whose meditations were delivered in the church after that date have had their meditations collected in the annual volume *The Shannon Nissa Bailey Powers Senior Meditations Collection* (PEA Press) and made available to the Phillips Exeter community free of charge. The editors hope in due time to gather these annual senior meditations (2011 to the present) into a volume of their own.

INTRODUCTION

*How can the places where we learn to know become places where
we also learn to love?*

—Parker Palmer

"Meditations" as practiced at Exeter are personal essays written, and
then delivered orally, within a community. Since this community, the
school, is generally both curious and accepting, the speaker can assume
goodwill in the audience; trolls, if any are present, bite their tongues.

Anyone paying attention to public discourse in our time will understand
how fundamental and how precious this assumption is. Both speaker
and audience are rewarded by it, since it creates room for openness,
for authenticity. Sometimes it is the disclosures themselves that remain
most ineradicably in the mind and heart; sometimes the way the piece
is written, the vehicle, becomes itself the stuff of memory. If you read
widely in this volume you will probably have both experiences.

Exeter meditations began in the 1970s. They are now spoken weekly in
Phillips Church; many more are written and spoken in senior English
classes. Generally a meditation is a fusion of remembrance and reflection.
Like other literary writing, meditations tend to find the universal in the
particular.

Still, the community is of course made up of individual listeners, seated
next to one another. We no doubt respond differently, even privately,
to much of what is said. As someone who has heard many dozens of
meditations over the past few decades, I recognize that some, necessarily
a smaller number, have become part of my own inner intellectual and

moral landscape. Perhaps the people sitting next to me have been more powerfully affected by different ones. (May it be so.)

For me the permanent ones include Richard Spalding's confrontation with failure and Drake Bennett's tribute to his mother (Volume 1); Christine Robinson's portrait of Eddie, a then homeless man she met and befriended in a faraway city (Volume 2); Sarah Pruitt's characterization of her father, Bruce, then a member of the History Department, thus someone well known to many of her hearers (Volume 2). With Volume 3, whose pieces have lived in me for fewer years, I have to muzzle myself in the face of such abundance: to read over the names of the writers is practically an incantation. Volume 4, its own storehouse of remembering, thinking, writing, is before you.

Like its predecessors this volume invites its readers to share in the school community's deep pleasure in the stories, and the conclusions drawn from them, that you will hear in the 36 voices included here. Each represents the joyful, contemplative or poignant memory of a young or an older writer. Collectively they embody one of Exeter's most distinctive, most essential cultural practices.

David Weber

MARSHALL MOORE
A Big Fish Story
January 31, 2008

ON FIRST LOOKING INTO CHAPMAN'S HOMER

Much have I traveled in the realms of gold,
And many goodly states and kingdoms seen;
Round many western islands have I been
Which bards in fealty to Apollo hold.
Oft of one wide expanse had I been told
That deep-browed Homer ruled as his demesne;
Yet did I never breathe its pure serene
Till I heard Chapman speak out loud and bold:
Then felt I like some watcher of the skies
When a new planet swims into his ken;

Marshall Moore is a graduate of Groton School and Harvard. He is father to three Academy graduates, Nick '03, Davis '05 and Tim '08. He lives in Exeter with his wife, Becky, who teaches English at the Academy.

Or like stout Cortez when with eagle eyes

He stared at the Pacific—And all his men

Looked at each other with a wild surmise-

Silent, upon a peak in Darien.

—John Keats

The air was heavy and moist as the creaky WWII-vintage twin-prop cranked to life. Two members of the fishing party sat up front with a clear view into the open cockpit. Randy, an ex-Vietnam fighter pilot, scanned the scene and raised his eyebrows. He leaned over to Christian, smiled and said, "You know you're in trouble when ... " "When what?" shouted Christian, barely audible above the engine's roar. "When the pilot is wearing fire-retardant gloves." Christian returned the smile. He had no worries. Starting in Boston, on through Miami, and now in Panama City he had struggled to make it onto any plane, twice engaging the services of the airport porters to wheel him to his departing gate by wheelchair. He was hurting, but determined, and happy just to be on the trip at all — the fishing trip of a lifetime.

For years, Christian's cousin, Ted, had dreamed about, spoken of and planned for this trip. "Wouldn't it be great if we could get all our favorite people in one place to fish for a week?" And to fish for not just any fish. To fish for black marlin. Ted thought big. The black marlin is the greatest sport-fishing prize in the sea — world record: 1,560 pounds. Black marlin are members of a group called "billfish," so named for having a long bill or sword for a nose that serves to slash or stun the smaller fish they feed on. Growing to more than 15 feet in length, the marlin can swim at speeds estimated by some at up to a remarkable 80 mph. But mostly, they cruise the tropical and subtropical Indo-Pacific oceans following warmer currents and schools of bait. They have a wide range, and are caught off coasts from Australia to Africa, California to Chile. The black marlin's body is blue-black above and a silvery white below. Marlin come in several flavors; black and striped are found only in the Pacific Ocean; blue and white are found predominantly in the Atlantic. Other billfish include the swordfish, which looks like a smaller, stockier marlin cousin, and the sailfish, a spectacular jumper with a much longer, floppy, sail-like dorsal fin.

On the end of a fishing line, there is perhaps nothing as exciting, challenging or indeed daunting as a marlin. Catching a "grander," or a fish weighing more than a thousand pounds, is rare but not unheard of, and such a fish can take several hours to reel up to the boat. Hemingway's Santiago, in his *The Old Man and the Sea*, catches a blue marlin grander off Cuba on a hand line (no rod or reel, just a square block of wood upon which to wind the line). He lashes the giant to his small craft only to have most of it eaten away by sharks on his way home. The marlin is powerful and acrobatic, and can leap clear of the ocean's surface many times during one battle with an angler. Marlin have been known even to jump right into fishing boats, with potentially lethal consequences. In Bermuda just a couple of years back, a captain named Alan Card and his grown son, Ian, the mate, hooked into an 800-pound blue, which leapt clear across the transom, gored Ian through the shoulder, and took him overboard. To this day, the 230-pound man has no recollection of how he "de-impaled himself" or how he got back in the boat. Miraculously, the fish missed all critical arteries and Ian fishes on to tell the tale.

In the old days, fishermen used to bring as many marlin as they could catch back to the dock to string them up, weigh them, and lord it over their buddies. Nowadays, it is the habit of most charter boat captains and fishermen to practice "catch and release." That is, once the line is reeled up to the point where a mate can simply touch the "leader" (the last 5 to 10 feet of line), the fish is considered "caught." It is then tagged with a tracking device, photographed and released, tired but unharmed, back to the depths. Special "circle hooks" first manufactured by the Japanese also have been designed to hook fish cleanly in the mouth, not down in the belly. Many fishermen are thinking conservation first and are feeling less of an urge to show off trophies by mounting them over their fireplaces.

Ted had put out an invitation to 45 friends for this trip. In the end, only seven were able to make it: Ted himself, Christian, Ed, Joe, Peter, Randy, and Steve. The men ranged in age from 40 to 60 and most were successful corporate types; men who had made it big on their own in America — dreamers of the dream, living the dream. Ted was the founder and owner of a large indoor sports facility. Called by some the luckiest man alive, he was the consummate angler. When fishermen come home with no fish, they say, "That's why they call it 'fishing.'" Ted always came home with a fish, or the first fish, the best fish or the biggest fish. Usually, all of the above. Ted, they said, had "the magic." He wasn't really a fisherman at all. He was a catcherman. Ted could go fishing with a stick and marshmallow in the frozen puddle of a Wal-Mart parking lot and return with a world-record rainbow trout. But Ted wasn't just lucky. Ted also was knowledgeable and prepared. Ted knew that there is a fine line you cross in fishing, and in life, when preparation looks like luck to the unprepared. Ted had not prepared for the Wal-Mart of fishing trips. Ted had prepared for a trip to one of the most prolific billfish fisheries in the world: the Pacific coast off Panama. Specifically, the group would be guests at the famous Tropic Star Lodge.

Despite best-laid plans, the seven men did not all know one another. They would become friends over the next six days by rotating through different partners on different boats each day out on the water. You can learn a lot about people on a boat over eight hours, even when you don't all speak the same language. Everyone has their distinct roles and places on a fishing boat. The captain steers the boat, looks for signs of fish, and decides when to move or where to stop. He also tells the mates what to do and when. The mates handle the bait, lines and rods, and actually set the hook after the fish bites. They help the guest move into what's called a "fighting chair" and hand the rod to him. The guest has two primary roles: 1) not to interfere in anyone else's role, and 2) not to lose the fish once the rod is in his hands. When you hook into a big fish, there is no time to start deciding what to do. Every piece of equipment, every piece of food, has its role and place. If you give an orange or an egg from your picnic lunch to a crew member, he will always accept it, even if he doesn't eat it at once. If a mate offers something to a guest, the guest should accept it. There is a plan, a process ... a positive karma on a good boat. If someone or something is out of place, or doesn't do his job at the right moment, the fish is lost. Losing a fish, then, is a statement that the boat was not prepared or that someone did not properly perform his job.

Christian had studied law, but after earning his degree had decided he wanted to teach and coach then possibly run a secondary school. He had taught and had been a school administrator but had fallen ill with Parkinson's disease at the age of 34 and so had turned to writing. He was wiry and athletic and had a good sense of humor. He had fished with Ted for many years both in fresh- and saltwater—but never for billfish. On this trip, Christian was awash in deep spiritual thought, looking for and suddenly finding patterns, reason and design in all things. He realized he was having a religious wake-up call, a moment of epiphany. Out on the boats, the debate played itself out inside his head. "Prove God," said a voice. OK ... If there was such a thing as coincidence, why not divine design? If one could believe in superstition, why should faith in a god be any longer of a leap? Again, the voice. "More proof, please. How about in the 'laws' of nature and physics?" Right. If we cannot see gravity, magnetism or the wind, how do we know they exist? If we cannot see God, does that mean He doesn't exist? Maybe we're just proving we don't know how to look, or what to look for. He or She is supposed to be pretty sophisticated, after all. From here it got silly. "For every action, there is an equal and opposite reaction." In that case, thought Christian, I should get thinner if I take a second helping of chocolate cake. "Two wrongs don't make a right." True. They don't make a left, either. "Opposites attract." Maybe for a while. But then, look at the divorce rate. From here, Christian's thinking totally degenerated. Was this part of the master plan? Thinking deep thoughts until you got silly? Christian called this part of the "debate" "The Big Ha-Ha." He started quoting Yogi Berra, the former New York Yankees baseball great. Yogi's Laws. "In theory there is no difference between theory and practice. In practice there is." And, "You better cut the pizza in four pieces because I'm not hungry enough to eat six." And, "You can observe a lot just by watching." And, "If you find a fork in the road, take it." And, "You got to be careful if you don't know where you're going, because you might not get there." Going nowhere now himself, Christian circled back to his favorite physical law: "All matter is conserved." His translation: "No matter what happens to my matter, I will always matter." He resolved that whenever he had a choice between coincidence and superstition, or design and faith, he was siding with design and faith. Between luck and God (with his luck), he was choosing God.

Ed was perhaps the most quiet of the bunch, the most caring and sensitive. He knew a little Spanish and had high regard for the Panamanian people, having lived in the country as a young boy. He was trying to put together financing to build an exclusive spa in Panama's mountains. On the second day out, his boat had wandered far south, almost into Colombian waters. Way out there in the middle of nowhere, he had mistaken a radio tower on an island for a statue of the Virgin Mary. As he turned and looked away, he mumbled to no one in particular, "Am I seeing things, or is that a statue of the Virgin Mary?" Just then, two rods bent over with tuna fish on the line at the same time. A "double." Most fishermen are superstitious. It is considered very bad luck, for example, to bring a banana on board a fishing boat. (The origins are varied.) Virgin or tower, what "it" was doing on a tiny deserted island a hundred miles from nowhere was a mystery. Still, at the time, Ed's sighting was a welcome harbinger.

Joe was a lawyer with political aspirations. A black man from Philadelphia, he had one foot in an old world, one foot in a new — a world he could feel, smell and almost taste changing in his direction. A world he hoped to take in his direction whether it liked it or not. At the same time, both of his feet were not in his normal fishing sandals. He had loaned them to Christian, who had brought his own boat shoes but, after the first day out, had deemed them too slippery on the deck of the diesel-powered Bertram 31-footers, 10 of which composed the Tropic Star fleet. Joe's father had taught him how to fish the ponds and reservoirs surrounding Philly with spinning gear, but Joe had taught himself the "fine art" of fly-fishing. He had even brought his own fly rod on the trip in the hope of coaxing a black marlin to hit the long fly called a streamer at the end of his line. Full of energy and bravado, Joe peppered his conversation with boasts, challenges and laughter. His personality was infectious. He boldly claimed the group's fishing-points trophy before any points trophy had even been announced as claimable. Oh. And Joe was prepared, too. He had a second pair of sandals.

Peter could have been called "over-prepared." He ran an airline duty-free catalog outfit. You know, the kind of place that advertises all those "must-have travel necessities." Like, *The all-in-one picture frame and... weather station*. Not for you? Well, there's always *The flying alarm clock*. "This digital alarm clock launches a rotor into the air that flies around the room as the alarm sounds. Hovering up to 9 feet, it will not cease ringing until the rotor is returned to its base." Here's a favorite: *The Big Foot Garden Yeti Sculpture*. Says right here, "Will have guests doing a double take ... sculpture of the mythical legend has been captured in quality designer resin, and is finely hand-painted for ... startling realism. Over 2 feet tall!" (Wait. Aren't the Big Foot sightings of a creature closer to 10 feet in height?) Not surprisingly, Peter was consumed by technology: cellphones, laptops, digital cameras, converters, adapters ... a new breed of soon-to-be dinosaur was literally eating him alive. Christian teased Peter for his collection, nicknaming this beast the "converto-digi-cama-laptor." Whatever was silver, black, new and clicked, hummed or buzzed, Peter had one in his hands 24/7, fingers whirring and eyes riveted — locked open. In the end, of course, "wireless," like the Yeti, is a myth. At night, Peter's bedside table resembled a mini Las Vegas strip, totally aglow with recharger lights of assorted colors. Wires everywhere. The guys kidded Peter that he was missing the whole trip, missing life itself in real time. Unconcerned, he replied good-naturedly, "No problem, I've got it all on disk." Logically, Peter became the trip secretary, archivist and historian. But perhaps his real value to the group lay in his ability to speak Spanish. On the day the two were paired together, Christian spent hours grilling Peter on Spanish vocab and pronunciation. Peter knew the language well. And if he didn't, he could just look it up in his...oh, here it is (page 32) *Pocket sized Lingo Voyager 12-language talking translator*. For his kind heart, and bulletproof ability to take a joke, Christian nicknamed Peter "St. Peter."

Randy was a big man, a man familiar with being in charge. He was the CEO of a multinational medical-equipment company. Besides having been a fighter pilot over Vietnam, he had been a football defensive lineman in college. An experienced deep-sea fisherman, Randy had his own place and fishing boat down in the Caribbean and flew his own plane to get there. He too had fished many times with Ted, and together they had some fantastic stories to tell. Once, they had gone out on Randy's boat and returned in a thunderstorm. They got back to the dock with lightning bolts flying all around them. Later, slouching safely into dry, comfortable chairs at the marina bar, they watched stunned as a single bolt shot out of the sky and struck amid the docks. The next day they walked back down the dock ramp only to find Randy's boat completely fried — a total loss. The lightning had hit his boat. About that same time, Randy had been diagnosed with cancer, only to find out soon thereafter that it had disappeared from this body. Coincidence? "Hello?" (The Voice.) God calling. Lightning never strikes in the same place twice?

Steve was a commercial real estate deal-maker in Manhattan. Cool, curious, intellectual, Steve represented the "calm, sage, wisdom" side of the group. He enjoyed deep conversation, and good-natured banter as opposed to the sometimes-ribald humor of the others. Steve had a wonderful sort of a delayed-reaction kind of laugh. Upon hearing a joke, he would first furrow his brow and process the words. Then, like a West Coast morning, the dawning would come from over his shoulder until fully beaming on his face. Steve dressed crisply, often wore a blue blazer even in the jungle heat, and was very organized. Having married a first-generation Cuban, Steve also knew some Spanish. Steve was a scholar, pointing out on the first day of fishing, for example, that the vegetation along the shoreline grew closer to the water here because this was the Pacific Coast — the calmer side of the world. Being paired on a boat with Steve meant a peaceful day of productive fishing and warm camaraderie.

After circling over Panama City and the Canal, the old plane headed south and now rattled on through puffy white clouds. Breaks in the cover allowed snapshot views below of dark-blue waters and small volcanic islands tufted with jungle. After 90 minutes, the pilot banked to the right and then sharply left. The plane began its descent. Through little round windows, the group could clearly make out the few buildings dotting the fishing lodge property, as well as the dock, the boats and the jungle — jungle everywhere. An airstrip now filled the view from the cockpit, a single short tarmac swath that stretched from the sea to what seemed an abrupt end in the jungle. No other planes on the ground, no hangars, no lights, no taxicabs, no refueling trucks, no tower. One plane, one trip, one day, one shot. The wheels squealed on impact, the engines roared, the little plane shuddered and slowed. Safe. At the jungle end of the runway the pilot turned, taxied back toward the sea and cut the power.

The place was primitive and mysterious but gorgeous — a giant step back in time, a scene right out of *King Kong, Jurassic Park* or the old TV show "Fantasy Island." Between the runway and the sea lay a wide stretch of black volcanic sand. On the far side of the runway sat a crude native village; smoke lazily rising from cooking fires. A small stream of children and dogs was snaking its way across the beach to the "terminal": a simple roof over a raised platform and one enclosed bathroom. Waiting there already were several other indigenous children who timidly sought to sell various hand-made trinkets — beads, pots and baskets — to the new arrivals, as well as to the party of fishermen headed home. Also awaiting the plane's arrival was a tractor pulling a large wagon full of benches. This trailer transported guests from the airstrip, through the jungle, to a small fleet of motorized dugout canoes that covered the final leg of the trip down a "lost" river, across a lagoon and finally to the actual lodge.

Perhaps most conspicuous among this curious meeting of "great white hunters" and dark mini merchants was an *abuelo*, a grandfather, a tribal elder or wise man. He stood apart from the others, closer to the nose of the plane in brown shorts and a faded yellow short-sleeved shirt. He was muttering incoherently with arms outstretched, frozen, arms that even at a distance one could see were scarred arms; arms with no hands. Was he begging for help, for money, for food ... for forgiveness, or just for some kind of attention? Was he begging at all? When was the last time he had held someone in those arms? It became clear that there was no emergency, but the sight of him was sobering and quickly replaced the "fantasy" in "Fantasy Island" with a cold jolt of reality.

The lodge was rustic but comfortable and very efficient, built to pamper serious fishermen and a couple of fisherwomen — not tourists. Eighty employees were on hand to serve a maximum of 36 guests, for a week at a time. Owned by Americans and staffed by Panamanians of both Spanish and Indian descent, the lodge was composed of a series of bungalows, an outdoor patio/pool/bar area, and an air-conditioned indoor dining room/kitchen/office and shop, all linked by a network of winding dirt paths. Every building had a veranda. Backed into the dock, ready and waiting, bobbed the 10 Bertram 31-foot sport-fishing boats with their small second-story towers or "flying bridges," each manned by a captain and two mates. The drill was simple: 5 a.m. rise and shine, 6:00 breakfast, 6:30 get on your assigned boat, 7:00 catch bait, 8:00 catch big fish, 3:00 head for home, 4:00 pool, 5:00 bar, 6:00 tall tales, 7:00 dine, 9:00 read, 10:00 bed. Repeat.

The rain forest surrounding the lodge was huge, wet, colorful and alive. Spectacular. Larger than life. Grotesquely oversized fan-leaved plants, fireworks of flowers bursting from the centers, parrots like biplanes, even some kind of prehistoric-sized cricket lurched around every line of sight. At night, the sounds (probably of mating and death, or both) were wild, yet freakishly calming. What eyes glowed pale and yellow in the nearby thickets? What in the food chain would not be there to claim its place in the morning? Lodge guests, well fed and carefree, bedded down in screened-in, air-conditioned bungalow bliss, and dreamed of "The Big One."

There are several methods used to catch marlin, but most frequently boats drag or "troll" a "pattern" of five or six lines at a distance of 5 to 50 yards behind the stern, at relatively fast speeds. At the end of each line is an assortment of live or dead baits, colorful lures and/ or hookless "teasers." Everything is designed to attract the fish's attention. Interestingly, billfish are curious even about the sound of boat motors. They swim into the pattern and start slashing and biting. Once a fish is in the pattern, other baits or a fly, for example, can be pitched back toward them, if desired. This fly-fishing would be considered more sporting.

The first day dawned warm and bright from over the shoulder of mountains behind the lodge. A light breeze blew with the sun from the east. The fleet got off briskly together, guests betting and boasting over the deep growl of diesel engines, coffee cupped in hands. First, the boats headed inshore to catch bonito, a sturdy, tuna-shaped baitfish of about 18 inches. The surface of the small bays around the lagoon was boiling with bonito and it did not take long before the requisite six baits were on board. They would be kept alive in tanks known as "live wells," then each actually sewn onto "circle" hooks and dropped overboard to troll behind the boats ... tempting snacks for the great black marlin. True to form, Ted's boat was the first to catch six bonito. The captain ordered the mates to reel in all lines, swung the bow to the west and pressed the throttle to full forward. From the plane, the waters around Panama City appear very shallow and muddy. But here, the continental shelf is said to drop dramatically to a depth of 5,000 feet, not far off shore. The big fish often run deep then charge to the surface when they see food. Just five minutes after heading out to sea, the captain slowed the boat. Instantaneously, the mates had three lures and two bonito hooked, tossed and swimming behind the boat in the pattern. It was 8:32. Just 60 seconds later, the captain yelled, "Marlin!" and line was screaming off a reel. Ted gestured for the rod to go to Christian, but his cousin demurred. It wasn't right. This was Ted's idea, Ted's trip, Ted's fish. There was no time. Ted grabbed the rod and the fight was on.

The instinct of any wild animal when presented with even the smallest inkling of a suggestion that it is to be hooked or caged or in any way deterred from proceeding freely with its wildness is to unconditionally and violently resist. To resist and to try anything to get away. Even fresh springwater in a boiling pot makes very angry noises and will try different methods of escape — leaping out of the pan or even morphing from its liquid state to steam. The trick to landing most fish centers on keeping tension on the line through the rod tip. Not allowing any slack in the line when the fish is racing toward the boat, and not forcing the fish back toward the boat when it is taking line off the reel means being patient and knowing when to reel, when not to reel and when to reel quickly. Ted was a master. The great fish thrashed and jumped — everything you see in the movies. It took 20 minutes to "catch" and another 30 to "release," the fish having made a second long run away from the boat after the leader had been touched. The captain estimated the black at 500 pounds. It turned out to be the biggest fish caught and released all week. And, a surprise, Ted's first black marlin ever.

After the day's fishing, it was Peter who found out. He asked someone what had happened to the *abuelo*. The answer was disturbing. Many years ago, when the resort was in its infancy, another fishing party had dropped out of the sky with their new technologies. One of their tricks was to fish with dynamite; just light a waterproof fuse and drop a stick over the side into the teeming lagoon, and fish would float dead or dazed to the surface. Easy. Magic. The villagers were awestruck. Frost wrote, "Poetry is what gets lost in translation." So too is danger. In the exuberance to catch fish, one imagines, the dangers of the dynamite were not adequately translated. The *abuelo*, then just a teenager, sat alone in his canoe and lit a stick but did not understand how dynamite works when not under water, or simply didn't see the spark catch. He tried putting fire to fuse again, but deep within plastic tubing, the first spark had already reached its mark. The dynamite exploded in his hands.

From here, for some, the trip took on a decidedly different turn — a different meaning, a greater awareness. It was as if the dynamite story had flashed a new harsher light on the world; two worlds really, the old and the new. It wasn't just about who was going to catch the biggest fish or about catching fish at all. Rather, the question became, "What was this expedition of outsiders, of know-it-alls, of foreign men, actually doing here?" What were these footprints, our footprints, in this jungle going to look like after we were long gone? What word, deed or even idea, not to mention disease or device, had been brought into this fragile culture that did not belong? Indeed, was it, too late? Had cultural contamination already irreparably damaged this small indigenous tribe? Certainly, the *abuelo*'s story would argue, "Yes."

With this uncomfortable realization came also the almost overwhelming understanding that this whole place, the rain forest, the village, the lagoon, was a sacred place: truly closer to an earlier age, closer to the beginning, to innocence, to paradise ... to God. Here was an entire ancient network of people, good people, smiling people, simple people who had been hired away from their native lives to work largely unseen all day and all night *inside,* cooking food, cleaning rooms, readying gear, fueling boats, catching bait, packing lunches, sweeping paths, just so others could enjoy going fishing. The world seemed wildly out of balance.

To level the moral playing field, the burden to serve or to give — just to do good and be good — abruptly shifted from the servers to the servees. And some guests were decidedly not bearing their burden. Compelled by a distorted view of what Martin Luther King might call "the fierce urgency of now," one man yelled across the dining room, "Hey you. More coffee!" It was more like "the fierce urgency of ME." Perhaps it hadn't dawned on the man that he was only one of 36 guests dining in the same room, or that the servers were all busy serving someone else's fierce urgency. Was it too much to ask the man to at least call a waiter by name? Every staffer wore a name tag, for goodness sake. Maybe he didn't speak the language? Here's a tip. Luis is Spanish for ... Luis. Or how about trying the word "please"? Please works well in any syntax. Like, "Hey you, more coffee, please." Or, "Please! Hey you, more coffee." Still not getting service? Try, "Coffee, please." At the bar one evening, a man from Texas pontificated about how his wife had traveled finally to Hawaii to find an appropriate "destination wedding" site for their daughter. They didn't want out-of-town guests to have to "deal with the Mexicans." He droned on as a Panamanian (native tongue Spanish but trained to serve in English) poured the Texan another whiskey. Was the Texan sure that his guests would more easily put up with Hawaiians? They too are brown. Had he considered that some Mexicans might actually have made it to Hawaii by now and might work for Hawaiian wedding planners? Another party of fishermen even complained that there were "no fish," implying that the lodge had not done enough to get fish to bite their hooks or was somehow responsible for their bad luck. The complaint came on the day that same party lolled around the pool bragging about having boated three large sharks, two tuna and a rooster fish, a good day by almost any measure. Sure, sharks are generally not considered sport fish, but what these fishermen meant was they hadn't yet managed to catch a black marlin or a sailfish. What they didn't say was that they had hooked but lost several sailfish. What was the karma like on that boat? Ever eager to please, the dockmaster sent word that the weather had been uncharacteristically sunny for this time in the year, and that the captains were praying for cloud cover and rain. When it rained the next day, the same fishing party complained that it was raining.

At a specially prepared banquet on the last night of the trip, the seven men, now close friends, were each presented with a diploma certifying the successful catch and release of at least one billfish apiece. Three had caught marlin and four, sailfish. The next afternoon the seven retraced their steps from the first day, canoes to tractor to plane. Once again, the children made their way across the sand to hawk their wares, this time while brusquely prodded by fatigue-clad, machine-gun-toting troopers who had mysteriously appeared from some hidden jungle base. And, the *abuelo* was there too, now sporting a light-blue baseball cap. Christian had been feeling poorly all day. He had needed assistance from a staffer, appropriately named Gabriel, to get into the canoe for the trip to meet the tractor. In fact, he had spent much of the week on his back and the entire trip trying to return the kindnesses that had been heaped upon him by the employees. Predictably, the more he had called people by name and used the words *por favor* and *gracias*, the more the staff had wanted to serve him. At first he had felt guilty. Later he felt blessed. By trip's end, he was feeling relatively comfortable about his "footprints." The adventure had been a wonderful, eye-opening, fulfilling experience. And, thanks to the staff and to St. Peter, he had expanded his Spanish vocabulary and knowledge of idioms significantly. Inside he felt good, energized, happy ... almost well.

Christian did not know what was about to happen next, but he had a strong feeling. When it did, for once, he was prepared. Christian hadn't taken his mind off the *abuelo* since learning his story and he didn't take his eyes off the old man now. After the plane had offloaded its newest gaggle of fishermen, the pilot restarted the engines and spun the aircraft around, ready to load Ted's party for its return to "civilization." As he did, turbulence from the props blew the *abuelo*'s hat off his head. Handless, his wrinkled, stumped arms groped fruitlessly in the dirt for the cap. Christian, recognizing that this was his moment, rose from a supine position on the wagon benches and walked toward the *abuelo*. He picked up the hat, dusted it off and returned it to the old man's head. He then gave the *abuelo* a hug, whispered *"Dios te bendiga"* (God loves you) in his ear, kissed him on the cheek and, slowly ... turned for the plane.

***

John Keats, in his famous sonnet "On First Looking into Chapman's Homer," is inspired to write after reading Chapman's great translation of Homer's *Odyssey*. He equates his inspiration and wonder to that of Cortez and his men upon first seeing the Pacific from a mountaintop in Central America. Mute, in awe, the Spaniards stare in the moment of discovery, "Silent, upon a peak in Darien." Of course, Keats didn't get it quite right. It was Balboa who "discovered" the Pacific. Still, the province of Darién in Panama is a striking piece of this Earth. It is the last link in the land bridge between Central and South America and remains one of the most biodiverse areas in the world. Today it is under threat principally from colonization and logging. To counter this, the Darien National Park was created in 1980. The Park covers 1.5 million acres along the Panama/Colombia border, and is the largest national park in Central America. The park is home to 770 vertebrate species, six indigenous cat species, and many reptile and amphibian species. The forests are also home to 2,440 plant and more than 450 bird species. An important bird-watching site is located near the Cana Scientific Station in the park's center. Here too the Spanish once operated the Espiritu Santo Gold Mine, which produced gold continuously until 1727.

The protected area begins on the Pacific coast, with mangroves and lagoons, and progresses through very humid tropical forest, to the rainforest canopy at the top of the Serranía del Darién mountain ranges, which are of volcanic origin. The Park also shelters various Indian tribes: Embera, Wounaan and Kunas. The Kunas have traditional settlements at the foot of the sacred mountain known as Cerro Tacarcuna, which rises 1,895 meters above sea level. Their language and behavior are in part directed by their relationships with wild animals and plants, and the symbolic and magical features they represent.

The only major resort in this vast area is the famous Tropic Star Fishing Lodge on the Pacific coast. More than 170 fishing world records have been set at the Tropic Star. If you are very lucky, you might catch a world-record fish someday. But if you are alert, patient and prepared, and are "always kind and good," you have the opportunity, on almost any day, to catch the Fish of a lifetime.

My name is Marshall Christian Moore, and you have been a patient audience. Thank you.

DIANA DAVIS '03

February 7, 2008

I have always had a very analytical mind. When I was 7 or 8 years old, I wanted a definition for love. I knew that my parents loved me, and I knew that my grandma loved me, but I needed a definition of love that could apply to every situation. I knew that my mother supported President Clinton and was glad that he had been elected, but did she *love* him? I came up with a working definition: If they died, you would cry — that means you love them.

That instinct to quantify emotion, the same instinct that makes love into a testable, measurable object, also makes me see friendship as a curve, time as an axis, letters as a fundamental link.

I met Rebecca in August of 1999, less than a month before I came to Exeter as a prep. When people ask us how we met, we always give the easiest answer. Do you know her from home? Do you know her from college? Yes, yes, we always say, because the truth is too complicated to hold the interest of a casual acquaintance. The truth is that we met in Costa Rica on a trip for families — her grandparents brought her and her sister from Vermont; my parents brought me from New Hampshire —

Diana Davis graduated from Exeter in 2003 and taught in the PEA Math Department as an intern during the year 2007-08. She is currently a mathematics professor at Williams College.

and somehow in just those 10 days we formed a bond of friendship that would last, even though distance separated us.

My prep year started with rain. In the fall of 1999, it rained for three days straight — Thursday, Friday, and Saturday, the first three days of class at Exeter. The bottom 6 inches of my pants were soaking wet, and as a day student, I had no change of clothes, no dry socks, no way to dry my shoes between cross-country and history class. The worst was when, hurrying across Front Street, jumping across the 4-foot moat at its edge, hunched over to keep the rain out of my eyes, my peripheral vision obscured by the hood of my raincoat, I walked through *the gate*. The *gate,* the brick archway that, I had already been warned several times, if you walked through it, you wouldn't graduate. It was an inauspicious start.

In many ways, my prep year is inextricable from the beginning of my friendship with Becca. I finished my homework during my free periods at school, so that when I got home I would have time to write to her before I went to bed. When the carpool dropped me off at night, I ran up the stairs to the kitchen table to see if there was an envelope with that characteristic handwriting and shiny return address label on my place mat. Sitting in the car, waiting to get home, our friendship was a frequency plot of when I received letters, carrying a probability distribution of whether there would be one today. The mail takes two days to get here and there's no mail pickup on Sundays, so no letters on Tuesdays. I got a letter yesterday, so probably no letter today. I sent her a letter five days ago, so two days for it to get there, one day for her to read it and send a new one, two days for it to get here, maybe I'll get one today. I never knew, but I could pretend like I was calculating it, quantifying it, minimizing the uncertainty.

As a prep at Exeter, I felt very small, and very on the outside. I was not a boarder, so I wasn't really part of Exeter, but I spent my whole day at Exeter, so I was never really at home. I did not belong anywhere. The days were long; the weeks were long — the classes themselves were fine, but the schedule was overwhelming. It was more than a month before the schedule seemed normal. It happened suddenly one afternoon as I showered in the gym after cross-country practice, this moment of clarity that the day lasted until 6 p.m. and that was normal. After that, the days were fine, but the weeks were still very long. One Friday night, after a week of trouble sleeping, I couldn't sleep at all. I kept thinking about the 13-day marathon of school that loomed before me: not only six days a week of school, two weeks in a row, but even a Junior Studies event on Sunday that I had to drive in special for. Around 4 or 5 o'clock in the morning, my dad decided that he would call me in sick to school the next day. I missed all of my Saturday classes and a cross-country meet, but by the end of the day my nervous breakdown was mostly over.

That afternoon, a letter came from Becca. In it, she wrote about the TV show she was watching, the catalog that had just come in the mail, how boring her bus ride was — not a memorable letter, really. But on the back, she wrote, "This letter is short and hand-written. I didn't have much time to write it. Just know that I'm thinking of you, and I miss you. Just know that, OK?"

How did she know? What was the probability that she would know, on Wednesday night, that she should write me a letter, to be mailed on Thursday, so that it would arrive on Saturday, just when I needed it most?

Our letters form an ongoing conversation lasting many years, with its own rituals and inside jokes, its own guidelines, its own rich history separate from the rest of our lives. Stripped of the dates and particular subjects, our letters written in 1999 are indistinguishable from those written in 2007, despite the former being a third of our lives ago. The words, the voices are the same. This parallel space of letters, being somewhat timeless and detached from the world, does not often intersect with actual time, which is why it was all the more miraculous that the words I needed came to rescue me on that Saturday afternoon in 1999.

I came up with the idea of "letter time" to describe the parallel time and space where letters live. One simple exchange — I ask a question, Becca answers it — might take two weeks, from the time I write my letter to the time I receive her response, but it is one moment in letter time. I could resent the delay of the mail, but I decided to embrace it as something that required us to slow down and think before writing. One summer day, when Becca was staying with her grandparents in southern Maine and I was at our cabin in midcoast Maine, she wrote me a letter in the morning and I received it that afternoon —just six hours after she had put pen to page. I felt like we had cheated, that this was a subversion of letter time. When she said "this morning," she really meant *this* morning. It made me uncomfortable; I couldn't think that fast.

This is deliberately anachronistic. We have telephones; we have email. But there's something magical about sitting down and writing a letter.

This fall I read a book called *Letters Home*, by a psychiatrist who uses letters in her treatment. When her clients are trying to deal with repercussions of childhood abuse, with their parents' unrealistic expectations, she does not ask them to *talk* to their parents about it; she makes them write a letter. To put ink on a page is a deliberate act, less prone to impulsive outbursts of emotion than the spoken word, or the typed word. In a letter, no one can interrupt you before you are finished. You can start a letter one day and come back hours, days, even weeks later to finish your thoughts right where you left off. And if you wish, you can revise your words until they reflect exactly what you want to say.

In my junior year of college I spent a semester at Mystic Seaport in Connecticut, and for my history research project I read old letters written by whale-ship captains to their wives on shore. Each day I went to the library, put on my white gloves and pulled from an envelope a stack of delicate pages from the 1800s. I was interested in letter time, especially the extended, danger-fraught letter time of the sea mail, which worked like this: a sailor writes a letter, addresses the envelope and puts it into a mail bag. When a ship is headed homeward, it takes the mailbags of the ships it meets and delivers them when it reaches land. When a ship leaves the harbor, it takes letters from sailors' wives, in hopes that it will meet up with the vessel carrying the sailors for whom those letters are intended. Since whaling voyages could take two or three years, it took months for a single letter to reach its recipient, and years for a question-and-answer exchange to take place — if the letter arrived at all. The ink is brown; the pages are cracking. The backhand script is difficult to read, but the words are eternal.

> My dear, my feelings are such as take away my faculty
> of expressing them, and were I present with you,
> silence perhaps might speak more than I can write.
> However, were we to give up all business for the
> indulgence of our affections, we should make but poor
> citizens, and worse husbands; so let us be content
> with the fortune all wise providence has caste into
> our laps, and rather than look back with grief on the
> happenings we have enjoyed, — look forward with
> hope, and fondly anticipate that which is to come. — So
> I remain your sincere and ever affectionate husband
> until Death.

There is something immortal about these words, written in cramped, dark quarters below the waterline of a wooden ship, thousands of miles from the one he loved.

Our world is similar, though we don't notice it. We no longer go on whaling voyages across the sea, but we send 14-year-old children around the world to go to prep school, we move across the country for college, we move across the country for jobs, always leaving loved ones, loved places — love — behind. Of course, we cannot give up all business for the indulgence of our affections. We move for the best of reasons, but we do not communicate in the best of ways. The letter-writers left in our world have white hair, address their envelopes with typewriters, have trouble walking to the mailbox. There is something about a letter that makes the distance smaller.

The distance is an essential piece of the relationship. What does it even mean, you might legitimately ask, to use the words "best friend" when you have never lived in the same place, when you have never even seen this person for more than a few days at a time?

In the summer before my senior year at Exeter, I went to Japan for six weeks. Becca and I had agreed that the distance was too far to send letters; the mail would be too difficult, too expensive, too slow. So the only communication she had from me was the weekly updates that I sent to friends and family on email. Now I saw the graph of our friendship as a step function: Becca's perception of me one day, and the next day, and the day after that, was based on what I had said in my message two days before. So all of those days, to her, were the same; there was a horizontal segment across all of those days. When I sent another message, it put the next segment at another height, and so on. You can see how it's a series of "steps," not only going up or only going down, but going up and down based on the content of my messages. This piecewise function was only smoothed out at the end of the summer, when we exchanged the journals in which we had been writing our letters to each other all that time.

For years, I hid my letter writing like a drug habit. After I finished my homework at night, I would sit on the floor on the far side of my bed next to the wall, my back pressing against the knobs of my nightstand. My mother required that my door be open all the way at all times, allegedly for circulation of heat, and she would stick her head in every so often and ask, "What are you doing? Reading?" "Yup." "What are you reading?" "A book." To myself I said: This is not a lie; I am reading the book of my own mind.

If addictions are hereditary, then mine skipped a generation and came from my grandma — my mother's mother. Every week, my grandma wrote three or four letters to my mother. She lived by herself in Nebraska, in the town where she had always lived, but we lived in New Hampshire, far enough away that she visited only twice a year, and so all the other times, she wrote letters. She wrote in blue or black ballpoint pen on unlined tablet paper, three letters a week, a page or two each, for decades.

Decades are a funny thing in my family. Everything seems to be separated by decades. My grandma and my mother and I were all born in years that end in 5: 1915, 1945, 1985. My grandma's son, her husband and eventually she herself all died in years that end in 7: 1967, 1977, 2007.

Over the decades, the letters got harder to read. When I was born in 1985, my grandma's handwriting was like that of any other grandma who had once been a schoolteacher: neat script in even rows. But over the years, the benign familial tremors her mother had came also to her, and her hands shook, and the cursive got tighter, with more sharp edges, and sometimes she had to cross out words and rewrite them above, neater.

But as the letters changed, so they remained the same, like multiplying both sides of an equation by a constant. My grandma told my mother what was going on in town: the town my mother had grown up in, that my grandma had grown up in, that her parents had grown up in. And because none of them really grew up *in* town, she always talked about the weather. My mother grew up on a farm, as did my grandma, as did her parents, all farms outside the small town of Tecumseh, Nebraska. So she talked about the rain, or the drought, and she told my mother which ladies had come to quilting, who had moved to the care center, and whose funerals she had set out plates for in the church basement.

If you make a stack of the letters I have written to Becca over the past eight years and press it down with your hand, it is over a foot and a half high. How tall would the stack be of four decades of my grandma's letters to my mother? Letters as a bar graph — measuring friendship, measuring love.

When you write this many letters, there is a certain order to them, certain rituals that you do each time. When Becca and I write to each other, we write the day of the week and the time at the top: Thursday, February 7, 2008, 10:10 a.m. When my grandma wrote to my mother, she wrote the temperature and the weather: May 17, 2007, a.m. 62°, overcast. Why? What does it matter what day of the week it was, what time it was, how warm or cold it was, or what the sky looked like? Isn't it just the words that matter, after all?

Maybe it started, for my grandma, in 1959. Her son, my mother's older brother, headed off to college at the University of Nebraska 50 miles away in Lincoln, and he was having a rough time of it. He was homesick, and he wanted to quit. So my grandma wrote to him every day. Every single day! What is there to write about, day after day? Maybe something like, "I'm thinking of you, and I miss you." And in any case, there's always the weather. And if she told him what she was doing, what his father was planting and harvesting, how many bushels of apples she had picked, how many cans of pickle relish she had put away for the winter, then maybe he would feel more connected, less far away.

So we put in this structure so that as you read the letter, you can think, "Oh, on that cloudy morning of May 17, there she was sitting at her kitchen table, perhaps looking out the window at the warm, gray day as she wrote these words," or "Oh, Thursday, 10:10 a.m., at the moment when she was writing that, I was driving from Exeter to Boston; I had no idea that she was writing to me then."

But that is not true. On Thursday at 10:10 a.m. you are sitting here, and on the morning of May 17, 2007, I do not know what the temperature was, or what the sky looked like in Nebraska, because that is when my grandma died.

When my grandma died, I was writing a letter to Becca. I don't know the chronology exactly, but I like to think that just when I wrote my name at the end of the letter, she took her last breath. It was late at night — I had just finished my last final exam of college, a take-home math test whose last proof I had written around 1 a.m.. And then I wrote to Becca, because I knew my grandma was about to die, and other than analyzing it mathematically, the only way I know how to think about anything is by writing about it in a letter. So I wrote her the letter, about my grandma dying, and went to sleep a little after 2:00, and around 5:00 my mother called to say that my grandma had died in the night. When in the night? We don't know, but maybe just at that moment when I finished writing about her death.

My mother did not get to say goodbye to her brother, who died in Vietnam in 1967, the summer after my mother graduated from college. She did not get to say goodbye to her father, who died a decade later of a heart attack in the night. But she did get to say goodbye to her mother, who died comparatively more slowly, seven weeks after being diagnosed with cancer. Seven weeks is a long time compared with the fast death of war or heart attack, but really it is a short time, especially when the person in question is 91 years old but mowed her own lawn, cleaned her own gutters, and who, when it was too icy to walk a mile outside, did 86 laps of her basement, and showed every indication of living forever.

But no one lives forever, and my grandma was dying, and so I decided to ... write her a letter. I would write about how great it was to talk to her on the phone each week, how much I enjoyed visiting her in Nebraska, how I remembered her teaching me to sew and playing "Amazing Grace" on the piano, how much I appreciated the dozens of quilts she had made for us over the years; I would thank her for saving money for my college education; I would assure her that I would be nice to my mother. It was going to be a great letter, but it was the last week of class in my last week of college and I did not have the time, and by the time I sat down to write my letter, my grandma, who had been self-sufficiently living by herself the week before, was sleeping in a hospital bed in her living room. I thought I did not have the time, but really, my grandma did not have the time.

I called my grandma about a week before she died. The last time I had spoken to her was about a month before, and then, it was just like any other time I talked to her on the phone. I told her about my math classes, about my thesis, about my races in spring track, about my plans to be a teaching fellow at Exeter for a year and then to get a Ph.D. at Brown. I asked her about what she had been doing, what books she was reading. When I could not think of anything else to talk about, I asked her about the weather, what the temperature had been, whether it had rained.

I had not talked to her since that time, a month before, until now, the last time I would talk to my grandma. I had to say something now; there was no letter time to wait and reflect, but the book of my mind, from which so many letters had easily flowed, was now blank, and I could not find anything important enough to say. And so, when the morphine slowed her speech too much, when small talk seemed inappropriate, when conversation became too difficult, I looked out the window and told her what I saw. "It's a beautiful day here, Grandma. The sky is blue, and the sun is shining."

ELIF TASAR '08
Reel Time
April 24, 2008

Enter any corner market in Spain and somewhere near the cash register you will find a basket of wooden bracelets called *pulseras de los santos*. Glued onto each of the wooden tablets are small oval stickers containing portraits of various saints. The stickers are shockingly nuanced and grandiose for their size, resembling miniature versions of paintings by Tintoretto or El Greco. In these portraits, the saints' garments do not rest on their frames, but rather drape and fold and swirl about in the wind. The backgrounds of their portraits are not static or one-dimensional but, in fact, are dynamic depictions of the heavens. Some are orange, some blue, some gray, and each is adorned with its own seemingly drifting celestial clouds. These saints are real characters with real histories, and, for the price of one euro, nearly every teenage girl on the Iberian Peninsula carries them around her wrist as a good-luck charm. For a year, I was one of those girls.

The problem with the bracelets is that, because of their low quality, the stickers are constantly falling off. In the eight months since I have

---

Elif Tasar graduated from Exeter in 2008 and from Stanford University in 2012. She lives in San Francisco and works at Tesla.

returned from Spain, all but two of my bracelet's 13 stickers have disappeared from their wooden plaques. Sometimes the saints turn up unexpectedly, stuck to my desk or bureau or the floor of a hallway that I pass through often. But for the most part, I never see them again. They depart and their destinations are unknown to and unsolicited by me.

Saint. My dictionary provides several definitions for the word, the loosest of them being: an extremely virtuous person. I do not like this definition, for it does not begin to encompass the number of individuals who have had the effect on me that all saints, I believe, should: the fundamental effect of bringing men closer to God, or to some higher state of spirituality. This is a loaded concept for someone who is not even certain what it means to believe in God. Certainly, I do not believe in "Mr. God," the father of Christ, a "bottlenosed judge in a wig," as James Joyce described Him. Do I believe in the Quran's Allah, the God that my brother and grandparents believe in? Maybe — it depends on the day. While I do not believe in the God that usually pertains to conversations about sainthood, I am cognizant of the many secular saints who have appeared throughout my life, impressing in me a sense of spirituality. I call them secular saints, for they are not particularly virtuous, nor are they figures of public veneration. They are not ethereal, but hued by strokes of earthly paint: sweat and tears and blood. Their vices are as sacred to me as their virtues, if not more sacred, for it is by virtue of their imperfections that they have affected me. In my portraits of them, they are encapsulated in cinematic frames of memory, what T.S. Eliot calls "still points," when our paths coincided between departure and destination.

Chapter 18 of the Quran is called "The Cave." One part of the chapter tells the story of the acquaintance of the Prophet Moses and a mysterious sage whose knowledge and wisdom are boundless. This sage's ever-fresh and everlasting knowledge have earned him the traditional title of "Al-Khidr," meaning "the Green One." In the parable, Moses asks the sage if he may follow him to acquire some of his wisdom. The sage responds that Moses will not have the patience to learn from him, for "how couldst thou be patient about something that thou canst not comprehend within the compass of [thy] experience?" Nevertheless, he accepts Moses' request. Subsequently, the sage commits a series of actions as dubious as killing a man, to which Moses vehemently objects. Only after the sage explains his motives and reasoning does Moses feel ashamed of all his protest. When my father explained this story to me, the idea that the ultimate source of wisdom might transcend the knowledge of prophets seemed revolutionary. It suggested that maybe the Quran itself could not offer all the necessary explanations, and that the conventional lines demarcating good and evil could be blurred.

My father then recounted a story of his grandfather fighting in the Crimean War for what was then the Ottoman Empire and is now Turkey. After a battle, my great-grandfather somehow found himself displaced, lost and starving behind enemy lines. For hours he stumbled through the barren, hostile terrain awaiting sure death. Out of nowhere, a figure appeared. He did not introduce himself but offered my great-grandfather help, promising to lead him back to his base camp. Though he did not trust the man, my great-grandfather was dying and had no choice but to let himself be guided. Sure enough, the figure returned my great-grandfather back to base camp and vanished just as he had come. My great-grandfather was nourished back to health and survived the war. For the remainder of his life, he was convinced that the figure who had appeared before him, the man to whom he owed his survival, was Al-Khidr, the "green sage."

How do we differentiate between enemies and those who dwell behind enemy lines? The sage that saved my great-grandfather was, at least to him, a saint, but he had to cross over to enemy territory in order to execute an act of sainthood. There is a line in Milton's *Paradise Lost*: "The mind is its own place, and in itself / Can make a Heav'n of Hell, a Hell of Heav'n." Perhaps enemy lines, Heaven and Hell, exist so that they might be trespassed. And perhaps by transgressing these boundaries, our minds can find a place where sacred and profane converge.

My great-grandfather died when his son, my father's father, was still a child. His war story was inherited from my great-grandmother, who lived from 1888 to 1978. When I think about the span of her life, the fact that she was born into an empire and died in a republic, I wonder whether she viewed her generation as preservers of a soon-to-be-lost history.

Though not in the historical sense, the span of my parents' lives is already equally impressive. The lives they have shaped for themselves in no way match the lives they were given. My parents immigrated to America from Turkey shortly after marrying in July of 1972. With two suitcases and $200 in their possession, they left their families and 24 years of familiarity to obtain master's degrees in electrical engineering at the University of Missouri at Rolla. My understanding of their trajectory deepened in Turkey over winter break, with the help of the rediscovered projector of an ancient Yashica video camera.

One morning over break, I roll out of bed and stumble to the kitchen, where I see a box of rolled-up film sitting on the kitchen table. My mother tells me that they are silent short films that chronicle my family's life from my parents' wedding through my brother's elementary school years. My grandmother has had the films in her apartment for years now and does not know what to do with them, as no one remembers what became of the film projector. At this moment, my 86-year-old grandfather interjects that he knows where the projector is. With great exertion, he lifts himself from his chair and walks over to a cabinet with his back hunched forward. I worry he will fall like he has so many times before. After minutes of fumbling through the contents of the cabinet, my grandfather pulls out a bulky object in a vinyl case. Sure enough, the metal mass beneath the case is a giant projector.

My grandfather has slowly been dying on the rocking chair of his study for nearly a year now. His sickness is the reason we have come to Turkey in December rather than wait until summer as we usually do. It is ironic that, of all the members of my family, only the eldest has remembered the projector, which proves to be not just an appliance but a vehicle of time travel, a means of reliving forgotten, or, in my case, unremembered memories.

My father spends the afternoon rereading a manual he read years ago, retuning his fingers to the grooves and buttons of a machine that has sat collecting dust for nearly 40 years. It is dark by the time he calls the family over to the dining table to watch the films. With the click of a button, the machine begins to whir and a little box of light appears on the wall, magically revealing my brother, now 29 years old, as a toddler. Within a few seconds, I recognize the setting of the film: Disney World. I have heard stories about how my parents would often drive from Michigan to Florida just to experience the American grandeur of the attraction park, a cultural splendor nonexistent in their cockroach-infested apartment in Detroit. But never have I considered that the way they looked then, the things they talked about, the things they laughed about, may have been different. There is a collective gasp around the table as my brother, younger here than his own daughter is today, teaches himself to walk on the cobblestone street next to Cinderella's castle, balancing his arms on either side as he scampers along.

The next frame is of my mother attempting to fasten my baby brother back into his stroller. *Baby brother.* It's strange to hear those words come from my mouth; I have never referred to my brother in the diminutive voice. My mother looks different, with long, curly, brown locks that grayed and were cut short before I was born. My brother sobs and wriggles and pounds his feet against the ground as she clutches him, begging to be released so that he can once again experience the newfound freedom of being transported by his own two feet. That must have been an exalted moment — when your body first permitted you to declare your autonomy.

We switch films, and the next scene is of my infant brother sitting in my father's lap. My father, with his scruffy black beard, giant square glasses, and bellbottom pants, resembles some unfortunate cross between a crazy chemist and Don McLean. He is tickling my brother's stomach, and a kind of tender giggling I have never before witnessed erupts across my brother's face. The tickling and giggling continue until my brother can no longer endure more, and retreats face-first into the depths of my father's lap. All the while the machine is whirring, whirring as the reel of film on the side of the projector spins, spins, spins. I cannot remember ever observing such affectionate interaction between my parents and brother in real life. I say real life, r-e-a-l, as if the life before me on reel, r-e-e-l, never took place. Truly, I do not know what happened to the people in these films. The duration of that life, that world of theirs, expired before I was even brought into existence. Reel time is time unreal to me.

A subsequent film displays my brother, about 4 years old, standing on the porch of a home I never inhabited, next to my mother's mother, whom I never knew. I have read that moving one's family and possessions three times in this country is equivalent to having one's house burned down. If that is true, about four of my parents' properties have been scorched since 1972. Of course, they had fewer possessions back then. And fewer worries. With each film is a new location, documenting my parents' many trips from one coast to another. Some of the films reveal familiar places, like Yosemite. But Half Dome's usual gray is tinged with sepia, and the smiling parents before me are far leaner and younger than my own. At the top of Nevada Falls, my father holds my brother on his shoulders and the two wave at the camera. Years later, when my brother was off at Exeter, I too would be carried to the top of this waterfall, and I, too, would pose as my mother took photographs of my father and me with a newer, digital camera.

My brother is as absent in the photo albums of my childhood as I am in the silent films of his, but the backgrounds of these portraits — Yosemite, Ankara, Disney World — are often identical. I think of the photographs in *Harry Potter*, whose subjects can enter and exit the frame as they please. Where was I when the rest of my family was posing in the films of my brother's childhood? Where was my brother when my parents and I were smiling for the snapshots of mine? Where were my parents in between those two chapters? In the darkroom, I suppose, developing the film of my brother's youth and preparing for their next project: mine.

Cameras capture still points, but don't account for change. And even the still points are incomplete as representations. There are no films or pictures, for instance, of the first time my mother left my father and me to work in Dallas to save money for my college education. I was 3. Nor are there films or pictures of the weekly airport drop-offs and pickups, or the teary phone calls, or the lonely Sundays that haunted my youth. There are no films or pictures of the moment when a gust of wind swept my father off the deck of a sailboat into San Francisco Bay, where he drifted between life and death for hours until the coast guard retrieved him. There are no films or pictures of the times my mother did not drive home and kiss me good night the way I'd made her promise as a condition of my parents' legal separation. The memories we elect to store via cameras differ from the memories that the lens of our mind stores for us.

The film ends with a click and the whirring halts. My grandparents, mother and I sit in silence as my father places a new film onto the reel.

And so the square on the wall lights up again and a new cycle begins. These frames contain my parents, along with my father's parents and younger sister, jump-roping at a picnic site on Mackinac Island, in Lake Huron, Michigan. The year must be 1972 or '73. I inhale to prevent the thickening in my throat that accompanies tears. The grandfather I know, who struggles to lift himself from his chair and who mutters insults at my grandmother as she hands him his myriad daily pills, appears before me strong and unwrinkled, a man not yet 50. He and the younger version of my grandmother jump in unison as my parents swing the rope. My aunt, barely 20 and dressed in a flashy, back-bearing top, applauds them from the side. My grandmother soon trips over the rope and all members of the family clutch their stomachs from the pain of laughter. I glance across the table at my grandparents, who are viewing the film with equal astonishment and awe of their former selves. If someone had then described to them the seven-day pill dispensers, the inhalers, the falls from tripping on carpet fringes, the emergency trips to the hospital, and the loss of fellow elderly friends that awaited them, still they could not have truly comprehended the process of aging. Likewise, if someone had told my aunt that she would give birth to two autistic sons, she would not have believed it. In fact, she and her husband, my uncle, refused to accept that their sons had disorders for years after they were diagnosed. But these realities do not pertain to my family members as they exist in the reel time of film, for they are in the prime of their lives.

What will I look like in the scrapbooks and home videos of my future? I do not know and do not want to know. I like to think that I, too, am in or am at least approaching the prime of my life, and that this peak will last for a while. I like to think that, by means of attitude and personal creed, I can dictate the duration of this peak.

So what do you do if your children are born with autism? If you are my uncle, you live smothered in the cynicism of your mind. You wake up in the morning and are lured out of bed only by the prospect of a cigarette. You kiss your 12-year-old son and, leaving him in the care of a longtime babysitter, drag yourself to work. Your elder son, age 23, is asleep. Soon he will rise and spend his day roaming the streets of Ankara, as he has every day for nearly 10 years. You have never known precisely where he spends the daylight hours, and by now you have stopped attempting to find out. Your wife has already left for work; she likes to walk rather than be driven so that she can spend this time of morning alone. You know this desire for isolation and are not offended by it — you feel it, too. You fight with her much less now, now that you have stopped trying to be content with the cards God has dealt you, now that you have stopped trying to forgive Him. You have accepted your wretched life. Still, every once in a while something happens, maybe your 12-year-old throws a fit in a particularly public place — the metro, perhaps. Whatever the occurrence, it rekindles thoughts that sear into your forced state of reconciliation as if to mock it. In such times, you cannot think beyond the irony that, while one of your sons is mute and the other cannot retain any information he is taught, your brother-in-law's two children are receiving the finest educations America has to offer. Accepting that life is not fair proves to be a self-renewing struggle.

My uncle Mustafa has been the subject of my family's criticism for years. His persistent negativity and hostile nature upset us. Really, though, I believe what makes us uncomfortable about my uncle is the doubt he engenders in us. We would like to think that we would do a better job in his position, that we could still manage to lead fulfilling lives. But could we? Who is to say that any of us could better handle a lifestyle demanding supernatural, saintly patience? My uncle disturbs us not because of who he is but because he is a reflection of what we might have been, or in my case, might potentially be.

My father inserts a new roll of film onto the reel. At first I do not recognize the figure who stands before me in the hallway of a distinctly Turkish apartment building, rocking in his arms a baby not older than a month or two. The young man is startlingly handsome, tall with jet-black hair. He nuzzles his nose against the baby's and makes faces to provoke laughter before glancing up at the lens. His eyes smile at the camera with the blissful confidence only a new father can possess. I know this because I have seen the poignant expression in those eyes only once before, a few minutes ago when observing my father play with my brother on film. That is real, that expression transcending the reel and the way I feel when witnessing it. It is real because I feel it, and that must make it love.

For these 70 or 80 seconds of reel time, my uncle Mustafa is the spitting image of the perfect father. In real life, I know that he is not. My family members and I regard him as a bad person because it is convenient to do so. Yet, in classifying my uncle we have oversimplified matters. Where does Al-Khidr, the "green sage" from the Quran, fit into all of this? Where does bad bleed into good? Where do the enemy lines, the Heaven and Hell, the past and the present, within us touch? Nabokov called life "a brief flash of light between two eternities of dark." A flash of light, a momentary awakening, a projection much like the flickering gallery of saints fashioned by beams of light upon the wall. These hagiographies, that is, biographies of saints, are not confined to religious texts but are fluid and fluctuating in film. These are private saints, flawed saints. But they are saints nonetheless, for they remind me of the fragility of life, the brevity between a man's first step and his first fall. They remind me, too, of the precariousness of naivety, the ease with which happiness fades into discontent. I believe that acts of sainthood are performed every day. This may be a maudlin theory. But if all we are endowed with is a flash of light, one tenuous still point between departure and destination, then why not exalt the mundane?

LAURA BLAKE '08
May 1, 2008

There is a room where moments knit together, so that a fabric is formed as the present loops through the past. The window is propped open with a stout, weathered Ancient Greek-to-English dictionary. You can hear peacocks cawing on the close and smell the first blossoms unfolding in Dean Kowalski's garden. In the distance, the hunched dome and scaffolded spires of the Cathedral of St. John the Divine rise into the cityscape.

I rise early to come here, the air blue and wet on my tongue as the street vendors open their carts for the morning. And the close just beginning to stir — the old orphanage, Synod Hall, the stone school all silent save for the rustlings of the choirboys who had once called these grounds their home.

I bend over my red Jenny text, long since out of print, curling my tongue around the syllables of the Latin language. Age 12 in this sunlit classroom where the distant rumble and whine of traffic meets my halting pronunciation and all the whispered, scribbled history of a word passes through my breath.

Laura Blake graduated from Exeter in 2008 and from Yale University in 2012. She is an MFA student in creative writing at the University of Montana.

Translation of an ancient language is both a fast-forwarding of time and a suspension of time. In translation we leap a word's millennia-long evolution in a momentary utterance of syllables. We speed through time, but we also suspend it, folding the present upon the past. We hunt for the heart beating within the word, its essence, a core that has survived all along the word's journey, reincarnated in varied sounds and appearances. And when we find this core, time can hang in a syllable.

And maybe in the same way that different letters and pronunciations wrap as a skin about the heart of a word, layers of time and place and experience encircle a life. As we live, we peel off past selves, examine them, adopt new ones. Our journeys, our translations of self, define us, teaching us to listen for the beat of our own blood, the pulse within our histories.

My favorite bed sheets growing up were printed with the alphabet. Each letter had a face and personality. M was rather morose, C squinted like a con man, Z was exotic, E obliging, U a bit sleepy. The alphabet became my companion. It was last to wish me good night as I shut my eyes and first to greet me when I opened them each morning. Long before I could piece letters into words, I knew their curves and attitudes.

So I learned to speak in the language of my family's small blue house with its sour cherry tree and stern arborvitae in the front yard. Before I could read or write or distinguish yesterday from tomorrow, the names of a world were whispered into my ears. Names for the doves who nested each year in the roof, for the hiss and plunk of summer rain, for my father's old canvas tent that my sister Hannah and I used to pitch in the backyard.

A blizzard came unexpectedly one March. Iced tree branches clacked in the wind and gleamed where the sun hit. The arborvitae curved under the weight of the snow until its peak touched the ground and the trunk splintered with a moan. Once the spring thawed, men came to cut down the tree and my mother planted hyacinths around the stump. Yet every time I saw the stump, I saw the tree, too; what had been and what was, present in the same column of air.

Literacy, too, splinters the past from the present, the self from memory. On the train to Philadelphia to visit Ellen and her daughter Abby, who is nearly 2, I read an article titled "Twilight of the Books." The author examines oral cultures where, he writes, "Words have their present meanings but no older ones, and if the past seems to tell a story with values different from current ones, it is either forgotten or silently adjusted ... It is only in a literate culture that the past's inconsistencies have to be accounted for, a process that encourages skepticism and forces history to diverge from myth."

As I sing the alphabet that afternoon with Abby, as she dances, tossing her beautiful little head back and forth, and cries out an elated "l-m-n-o-p!" I cannot help but wonder what jangling ring of keys I am handing her with these 26 sounds. What doors will letters unlock in her? What doors will they shut for good?

It is, I think, no coincidence that the words *transfer* and *translate* share a common Latin root. For as we transfer ourselves, literally bring ourselves across, to a new place, we must also somehow translate the past self into the present self, stripping off an old skin, growing a new one, clinging only to our bones and blood.

So as my family sent the furniture by moving truck and packed Deedee's espresso cups with the thin gold handles, all of our books, and both cats into the car for the two-day drive to New York, we were both transferring our possessions and translating ourselves.

New York spoke in a different tongue. The vibrato of a young woman's voice spilling out the window at 2 in the morning. The wail of ambulance sirens on the way to St. Luke's. The whoosh of wind and wings as pigeons took flight. Even letters were not the same. "A" could be both indefinite article and 8th Avenue express. Have you ever considered how much confusion, how much paradox lies in the phrase "The A"?

It was here that I began to formally study translation, in Dr. Vitale's classroom on the third floor of the Cathedral School of St. John the Divine. The Latin language was difficult at first, with its cases and principal parts, but over time it gave itself to me. I learned to love the precision of a verb form, the clean units of clauses, the firm pattern of declension.

There was a neatness to Latin, so unlike the sprawling noise outside or the shattered sound inside when I woke at night to hear my mother's voice crack *When was the last time you said you loved me?* Disjointed, fraying, messy syllables. I wanted the cleanliness of Latin forms. I wanted to wash all the dishes after dinner. I wanted to knit in even rows, tight stitches so that the holes forming the fabric were almost invisible. I wanted to sit inside the Cathedral and decline nouns in my head as the chaplain spoke.

One year the Cathedral caught fire. Stained glass saints melted in the heat. Some exploded into hundreds of jeweled fragments — St. Francis in shards across the pavement. The tapestries filled with soot. Have you ever seen a *church burn*? There was so much ash. For a year it filled your nose, your mouth, bitter, parching. I carried the smell of burning home on my navy school sweater, and to me it was good, fierce, an honor to smell charred.

It was a sharp smell, sharp like the corners of an ablative absolute. It covered the scent of my skin until I smelled the way Latin smelled. The way, I thought, scholarship smelled: the blazing, consuming drive to memorize, analyze. I could make this fire, this language my own. I pored over an Exeter guidebook, in love with the idea of a place where

42

autumn leaves blew in the sky bright as popping sparks and snow fell like cold drifts of ash.

Prep year I read Caesar in Latin. He marches. He camps. He kills many Gauls. Orgetorix is up to his usual shenanigans. The text is factual, historical, numerical. Snow sticks to the sides of buildings in blank, unrecognizable continents. My mother calls to ask how I am. *Fine*. Right before I hang up she tells me she is lonely, without Hannah and me. *It's quiet here*, she says.

Over the telephone, I cannot see how her shoulders hunch like mine or the way her mouth purses when she is concerned. I cannot even envision where she is standing or sitting, if the cat is in her lap, whether the apartment is neat or messy. I listen to the series of pitches that define her voice, flattened by static in their transfer along loping telephone wires. And I am angry at her, for the break in her voice that I hear as weakness, for the part of me that she holds in her shoulders and lips, for the guilt that splits me across the miles between us.

I began, that year, to scratch at my skin until I could peel it away in pieces from hidden places — my scalp, my feet, my back. My cuticles were a bitten mess, ragged and bleeding. I did not cut; that seemed too woefully adolescent. I bit and scratched. There were dreams, too, mostly in the winter, that left me exhausted and ashamed in the mornings. One night I dreamt that I pulled my stomach away in chunks and found nothing inside but the blackened, cobwebbed insides of a rotten orange.

I read recently that cuttlefish have phenomenal skin. It changes both in color and texture to camouflage them in their surroundings. If you drop black rocks into the sand where a cuttlefish rests, it will almost instantly display dark blotches upon its skin. A cuttlefish can even show one pattern on one part of its body and another pattern on a different part.

The summer after prep year, my mother, sister and I leave the apartment leased in my father's name. I go to be a CIT at summer camp in Vermont while Mom and Hannah move seven blocks uptown.

I received two letters from home over those two months of summer. My 15th birthday passed unnoticed, though I received a strangely acrid, fragmented letter from my mother a few days later. I learned life-guarding and CPR, puffing breath into the plastic mouths of Annies, thrusting my palms hard into their chests.

Only months later did I learn from Hannah how the days had stretched brittle with heat. How my mother had hardly slept and refused to eat. On a white wooden bench outside a bookstore, there is accusation in her voice. *You weren't there.* And I say to her, *You can always leave. There's always a choice.* And she just looks at me, because we have both grown more fluent in silence than in speech.

We never unpacked the 123rd Street apartment all the way. I kept meaning to do my boxes, but it was easier to stack them at the foot of the bed and try to ignore their hulking posture. Maybe I did not unpack because the space felt so temporary, a parenthesis in which to learn to live as three instead of four, a parenthesis in which to acknowledge failure.

Failure. Dr. Vitale could spend an entire class searching for the right translation of a word. He rifled through stacks of dictionaries hunting down etymologies, salt-and-pepper eyebrows leaping over the rims of his glasses. And sometimes, an hour up, he fell back into his chair defeated by a break somewhere in the lineage of the word, and I knew then that the word was untranslatable.

My grandfather grew up speaking a different language, German, until his native country betrayed him. When he came to America, his English vaguely accented from years in a British boarding school, he enlisted in

44

the Army and changed his name from Blach to Blake in order to erase its Germanness. And so the name that has been passed down to me is an invented one, cut loose from the roots of it ancestors.

What was lost in the changing of a name? What story slipped away in the lengthening of a vowel, the softening of the harsh "ch" into the mild "k"?

A month after Pa's death, my family went to visit the house he built where Cathy, Ish, Christina, Granny, Pa and Dad used to spend the summers. We were, I suppose, trespassing on private property, but the owners of the house had long since left Long Island for the winter. The house was shaped like a picture frame, and looking through it I felt as though the lapping December waves were made up of a series of stilled images, blended so perfectly together as to give the illusion of motion.

The walls of the house were made of glass, and I could see the life inside, frozen like a museum diorama: seashells, bookshelves, blue and orange tin cups hanging over the sink. Light shone off the glass bright as off a glossy photograph. And I felt no ownership of the wooden porch or the twin bunk beds; all I could claim was the light off the glass.

Can we ever inherit more than reflection? I remember Pa's books and the way he gave them away, slowly at first, then in great spurts. He had thousands, and I do not exaggerate. Books on cubism and ancient Egypt, yellowing stacks of *Life* and *Vogue*. Some were inscribed in a particular sort of script — a mix of artistic mess and analytical neatness, always in black ink — that you do not see anymore. *For Peter*, then some witticism or quiet joke, a burst of affection, and a looping, scribbled signature.

Here, take this one, he would say, shoving a stack into my hands. *No, Pa, we can't really. No take it, I insist.* And as he stacked the pile higher, my father quietly looked through them, separating the ones he knew once mattered from the rest.

Maybe we should have taken them all, accepted the gifts of words he pressed on us. Because one snowy night the roof collapsed in his assisted-living apartment, not above his bedroom, thank God, but above his bookcase. He woke from the crash to find the volumes buried under crumbled plaster, shattered wood, and still-falling snow.

My mother did her best with them, freezing the drenched pages then carefully drying them out, but in many places the ink had bled, inscriptions dissolved, letters collapsed into black rivers, the past running off the page.

In the car with my mother on the Mass. Turnpike, another September. She is a good driver, and I watch her hands grip the wheel, steady and confident. I remember how her skin grew itchy, red and puffy one summer. When she told her doctor that she was a rare-and-ancient-books librarian, her doctor almost laughed; what do you expect when you work with moldy old books? The rash was some ancient fungus, the spores preserved between the pages of an old manuscript. No modern ointment could help. She just had to wait it out.

But now her skin is smooth again and the veins branch over it like the highways crisscrossing the road map in my lap. Her blood flows blue with all her stories: dreams of becoming an archeologist, a summer spent teaching herself violin, and so much more than I can ever know.

I realize then that there is no such thing as a true synonym, either within the English language or between languages. Each word has been breathed full of life by its own set of lungs, filled with more breaths than we could ever count. And as we speak, as we choose one word over another, we cause two histories to diverge. In writing, in speech, we must breathe our thoughts into one word, leaving another to its own trajectory.

At school it hurt to shower, though I did so every day, worried that the skin might become infected. But I could still smell it on me everywhere

I went, the smell of blood and scabs, of flesh trying to heal. One day in the shower the water stung so badly that I began to cry, and I knew that I could not continue to exist scabbed, mottled, trying to inhabit both the skin of a student and that of a daughter, a sister, while in reality possessing neither truly.

I washed my body with my own tears, let the salt flow over my face, my neck, my stomach and hands.

In the spring I cut my hair short, amazed to watch the strands fall into my lap in commas and apostrophes. And I think, *I am paring away the unnecessary, trimming pauses, clipping hesitations.*

I have kept almost every letter I have ever received. Postcards, birthday cards, pen pal letters — I saved them all in shoeboxes and folders stacked under the bed. But last June, as we packed up again, this time to move to Washington Heights, I threw them all away. Perhaps it was the abandonment of Morningside Heights, that neighborhood cradled between Riverside Church and the Cathedral of St. John the Divine. Perhaps it was that senior year was beginning, that the inside of the cathedral was blocked off for cleaning, that the last time I had seen Dr. Vitale he had asked me what I planned to do with myself and I came up blank.

As I sorted everything into piles — recycle, give away, throw away — I felt a satisfied efficiency. I admired my ability to shed possessions. I watched Hannah carefully pack her notebooks, photographs and sketchpads. *You're taking all that?* I asked. *Don't throw that away!* she cried. *Why? It isn't **necessary**.*

Fall term I forced myself to meet the necessities from one day to the next. Burnt cups of coffee, days when I did not stop to eat anything until 4 o'clock, not calling my parents and, if I did, solving math problems while I listened with half an ear.

And I was proud. Proud that I did not **need** sleep and food the way other people seemed to. Proud of the ache in my body that never went away — the burn in my chest, the pain in my back. Proud that my light was on long after those in Hoyt and Abbot had been shut off. Proud that I did not cry once all term.

And I believed that *this* was living bravely.

It happens in the library of all places, the last day before December break. *Hey Laura,* he calls out. *What do you think of the Manhattanville Project?* And as I listen to a boy I hardly know extol the benefits of Columbia's expansion into Harlem, I find myself more lost than I have been in a long time. As he speaks of "progress," I see pink fliers from the block association taped onto the door. I smell the cigarette smoke drifting through the windows as Piña unraveled the day in conversation on the stoop. I hear the breath sputtering in my mother's throat as she slid her finger through the top of the envelope containing the lease renewal. Among the texts that have so empowered me in reasoned discussion and debate, I see the frailty of my elegant proofs and analytical essays, even of my careful poems and stories, against the tide that has swept through my family again and again, washing us up on new shores. The library windows seem to look out not onto the neat corners of Exeter, but onto my view of 181st Street, where the windows across the street frame an old man rubbing his bald head and a crescent of a woman leaning in her window frame, a second moon. In the collision of where I am and where I come from I find myself inarticulate, unable to translate the grating in my chest into clean reason, argument.

I know then that words are not clean. They are as dirty and cracked and beautiful as the roads they travel.

The bus ride home that night stretches for 10 hours; we are driving into a blizzard. I think of how the tracks we leave on the highway are filling with snow, our footsteps erased from sight, remembered only by the road. And I wonder how much time I spend in transport. If I added up the hours, minutes, seconds I spend on subway platforms, buses, car rides, planes, how long would it be? A week? A month? A month of my life spent in transition, translation.

At the summer camp where I work in Pittsford, Vermont, one of the main ethics among the staff is the idea of *the life of the open road*. I have been thinking about what it means to live this way. Because it is on the road, in the act of translation, in the shallow, gray light between night and dawn, the moments of deliberation between Latin and English, the raw period between one skin and another, that I most often find myself balanced within both past and present, folding time in two.

It can happen as I drive past an unimaginable town or an abandoned military base. It can happen as I wind a warp for a loom, or peel an apple into the sink, or walk along a sidewalk and feel, in a tugging instant, how many feet have beaten the path before me. And *then* I can feel the pulse of the road echoing in the rhythm of my steps.

But an echo is not enough. This is the open road, but not the *life* of the open road.

When I graduated from middle school, Dr. Vitale gave me a *Roget's Thesaurus*, sixth edition. The word thesaurus comes from the Greek θησαυρός meaning treasure or treasury. It is a treasury of words, of meanings, of bridges that almost span the distance between Latin and English, the past and the present, who I am and what I say.

On a bookplate pasted to the inside cover, Dr. Vitale carefully typed a line from *The Aeneid*, Book IX: *Macte nova virtute, puer: sic itur ad astra.* Or, loosely, *Well done, with new courage, boy; thus is the path to the stars.*

Late nights, as I rifle the pages, searching for the right syllables to translate a poem or craft a story, those words are a charge. They demand the courage to seek the synonym that can never fully exist, to trace an etymology that breaks, re-emerges, trails off into a dead end, and to breathe my own voice into the words I have inherited.

The language I speak is English, not Latin or Greek, as proficient as I may be in their respective grammars. I will always be bound to these words, these sounds, these 26 companions. Yet I am bound, too, to all the languages that flow into English like veins — Latin, Greek, Old English — converging, diverging, circulating with a single pulse.

As the bus rolls through snowy hours, I watch dusk shadow the highway, now blue and branching. In the window, my reflection layers upon the road unfolding ahead.

ANNA CONDELLA '08

As Ships Go

May 15, 2008

As ships go, she was a beauty, and no one of her time would deny it. Perhaps she was vain — a fourth massive orange steam vent added to the three she already had for no purpose other than to make her look more impressive — but she had grace and power and cutting-edge technology to make up for it. If I had been alive then, I would have gladly sold all I had for the opportunity to be onboard, and taken a chance on a new life across the sea. Figures something as simple as faulty rivets — miniscule dots in comparison with a hull the size of a city block — would take her down.

She sank on the last leg of her journey, in the dead of the night, in glassy water and deadly ice. Fifteen hundred perished with her, and their stories have haunted me since the time I first read them when I was 8 years old. Someone thought the tale of the *Titanic* would make a good learn-to-read story, someone who must have thought second-graders would zoom in on the massive sinking ship and just think, "Cool!"

Anna Condella graduated from Exeter in 2008 and from Princeton in 2012. She is now a medical student at Columbia College of Physicians and Surgeons, applying to emergency medicine residency programs.

I didn't. In a nutshell, I became obsessed, reading every book I could find on the story of that grand, broken lady. My family, probably glad I'd found something other than Power Rangers to cling to, chipped in, clipping newspaper articles, mentioning documentaries, getting picture books. My favorite was a gigantic, red-rimmed book with meticulously detailed cutaways of each section of the ship, from first class to steerage. Oh, but she really was beautiful.

She sank off the coast of Newfoundland, so many miles from shore, two days away from reaching her destination. I knew the spot so well from my reading that I saw the red X on every world map I looked at, but at 8, I hardly could have dreamed that I would look down on it one day. August of 2002, when I was flying away from every familiar landmark of my 12 years of life at 700 miles per hour, I flipped to the little "World Map" channel on my in-flight video screen in a desperate attempt to figure out where I was. The little pixilated plane was there, right there, so perfectly positioned over the spot of her sinking that I could do nothing but stare at the screen for the next few minutes, until it finally shifted farther west and I could breathe again.

There was something surreal about being thousands of feet above a choppy surface that hid, thousands of feet below it, the ruined hull and scattered belongings that were the only remains of the beauty and the hundreds of souls that slept with her. Normally, thinking about the long drop and vast ocean below the plane caused me to shiver, but here, on this spot, I felt an old, deep calm instead. I could have been above the ocean or below it; I would have been happy to find myself nothing but silt and bones in the murky depths, swaying gently with the current, with no concern for the future or the affairs of a world that had continued without me. A little morbid, perhaps, but I think it was appropriate, given that at the time, my world was ending.

It wasn't that special of a world, as worlds of sixth-graders go. Though my family had done a little moving in the past, we'd been comfortably settled in Ridgewood, New Jersey, for six years straight. I loved books and the Discovery channel as much as Nickelodeon, the Backstreet Boys and Bagel Bites. I was looking forward to learning to drive in New York City without getting caught, and having house parties in living rooms designed by Martha Stewart. Our home was in walking distance of all the schools, and a block from the library, sports fields and town pool. I had friends of different types, from my soccer team to my bandmates, and we had sleepovers and movie nights and pinky-promised to be friends forever. I was (happily, ecstatically, contentedly) typical.

The less said about the decision to move to England, the better, as I don't remember much at all six months before and after the event. I know that beforehand I pretended it wasn't going to happen, so well that half my friends weren't aware I was moving until a few weeks before, and I know that afterward our tiny London house was so full of fury, my parents weren't sure we'd make it a few months, let alone three years. My father couldn't find his type of job in America in December of 2001, so he looked elsewhere. As logical as this all sounds, it didn't quite make sense to his three daughters, and still doesn't to two of them, if my sisters' reflections on the experience are anything to go by. Maybe they had more to lose at the time; maybe I just gave up on my old life more quickly. Tess, 15 back then, never ceased asking my parents when it would be time to go home for good. I was more convinced of the finality of the journey, that once over the ocean I could not take for granted that I would ever make it back.

Immigration was not a new notion to my family, as both of my mother's parents were children of men and women who left Ireland, some in the dead of the night, for a new life in America. Some of their siblings chose a shorter but no less momentous journey, like Bridie, who traveled to London, England, more than half a century ago to start her new life. She was one of the first people we visited once we had settled our belongings there, and these visits soon became regular.

Her lined face and silver hair were ethereal in the sunlight of the only window to the room in which my cousin passed all of her days. She refused all nursing homes, preferring the living room of the house she'd lived in since the days of the Blitz. Her company was two cats, the TV and the caregivers who sometimes came and sometimes didn't. And, once a week, my mother and whoever else in our family who wanted to come.

Those Sunday visits were somewhat like going to church. There was a feeling of obligation, of course, because she may have been a distant cousin but she was still our blood, and afterward we almost always felt better for the trip. It helped when she was in a good mood, because for her age she still had a sharp mind and a quick humor. I don't think I ever fully appreciated what good patience and optimism it must have taken simply to smile as often as she did, let alone crack such jokes. Our conversations were usually light and uncomplicated, but sometimes they ventured into more painful territory.

"I don't know," she said quietly to my mother, one rainy Sunday that has never left me. "I just don't know why I'm still here, Mary."

I once went on a retreat for kids who naturally slipped into the role of counselors and comforters for others our age. They told us that if one of our friends ever started talking like that, we had to go and get them help. Meanwhile, we should remind the despairing party of all the good things they had to live for.

My mother leaned into Bridie and took her hand.

"You just have to let go," she said.

I'm ashamed to say I still don't know for certain how I am related to Bridie.

My parents always called her simply "our cousin," though as she was well over 90 when she passed away two summers ago, our relationship was clearly not as simple as that between the children of my uncles and me. She explained it to me once, and I understood that the defining factor was that my great-grandmother was her grandmother, but where precisely our bloodlines diverged after that is still a mystery to me.

Bridie's relationship with her family always was tangled and painful, from the day she was born an illegitimate child in Catholic Ireland. Her past contained stories of tragedy and love and misunderstanding to rival that of *Romeo and Juliet*, stories I will never know because I never asked her. They were over by the time I met her, and the bits I know I gleaned from my mother and grainy photographs. She grew up in a coastal town in southwest Ireland in the early days of the 20th century, ostracized from homes and friends for a crime she didn't commit. I've been to the house she was born in, run through the pastures she knew as a child. Rolling and rocky, they looked west onto the endless Atlantic.

I can see her in those pastures, gazing out, watching the grand luxury liners sail for an impossible horizon. Out in those fields, she was free from judging gazes, chores and undeserved reputations, free to be an innocent child. Feet squishing in the boggy grass, fingers twisting in her dirty dress, she dreamt of leaving everything she'd ever known to take a chance on a new life across the sea. She imagined being on a great lady with four impressive steam vents and faulty rivets, of joining in that voyage that surely led to a brighter future.

As a child, I read a picture book about a great sinking ship that haunted my imaginings; as a child, did she read the headlines screaming "TITANIC DISASTER" and gather her own ghosts? The majority of the dead were steerage passengers, and the majority of the steerage passengers were

Irish immigrants. Her dream, at the bottom of the ocean, with 1,500 dreamers like herself — is that why she turned her back on the western horizon, and never crossed the ocean as her brothers and sisters did?

One night half a year ago, I made the worst decision of the entire summer: I watched the 1997 movie of *Titanic* for the first time. Alone, save for our poodle, Sophie.

My mother came home to find the credits still rolling as I bawled into Sophie's dark, curly fur. I'd dragged her into my lap somewhere between the car scene and the iceberg, and she'd been patiently waiting to escape all evening. When Mom sat down next to me, she broke for freedom and I sobbed into my blanket instead.

"Oh my God, Anna, what's wrong?" my mother asked, horrified.

"She let him go, Mom!" I wailed. "She said she wouldn't and she totally pushed him into the ocean! After he spent a whole hour of the movie saving her!"

"Oh, honey," my mom said even as she cracked up laughing. "He was dead by that point!"

This only made me cry harder. Sophie scratched the door, trying to get as far away from this madness as possible. Mom sighed.

"See, when you were little, I would just get a magazine and point to Leonardo DiCaprio and say, 'Look! He's not dead! He's fine!' I guess that wouldn't work anymore, would it?"

I sniffled and shook my head. "She still let him go."

Bridie died in the summer, a year after we moved back. I was in Spain, on the abroad program, paying two euros for an hour of Internet in the local *locutorio*, and I heard by email. The last time I'd seen her, Mom and

I had tucked her into bed, and she had thanked us in such a beautiful way that I left the house in tears, because we'd all known it was goodbye, a last goodbye, as well. My mother's email said something about her being at peace, and I hoped-prayed-knew that to be true. I remembered Bridie asking my father to attend her funeral when it came, but the email said that neither of them could make it.

I didn't know how to mourn in that sunny country. We were staying in a town on the northern coast, a popular vacation spot, with seven beaches and great cruise ships sounding their horns every morning as they sailed into the harbor. Our group went to the beach that afternoon as usual, one with wide, crowded sand and the warmest waves I'd ever felt in the Atlantic. I waded into them, and looked across the water to the horizon. From that point on the northern coast of Spain, it was at least several hundred miles to London. I entertained a few crazy thoughts of running for the airport or jumping on one of the cruise ships to make it back in time. I thought of a funeral with no mourners.

One of the first nights back in Ridgewood, my parents took me to dinner at Janice's Bistro, a little restaurant that used to be Sheridan's Café. Before we moved, it served the best grilled cheese and chocolate malts, a favorite lunch I had grown up on. Now, instead of twirly stools and coat racks at every booth there was low mood lighting and dark-green tablecloths. Over a bowl of ravioli, my mother took my hand and asked me the question that belied my parents' biggest fear.

"Do you regret us moving to London?"

I looked them both in the eye and proceeded to tell them, with a conviction I wasn't sure I had, that it was the best thing that had ever happened to me, and that they shouldn't waste a night feeling guilty over their decision.

After all, they'd done everything they could to make it seem like those three years had never happened. We moved right back to Ridgewood, New Jersey, into the same house, with the same furniture and neighbors. I had my old bedroom back, and waiting for me, my old friends and school. Unlike my sisters, who were at college now, I had the chance to go back, settle myself again in the comfortable world of the suburbs.

But that world had continued on without me for three years, and I felt like a ghost when I came home. The buildings, the shops, the places I knew were all there, but the people were gone, replaced by friendly, awkward strangers. I could have given it time; I would have adjusted, I'm sure. Instead I visited a boarding school in New Hampshire I'd never heard of before my parents told me to apply, and liked its hot chocolate so much I decided to stay and take a chance on a new life.

I think that what haunted me about the *Titanic*, since I read her story in that little book, was the notion that she could have been saved, that all those deaths could have been prevented. I imagine that somewhere along the line, a choice was made that should not have been, that had only the rivet-maker or the captain been more informed, or thought longer on the consequences of their actions, the outcome would have been different. I believed that choices with such magnitude behind them should be more difficult, that everyone should realize what they are getting into before changing the future.

In truth, though, these grand decisions come down to simple things in the minds of those who make them, as they must if they are ever to be made. In the end it is just the sufficient number of lifeboats versus their aesthetic appeal on the deck, or the salary of a job abroad versus the difficulty of life in a new country, or the taste of hot chocolate versus the comforts of an old life.

When a choice that was made becomes hardest to understand is when you cannot ask the person who made it how they narrowed it down, when you failed to take the opportunity to look them in the eye and ask, "Why? Why did you never cross the sea to your family? Why are you here, alone, why wouldn't you leave this old house, these ghosts, and start again like I did? Why wouldn't you let go?"

For almost a century after the *Titanic* sank, it was thought that she had sunk intact. Though survivors, eyewitness accounts of the tragedy, insisted that the ship had broken as it went under, the majority of shipwreck buffs and scientists were certain that she was waiting somewhere on the bottom, whole, as though her presence had simply passed from one world to another. But when they finally found her, so many miles from home, off the coast of Newfoundland, and their brave little submersible descended through the murky water, the first things it came upon were bits. Suitcases, dishes, and maybe the odd fragment of the hull here and there — the screen displaying what the submarine saw was filled with only scraps of what she once was, spread out a mile square on the ocean floor. Even her main bulk was split, halves resting separately, 60 feet deep in silt that swayed gently with the current. It was then that they realized they could never know how she truly looked whole, that we can never see for ourselves how her life was, or why she ended the way she did. All that is left are fragments, broken dishes, grainy photographs, and stories gleaned from those who knew her in life, all resting below one surface or another.

DAVID WEBER
Four Tattoos

October 2, 2008

Three months ago, after teaching high school English for 38 years, I retired. There's an old *New Yorker* cartoon that shows a 40-something suit at a cocktail party, saying to a poised, well groomed woman, "Market research is merely what I *do*; it isn't who I am." Having set aside what I did for so long, I have been thinking a bit about what I have lost and who I still am.

In June, about a week after I retired, I dreamed that I was giving a public lecture about my childhood summers at my grandfather's farm 50 miles north of New York City. When I woke up, at first I thought this dream was about how my childhood in that place, and later my wife's and my wedding in the living room of the farmhouse, had mercifully shaped me, had partly defined me. But the lecture itself was intensely boring, numbingly boring, even though the farm will always matter to me. In the dream I violated every idea about writing that I have come to understand

---

David Weber is a writer and editor based in New Hampshire. His poems, reviews and essays have appeared in various local and national publications including *Independent School*, *Chronicle of Higher Education*, *The New York Times* and *Bird Watcher's Digest*. He compiled and edited *Civil Disobedience in America* (Cornell University Press, 1979) and is lead editor of *A Book of Meditations*, vol. 3 (Phillips Exeter Academy Press, 2009).

and that I tried to teach my students. Why this palpable ineptitude? Was it a dream about the farm, about the idea of failure, or about retirement?

When you retire you come face to face with serious trade-offs. On the one hand, you — I — suddenly have a new experience of time. Even on days when I seem to have a lot to do, I still feel that I do have enough time for whatever the work or play is: kayaking. A movie. Doing the *Times* crossword with my wife; or editing, reading, writing, talking to people about their writing projects or mine. If I get distracted or slowed down by something, the delay isn't very stressful. I have few real deadlines now, and I appreciate their near absence. While I was teaching there was an endless current of deadlines that I tried to acknowledge as they rushed past, and I almost always felt that there wasn't nearly enough time to get everything done. Some of this was no doubt self-pity, and some of it was my gross disorganization, but a lot of it was the daily experience of any halfway responsible teacher. Thoreau, whose foray into teaching was brief and quickly repudiated, says, "I love a broad margin to my life" — and I have always wanted one, too; but like most people in serious schools, I have only rarely had one. Retirement, in theory, comes with a broad margin attached. For many people, some of them perhaps fortunate and some not, retirement is *all* margin.

But if retirement brings you a margin — even a narrow margin — it is a margin that you pay for. To obtain the margin, the time, the freedom, I walked away from the role that had publicly defined me since I was a graduate student. For 38 years, along with a lot of pleasure of many different kinds, I usually felt over-occupied; but I had a coherent and satisfying sense of who I was trying to be. I believed in, valued, loved the work, especially the conferences with students about their papers, and the papers themselves, and the common commitment shared with colleagues. I didn't love the pace. But to obtain the margin I would have to give up this good work. And losing the work wasn't the half of it: I would have to face invisibility, anonymity, even irrelevance. And I would have to face a marker inescapably related to aging.

Later in the summer, as everyone else was heading back to school, I had two more dreams. In one of them I had been invited to teach Spanish 110, Spanish being a language I have never studied and absolutely do not know. Despite the obvious and severe disadvantages for my prospective students, for me the dream wasn't a nightmare. On the contrary, it was rejuvenating and exciting. I was spinning off rationalizations like a supercharged revolving lawn sprinkler — I can fake the accent! We'll learn it together! It will all be fresh!

In another dream later the same night, I had been appointed a Unitarian minister in Walpole, New Hampshire, a town where I have never been. At least I am a Unitarian; but I had had no ministerial training and had never met the congregation. All three dreams — the anaesthetic lecture, the inappropriate Spanish class, the wild leap into the ministry — now seem to me to be images of the loss of an actual vocation, unconscious warnings that the price of a Thoreauvian margin could be functional nonexistence. Who could I be if I didn't have something real to do? In the epilogue to his masterful memoir, *Covering*, Kenji Yoshino describes a friend who has horrified her parents by having a small tattoo of a blue star placed on her shoulder, where it will be visible above her wedding dress. She cherishes it as an ineradicable reminder of the poetic self she is subordinating as she enters medical school. The tattoo insists on the reality and value of aspects of self unconnected to her public role, her paid work. Do I need a (metaphorical) tattoo now? Of what?

During the summer I spent many hours talking and writing to people on behalf of my extended family's effort to protect our farm in perpetuity, to preserve this hilly, irregular land that now belongs to 81 first, second and third cousins. So I have been thinking about whether being a member of this extended family, a part owner of this idiosyncratic farm, amounts to an aspect of identity that might compensate for the absence of publicly recognized work. Whether or not you are what you do, you are also, usually for both better and worse, the child and grandchild (and cousin) of particular persons. When I left the classroom, I did not set aside my relationship with the farm, with my family past. The land, 125 acres, was purchased in the 1790s by my grandfather's great-grandfather, who farmed it and opened a store. It has half a mile of frontage on a somewhat murky lake; it has a long waterway we call a pond; it has 50 acres of woods; it has foxes, deer, 40 or 45 species of nesting birds; *and* it is the location for an endless struggle between two of my relatives who raise organic vegetables there and never collaborate on anything. Neither my wife nor my daughter has been at the farm in years, because the family conflict there is so distressing.

When I visit I stay in a nearby hotel. But I keep going back — for the land and the birds and some of my cousins — and this year I have spent perhaps a hundred hours trying to obtain funding (from the state, the county, the town, regional and local environmental organizations) that would allow us to avoid selling the farm to a developer. The town and the county and the organizations have all supported us. Now it's up to the state, which has a Farmland Protection Program under which owners get substantial payments in exchange for a legally binding promise that the land will never be developed.

If the state says yes and the family, the 81 cousins, agree to use the payments as an endowment for the farm rather than as cashable personal checks, I will probably be there more than I have been since I was a teenager. Though farms absorb energy endlessly, just as schools do, I would still have a margin, even a broad margin, since I would be choosing my own tasks, like improving the trail to the lake, and no one would be depending on me from day to day. I won't know for a few months how this has turned out. But in any case this whole experience has heightened my sense that being from "there" is one strand of who I am that is not dependent on my career, my vocation. So my first tattoo might be an image of the farmhouse.

To say or to assume that what you do is meaningful only in terms of your primary work leaves out a lot of other things. Many, probably most, of my students knew this already and identified themselves even more closely with their extracurricular commitments than with their course-based learning, their ostensible work. For several years I have been a board member of a nonprofit organization that seeks equal acceptance for gay, lesbian, bisexual and transgender persons and their families. I attend monthly meetings, I ask people to give $10 a month to support the organization's work, I have testified several times before legislative committees. I can tell that this unpaid, volunteer work has something to do with who I am, because often when I meet someone for the first time and gay issues enter the conversation, the person either embraces me because the work seems important or backs way off because he or she finds the work weird. The ones in the second group, being uncomfortable with the whole topic, can't decide whether it's weirder if I'm gay or weirder if I'm not gay but work for such an organization.

Though I don't get paid in dollars (instead I, too, write a monthly check), there are other rewards. State law is different and more accepting than it would be if this organization didn't exist. I meet people whose friendship I value and whom I would probably never have known if I hadn't been involved with the organization. So my second tattoo could be our logo: an equals sign beneath two linked wedding rings.

The remaining tattoos can be described more simply, but first I need to acknowledge that no one can convincingly think or talk about retirement as though it were a given. Too many of my colleagues by far did not live to retire, and others did not have a retirement of any length. Four of my departmental colleagues, all teachers who were part of the bedrock of the school, died in their 50s, two more in their 60s, both of them younger than I am now. So whatever good cheer lives in my description of my own experience, it is tinged by an implicit awareness that I am talking about one of life's starkest inequities, and that I have been lucky. In the terms of Jane Kenyon's unforgettable poem, it (that is, my being permitted to imagine this next stage of my life) might have been otherwise.

There are two more tattoos. On interstate highways you can sometimes see cell towers whose physical equipment has been painted and shaped to make them look as much as possible like very tall white pines. In this poem the speaking voice is supposed to belong to the tower:

WHAT THE CELL TOWER SAID

(New Hampshire, I-89)

Consider an alternative

to your understandable cynicism.

So I'm fifty feet higher than any

of the surrounding firs and spruces;

so my ersatz branches are horizontal

and my rigid lines of, well, needles

look like mechanized brushes waiting

to beat the dirt out of someone's rug.

If I were trying to fool you

I would be shameless, but I'm only after

a trick of the eye. In this quadrant

all you can see besides me is the others,

the residual forest, the uncluttered sky,

so if I were just rods and wires

there would be a kind of visual rape.

But steeped in the trees' deep color

and endowed with a loosely parallel form,

I can get your eye to say not just "metal" and "fake"

but "conifer"; it can't help itself. Think of me

as a gesture of respect

for the order being violated:

not derisive, but elegiac.

Every now and then in my retirement I will probably write something, and in any case I will always be a reader for former students or other writers who still want to make use of me in that way. So, as an economical symbol of things having to do with writing, my third tattoo might be a semicolon.

And unless it is to be somehow an engraved photo of my wife and my daughter, or a larger series of images on my chest that includes both my family and pictures of friends, then the fourth tattoo should be a catbird or a cardinal. These perky birds live in the trees and shrubs around our yard and entertain us with their posturing and their inimitable singing. In the margin (of whatever size) that I have now, I will do more birding and kayaking than when I was teaching. So here's another poem, perhaps a prophetic one:

BIRDING IN WINTER

This year the Christmas count takes place in wind

below zero. We huddle on the dunes

in our hoods and parkas, then do what we can

from the car. Bless the waterfowl for being

big: the loons and mergansers, herring gulls

and black-backs are unmistakable even

through a windshield at close to a hundred yards.

Before lunch we shame ourselves into action:

we will check for songbirds in the frozen

junipers and along the wood's edge beyond

the friendly road. Ice forms on our lashes;

our sniffles stand in for the notes and calls

we imagine in the deserted branches.

As we grow anxious about frostbite and begin

to doubt our sanity, a noiseless mockingbird

flies past and away from us. Did it follow

us here from its haunts near the house, mocking

all the way? We shrug and add it to the list.

We are ready to celebrate doves

and house sparrows, to enumerate starlings.

The other teams have been braver, done better:

Nashville, kestrel, dunlin. We buy coffee

and imagine next year.

TATIANA WATERMAN
To Make a Self

October 16, 2008

A physicist giving a meditation — you should probably ask for your money back now. If you'd rather stay, I'll speak about language, poetry and identity.

Statisticians tell us, in a *Time* magazine survey, that the first five questions one has in mind upon meeting a stranger, ranked in order of frequency, are: name, age, occupation (i.e., money), family status (married, children) and place of residence. Place of origin ranks about 10th. In polite company, age, money and family status, if not broadcast outright, are ferreted out during the first five minutes of the interaction.

When people first meet me, they can make a reasonable guess at my age, and then after I speak a few words they notice my accent. I play this little game with myself: "How many seconds, rather than minutes, will it take for the below-10th-ranked question to be asked?" The question usually comes as soon as I utter my first complete sentence: "You have an accent. Where do you come from?"

Tatiana Waterman teaches in the Science Department. She came to Exeter in 2004.

For a while I was not sure if this should bother me — since there are two kinds of curiosity, and I always allow for the benefit of the doubt on the good side.

When I was younger, I would get angry when such a question entered the initial give-and-take with a stranger. The reason was not just personal annoyance. My best college friend, 10 times smarter than I am, was repeatedly dismissed as not very bright because she has a Southern accent; my first-ranked physics classmate in college did not land his dream job because of his heavy Staten Island accent; my almost-last-ranked classmate got a leg up in the job market with his British accent, even though he lacked entirely too many skills. (His first employer had to let him go after a good amount of investment in his training. So did his second employer — justice served.) I would fume, and in my mind I'd scream silently about my friends' perfect-800 SAT scores and flawless syntax, calculus prizes and incredible creativity, or about idiocy or the accident of childhood residence. I'd get absolutely indignant at the injustice. What bothered me most was that stereotyping brought disadvantage to talented people — financial disadvantage on top of everything else; I cared about money then.

In moments when I sensed a bit of indifference or hostility from the person asking me "Where are you from?" I would answer coldly: "I have an accent in all three languages I speak. How many languages do you speak?" What did the offending stranger have to offer, to counteroffer — ha! But I was in my 20s then — young and rude. Now, older and mellower, I still ask what other languages does my new acquaintance speak, and if they don't speak the ones that simultaneously corrupted my language-making muscles when I was young, I offer them a $5 reward if they guess correctly, quite sure that they won't have the ear for this detective work. Invariably they guess Russian, from my first name. I have yet to lose a bet! (By the way, I know only four Russian words: *mir*/peace, *kneega*/book, *zemlia* /earth or place, and *spasiba*/thank you.) The ones whom I select for the $5 bet, and who take me up on my offer, belong to a stereotypical group — you can guess the characteristics of this group.

If physiology data are to be heeded, it is increasingly difficult to learn a language the older one gets. At the age of 30, I had no business starting to learn another language, but in order to impress my in-laws, I started learning Scottish Gaelic.

The truth is I had fallen in love with Gaelic when I first encountered it in the northwest of Scotland, in pubs, listening to its internal rhyming of poems and songs, without knowing what the meaning of a single word was — maybe that's why I was free to pay attention to its musicality.

My brain had filed away the sounds of fiddle, whistle, drum and clinking tableware at the pub; it had filed away the smells of salt air before ducking indoors to smell the peat fire; and it had filed away the taste of locally brewed stout (much different than the taste of the product bottled for shipping long distances). And so my brain retrieved these sensory memories from its crinkles involuntarily every time I'd listen to a Gaelic song or poem, no matter where I was. So, with my judgment and brain addled like this, I bought the best teach-yourself Gaelic course materials I could find, and started learning.

In addition to its musical flow of vowels in poems, the syntax of the language appealed to my physics brain. It was unlike anything my synapses had encountered in French, Greek or English. A syntax so ancient that its roots are lost in the linguistic paths that branch off from the first-generation Indo-European dialects. And every now and then, I would come across Gaelic words or roots that have the same meaning in Hebrew or Homeric Greek, and my heart would skip a beat. I was liking this as much as I like physics research: This language-learning was a time-travel detective tour; a supercollider of sorts that required very little to reach back in time.

My most memorable encounter with Gaelic did not happen in a pub, or listening to Sorley MacLean's poetry set to music, though. It came from lesson two, "common verbs," in my grammar book. To answer the question "What language do you speak?" you reply *Tha Gaidhlig agam.* "I have the Gaidhlig." Not "I speak" it — I "have" it. I was annoyed — the book came highly recommended and I had already found a mistake in it. Ugh! I had just learned the verbs "to be" and "to have" in chapter one, *and I* am an *A student.* I checked the dictionary. Perhaps there is a similar spelling of the verb that, inexperienced as I was, I took for "have." Nope! There was no doubt, the word was "have" and not "speak." And there followed another example: *Tha Sassuinach agam.* "I have the English." "Awe ... how quaint," I thought, remembering what language teachers always insist upon: that language reflects culture. Language is to be had inside the speaker. Two lines later, sure enough, there was the word for "to talk" (*bruinn*) — the making of sounds with the mouth — and the verb "to say" (*abair*) — the conveying of information with language.

A few lines later there was another surprise: different verbs to ask about origin precisely, for the different degrees of depth of information (where were you born, where do you reside). This needed cultural explanation. Indeed, explained the natives, the language reflects the people. You may not stay in the place where you were born, because there is no prospect for making a living there. So you may say where you were born, or where you reside long term. *Ruchag mi as ann Glascho, ach fuirich mi as ann Chanada.* "I am a Glasgowegian by birth, but a Canadian by residence." Precise coordinates and involvement: born in one place, but living long-term in another. These shades of meaning have evolved in the language to tell about local influence; about upbringing; about uprooting; about the heartache of immigration as part of the culture.

But the one phrase that had me mystified was *co leis?* "Whose are you?" Whose are you?! What?! I was more than puzzled, and a bit worried. In a place where everyone knows everyone else, and most people are part of the same extended family, this can cut both ways. If you come from a good father and mother, you are starting with good credit; if not, the dismissive *"Och, I kent yer faither"* can be a burden all your life.

From that moment on I started decoding under a new light the question that a stranger puts to me after detecting my accent. Does it matter where I was born? Where I lived the longest, where I had to move for a job? We do not have much choice where we are born, but we do make the decision to move, for education or work. What do these choices do *for* us? And what do they do *to* us? And what about "Whose am I?" — how do I answer this question for myself?

I am, of course, my ancestors'. My grandparents, by their example, left me a legacy of reaching out with love to others, no matter how hard the times; of commitment to social justice, at some cost to myself; and of forgiveness, in order to be whole. Like a "to do" list, they left me a "to respect" list. There are three items on it, with conditions: Have respect for intelligence only when it comes with humility; for wealth only when accompanied by charity; and for families who stay together through the generations, because it takes a lot of hard work to do so. They also left me a list of what to avoid: fights at all cost, and unscrupulous people, lest their ways rub off on me. And a list of what to seek: the small pleasures of simple meals with friends; song and dance; spontaneous, unplanned searching for joy in nature.

More immediately, I am my mother's and my father's, with modifications. My mother likes pretty things and security. I do, too, but I would not sacrifice time and energy to possess pretty things. And I am willing to give up security if there is a reasonable prospect for exciting changes; security could be boring.

From my father I inherited the love of baseball and math, music and literature.

I am also my colleagues' and my students' — their actions, of kindness, of courage, and of giving, rub off on me by our association, and influence me as I reflect on their gifts, and as I analyze my shortcomings.

So in this sense the answer to "Where do I come from?" is certainly not a dot on the map. I come from certain people and their influences.

But that's half the answer to the question "Whose am I?" and, by extension, to the question "What is a self?" and "how I made mine." The other half of the answer is: I am also of literature, of authors whose writing held a mirror to my changing self while their writing changed me. In stories and poems I found solace, inspiration, answers and, most important, *questions*; questions that the people around me did not offer me because they could not — they did not have the talent or the intelligence to do so. Like a parent, literature nurtured me and loved me. Like a young child taking from her parents, I am forever the one-sided taker, not expected to give back anything in return.

Yet, the dot on the map does have something to do with the making of my self.

A week after my sixth birthday, I saw tanks rolling on the street by our house in Greece. It wasn't a celebratory parade. A military coup gripped the life of the country for the next seven years. Many books came off the shelves and were hidden in boxes in the attic — and even that was dangerous; they were not quite burned as in the Middle Ages, but close enough. One did not discuss these books, for fear of being branded unfriendly to the government. They were classics and quite innocent books of fiction, love stories and travelogues; telling about the islands, the sea and the sunlight of the Mediterranean. There was nothing revolutionary in them — just love of nature and the pleasures of life. The travelogues of Kazantzakis about England, Egypt and China were my favorite. I could not figure out why they were dangerous. My father explained simply that when people are reminded of free travel and happy times, they start desiring them, and start realizing that their condition is not so good, and might want to change it. Instead of stuffed animals, my father would stash a forbidden book by my pillow for bedtime reading.

Music of certain composers was prohibited — songs with lyrics by Nobel Prize-winning poets. Poets who celebrated nature, life and liberty, but not quite the pursuit of happiness. No one does laments better than the Greeks. Perched at the crossroads of invaders from every direction, and on infertile soil, the Greeks know a thing or two about misery and death — and they celebrate it ... with song.

The song we heard a few minutes ago would have landed us in the local police station for interrogation. Even though it just talks about a mother's memory of her absent boy — immigrant, dead or in jail, we don't know, it doesn't say — the generals wouldn't want this notion to linger in our minds. There were too many jailed and missing sons. Freethinkers were a danger to the ruling junta. In the place where democracy was born, the country went silent — fear, the need for survival and forgiven bank loans, if you voted for the generals to stay in power (with money from foreign aid in the U.S. budget), were incentives enough for a submissive silence.

And from that incident in a country's history was born my love for freedom, a freedom guaranteed by laws and by a constitution. I did not have tugs of nostalgia in my heart to make me look back and be homesick for the place of my youth. Home became any place where I was free to think and talk, and felt secure in that freedom.

Books and music were my defiant way of making a self, just as I wanted it. I was lucky to learn about life and living through the poetry assignments of my American teachers, safely out of reach of government-issued curricula, in an American boarding school, in Greece. In poetry I would both lose and find the self I was slowly making. Poetry was the best redress for this only child; and literature became a self-therapeutic instrument in the hands of a headstrong girl in a male-dominated society.

"The nobility of poetry," says Wallace Stevens, "is the violence from within that protects us from a violence without. It is the imagination pressing back against the pressure of reality." My friends drove drunk; *my* reckless behavior was to read the forbidden books, and tell about it. And to blast the forbidden music, in my room, with headphones on ...

The poem "Meadowsweet," by Kathleen Jamie — a Scottish poet who is exactly my age — summarizes the role that poetry played for me in my making of a self, while I was growing up.

MEADOWSWEET[1]

Tradition suggests that certain of the Gaelic women poets were buried face down.

So they buried her and turned home,

a drab psalm

hanging about them like haar*   (*Scots word for "thick fog")

not knowing the liquid

trickling from her lips

would seek its way down,

---

[1] As Kathleen Jamie explained in a reading of her poem, meadowsweet is a cream-colored wildflower, which is the symbol of love and marriage in Ireland — good looks, but acrid smell ...

and that caught in her slowly

unraveling plait of grey hair

were summer seeds:

meadowsweet,* bastard balm,*   (*common names of
                                  wildflowers)

tokens of honesty, already

beginning their crawl

toward light, so showing her,

when the time came,

how to dig herself out —

to surface and greet them,

mouth young, and full again

of dirt, and spit, and poetry.

So, where am I from? If home is the place where they have to take you in when you knock on the door, I am "from literature." And whose am I? "Of literature" again. Poetry gave me the material to make a self.

But how well-made and how bulletproof is this self when the question is asked about my accent?

What do we really want to know when we ask a stranger where they come from? Why do we ask? What does the tone of voice of the question do to one's psyche? To one's confidence?

Our reptilian brain certainly wants to classify friend or foe — same or different, for fight or flight. What about the finer details? What is it that we want to know about the stranger when we ask personal questions?

My nonscientific hypothesis is that we ask because we want to know if the other person is a kindred spirit. A dozen millennia ago, coming from the same place was probably enough to signal common traits, views and experiences, and possibly survival skills. If you came from a river valley, you probably were a useful addition to the village group, because surely you knew how to grow food. A mountain person might not be as useful, if hunting was not the mode of feeding the village. Well, these qualities aren't essential for belonging anymore; but the question, a caricature of stereotyping, still remains, still stamped in our brain, still valid in our soul. Are you like me? Can I trust you? Do we think alike? There is this bright moment of kinship when two strangers discover things they have in common. "Me, too!" is the eager, high-spirited, gleeful answer.

So when people ask me about my accent now, and where I am from, I try to suppress the "map" answer. I gauge the questioner, and I either offer the $5 bet, or I start talking about my favorite writers. That's what I would like to know in return about the new acquaintance — whose writings made the self of the person sitting across from me? Who are their favorite poets? Why? So I can share a "me, too" moment, and know that we indeed are from a common place, and put the reptilian part of my brain at ease.

I confess I am equally guilty of stereotyping, instinctively, for a few moments, when I first meet someone new. When I hear a Southern accent, I react automatically with a feeling of comfort, trust, and security, because when I first arrived in Virginia, in the '70s, it was that accent that welcomed me in the land of Jefferson (who, by the way, was a book lover with the biggest private library in his time). And I freely admit that when I arrive back from overseas travel, the announcer's voice at the airport, in perfect American English, reminding me not to leave my luggage unattended, fills me with the emotional security of freedom, guaranteed constitutionally, even though the announcement is about danger.

I am home.

Thank you for listening — or, in Greek: *Ευχαριστω που ηρθατε να μ' ακουσετε*. And in proper Gaedhlig: *Tapadh leat arson thig sibhse a-seo an-diu. Beannachd leat.* Thank you for coming today. A blessing with you.

TOM RAMSEY

January 22, 2009

Good morning, and thank you for coming.

The music this morning consists of two songs from the musical *Hello Dolly*, both of which also feature in the recent Disney-Pixar film *WALL-E*. The song you just heard is "Put on Your Sunday Clothes," a song that WALL-E replays for himself as part of his nightly robotic bedtime routine, and the concluding song will be "It Only Takes a Moment," which introduces the svelte space alien who is the robot WALL-E's love interest in the film, as well as WALL-E's dawning consciousness that he can change things in his postapocalyptic world.

Robots, moments of awareness and the possibility of renewal all have something to do with the theme of this talk. Space aliens, love interests and "Hello Dolly" unfortunately do not.

I wanted to do this meditation out of gratitude for the sabbatical I enjoyed last term. People tended to ask me two questions about my time off. When they asked me how it was *going*, I replied that whoever had come up with the idea of a sabbatical was a pure genius. It was several weeks before it hit me that of course it was *God* who came up with it. Exodus, chapter 20:

Tom Ramsey came to Phillips Exeter in 1998, having taught previously at Trinity School in New York City. A former dorm head and affiliate in Hoyt Hall, he teaches in the Religion Department, advises several clubs, and enjoys coaching club golf every spring.

"Six days you shall labor and on the seventh rest." That doesn't take away from the fact that the Academy is generous enough to provide faculty with the opportunity to actually do so on a regular basis.

When people asked me what I was *doing* on my sabbatical, my initial reply was usually "as little as possible." But when pressed for details, I quickly came up with a list that went like this: I was here on campus one day a week to attend fac/proc meetings and do dorm duty in Hoyt. I was in Cambridge two days a week visiting religion classes at Harvard. I made several trips to Maryland to visit my parents. I took a weeklong course in Barre, Massachusetts, about Buddhist psychology. I attended a conference in Chicago, and I did lots of reading and a little writing. At this point, everyone was generally satisfied, and we went on to talk of other things.

In the kinds of interactions we have here every day — with one another and indeed with ourselves — a shorthand list of activities is helpful. We want to know and we want others to know what we are doing. We become accustomed to identifying our activities, grouping them together into meaningful units, and tying them to a context and a purpose for easy communication. Over the course of the dozens of daily interactions we have with other people here at Exeter, this process of editing our experience becomes habitual.

Do you ever notice, however, that after just a day of answering the question, "How was your vacation?" your vacation has become that short list of activities, and the next thing you know it has simply disappeared? What happened to it? Where did it go? And how do we so quickly find ourselves once again in what my students call the Exeter bubble? Does it have something to do with that process of self-editing?

And then, once we *are* back in the bubble again, why is it so hard to recover the quality of that vacation or that three-month sabbatical? Is it ever possible, in the midst of what we are doing, to recover something of that vacation or sabbatical frame of mind — to live in a way that is continually renewed — or is it lost forever, at least until the next vacation?

To start, let me make a public confession, and in a school like Exeter, the church may be the only place where we can admit to a sin like this: During my sabbatical, there were times when I simply did nothing. In part, I'm referring to those hours I spent drinking coffee at Au Bon Pain in Cambridge, or those wonderful Monday mornings when I would retrieve the latest copy of *The New Yorker* from my P.O. and sit down and read it cover to cover. Now that's luxury. But that kind of thing is not outside the realm of what might be permitted on a sabbatical. So, I really mean to talk about two moments when I truly managed, and realized I'd managed, to do absolutely nothing. And after I tell you about them, we'll come back to the Exeter bubble — how we get into it, and how we might get out of it without actually taking a vacation.

Moment number one: the first week in November, somewhere in the woods of central Massachusetts, about 11 o'clock in the morning. I've been sitting for the last two hours in a lecture given by Andrew Olendzki, Ph.D., Harvard University, resident scholar at and director of the Barre Center for Buddhist Studies. This morning's topic: consciousness, as described in the earliest Buddhist texts of the Pali canon. Two hours of precise analysis of how the mind creates a sense of reality out of sensory and mental input, with contributing insights from contemporary neuroscience. It's time for a break. I stumble outside into the sunlight and make for a path I'd noticed earlier. It's a beautiful fall day. The broad path leads invitingly into the woods with a promise of legs stretching and mind relaxing.

I enter the path, stepping confidently over a few roots and stones, heading downhill along a low rock wall. Within minutes, however, the path turns, passing over the wall, which is now just a jumble of stones, and heading into what must have once been a meadow but is now a nest of thorns, sumac and high grass. I'm still stepping along, brushing aside grasses to see the path that disappears in mud under my feet, carefully holding aside long branches of thorns, ducking my head at the same time, my heart pounding a little with the sudden slowdown, my breathing quick but regular, a smile on my face at the recognition that my brisk walk has turned into a bit of a slog, and when I finally stop moving altogether — perfectly stuck, unable to do a thing — the recognition that I have not only been walking, ducking, breathing, smiling, but also that I am singing quietly to myself "Put on Your Sunday Clothes" from the musical *Hello Dolly*, while thinking to myself about the movie *WALL-E* and the part where the hero cheerfully hums that song as he goes about his daily robot routine. I had probably been singing to myself since I stepped outdoors.

It comes to me vividly at that moment of stillness, a certain insight I have had a few times before — an insight shaped and clarified by Andrew Olendzki, Ph.D. — that we are constantly busy, even, like WALL-E, robotically so. At every moment, our hearts are beating away, lungs breathing, blood circulating, nerves tingling, eyes seeing, ears hearing, nose smelling, neurons firing, vocal cords humming, mind thinking thoughts, and on and on — a continuous whir of simultaneous activity motivated by God-knows-what. We are hardly aware at a conscious level of almost any of this going on — how many of us are aware right now of sensations in our left foot? — and yet at certain moments — for example, when I mention the sensations in our left feet — we are suddenly aware of them. But when we are running around, going through our WALL-E-like days of activity, we're unaware. It is only when we stop — stuck in the bushes, sitting in silence, taking a sabbatical — that we see what is happening, that we begin to understand how constantly and continuously we construct our experience of the world.

Moment number two: an afternoon with Dr. Wilbur Ramsey, familiarly known as Webb. Dr. Ramsey was born in 1920. His father was a restless soul who moved from small town to small town in West Virginia, Pennsylvania and Maryland, and Webb attended 13 different elementary schools. When Webb was 16, the family moved to Towson, Maryland, near Baltimore, where Webb met and later married Virginia Haile, with whom he had four children. In the late 1930s times were hard, jobs scarce, but everyone at some point will need a dentist, so Webb cut back on the English literature classes he loved and enrolled in the dentistry program at the University of Maryland. After a stint in the Navy in World War II, Webb returned to teach at the university, where he became head of the department of prosthodontics. For the next 47 years, his days, evenings and Saturday mornings were spent at the dental school, where he taught and maintained a private practice, and gave free care to anyone who came in for help but could not afford to pay.

He kept working at the university well into his late 70s. When he retired, hundreds of his colleagues, students and patients showed up for his retirement party. Now in their late 80s, Dr. and Mrs. Ramsey live in an upscale retirement facility with independent-living apartments, assisted-living units, and skilled nursing and dementia wards.

When you visit Dr. Ramsey today, you will not find him in the apartment with Mrs. Ramsey. Instead, turn left in the lobby and go down the hall. You'll need to go through a door opened by a keypad. The floor is beautifully carpeted and the walls tastefully decorated — think Amen Hall with flowers and artwork. And, like Amen, each resident has a single room. Dr. Ramsey's room is at the end of the hall, near the nursing station. Like the other residents, his name is on a plaque on the wall beside his door. As you enter the room, you loudly call out his name or relationship to you, as the case may be — "Dr. Ramsey!" if you are a nurse or former student, "Webb!" if you're a friend or colleague, "Dad" or "Grandad" if you are one of us, his children or grandchildren. In any case, however, the answer you get back is the same — a playfully gruff reply — "Nobody here by that name."

He has always favored an understated kind of humor. A witty and well-read man — the only person I know who ever did a *New York Times* crossword puzzle in ink and only filling in the "Across" answers — he preferred the backwoods idiom of his childhood. After a meal at a roadside restaurant, for example, he often remarked about the food, "Well, it was mighty good, what there was of it; and there was plenty of it, such as it was." He also cherished the little classical learning he had; a sign on his door at the dental school was a Latin quotation: "*Omnia mutantur, nos et in illis mutamur.*" All things change and we change with them.

When the voice says, "Nobody here by that name," you go in anyway. Dr. Ramsey, Webb, Dad, Granddad, sits or lies on the bed. He sees you only as a shape and color, because macular degeneration has degraded his vision. You really have to speak up, because one or both of his hearing aids might not be properly inserted in his ears. He makes you feel welcome, though, no matter what your shape or color, and whether he's heard your name or not. He always responds to people cheerfully. It becomes clear after only a minute or two now that he probably doesn't know who you are — whether he hasn't heard your name in the first place or forgotten it subsequently, it doesn't matter.

I talk with him as long as he is willing and able. Usually he wants to lie down. His favorite nurse and I cajole him into taking a walk down the hall, which takes a while, and he needs to stop and rest. Other residents of the Alzheimer's wing are doing the same thing. They wave to us or not, say hello or not. Back on his feet, Dad moves down the hall. He peers at each plaque on the wall and asks, "Is this my room?" But when he reaches his room, he knows what to do, and makes for the bed. We sit there together for a while. I hold his hand. He lies down and takes a nap before dinner. Sometime in there, I leave.

Despite his hearing and vision loss, my dad is oriented to the space around him. What's disappearing with the progress of his dementia, however, is his orientation in time, and consequently, his sense of self. The two seem to be closely linked. A neurologist I heard this fall said that Alzheimer's particularly affects those areas of the brain that help us coordinate past, present and future, and with it our sense of a continuing self that endures throughout. My dad, in an important sense, is gone. He is losing the sense of self that is the basis for his identity, a sense of himself as something that persists in a story that links past to future. His greeting to us, "Nobody here by that name," is poignantly and ironically true. This is hard for everyone. We mourn for the self that he has lost, and to the extent that our own sense of ourselves is bound up with his knowledge of us, we mourn for our lost selves as well. "All things change and we change with them."

When I sit with my dad on the bed these days, there is an odd peace. It is a wonderful thing to sit with him, because there is no pressure to be or to do anything in particular. The days of living up to my dad's expectations are a distant memory. The future is radically uncertain. Without the momentum of the past or the urgency of the future, there is just an open space that is not unlike moments in meditation or intense athletic activity, or in singing or drawing or playing the piano, when the sense of yourself doing what you are doing gently fades, and the activity itself is just happening. It is as though, in the absence of past and future and the resulting emptiness of one's self, the present comes unmistakably alive.

These experiences and others like them this fall — those moments of not doing anything — helped me to understand ideas I was reading about.

During my sabbatical, I did not set out to read systematically — instead I read rather randomly: fiction, nonfiction, philosophy, religion, etc. But I found that much of what I was reading had something to do with the nature of consciousness — what it means to be a conscious person, with a sense of the world and of one's self. Moreover, I found a remarkable consensus about the nature of consciousness, whether I was reading postmodern philosophy, Buddhist psychology or popular neuroscience. That consensus, as I understand it, is that we human beings are as much agents of our reality as we are participants in it. We construct our reality more than we generally are aware of. Our *sense of a world outside of us* is a kind of construct made up of sensory experience shaped by our past and by our mental processing. So too, *our sense of being a self* distinct from others with a continuing story enduring through time is a construct. Both of these constructs, world and self, are extremely useful. Without them, we could hardly find our way out of bed in the morning, let alone play basketball, do calculus or have a conversation in the dorm.

At the same time, we can benefit by recognizing the constructed nature of our reality. It is easy, as we all know, to get lost in the Exeter bubble. This isn't *just* because Exeter is what sociologists call a total institution, where all our needs — for food, shelter, companionship, work and recreation — are met on one 640-acre campus. It is also because our mental worlds are like total institutions — even if we wanted to, we cannot get outside of our own sense of reality.

But what does seem to be possible, in my experience and in the experience of other people I know, have met or have heard about, is a kind of mental sabbatical. In moments of non-doing, even in the midst of the action of our lives, we can get a glimpse of how our reality is constructed. Life sometimes gives us such moments of insight whether we want them or not — moments when we find ourselves "in the zone" while playing a sport, or when we suddenly stop what we are doing for some reason. It also appears to be possible to seek out and to train ourselves to be more accommodating to such sabbatical moments. Maybe that is what happens when you pray or meditate — you are practicing opening yourself to such moments. Maybe that is why you come to Meditation in Phillips Church on Thursday mornings.

Finally, what is the value of a sabbatical, of those moments of not doing anything, or of our presence here today? I can only describe it as introducing the possibility of renewal. At the very least, you will leave this hall today somewhat refreshed, even if you only had a good snooze and a snack in the Stuckey room. We won't necessarily save the world as a result of our moments of non-doing, as WALL-E did as a consequence of his moment of awareness, but we are in a way renewing it. By undoing the activity of the world — however fleetingly — we open the possibility of beginning again as new people in a new reality.

Thank you, again.

LANE PERTUSI '09

Sparrows

May 29, 2009

"There is special providence in the fall of a sparrow." — *Hamlet,* 5.2.220

Rain runs down the window of the car I sit in. It is my eighth-grade year and we are driving to New Hampshire to visit a boarding school where I have been accepted. The highway looks like a mirror — greasy with rain. At the moment when we lose contact with the road, I will be thinking that in one single drop of water there may be one sextillion six hundred and seventy quintillion four hundred and six quadrillion forty-two trillion three hundred and two billion one hundred and fourteen million three thousand four hundred and two molecules. In one rainstorm there are millions upon millions of raindrops. These numbers are inconceivable to me. My family and I are listening to the third song of the second disc of *The Sopranos* soundtrack, speeding along at 60 miles per hour, blind to so many numbers.

Computers store digits in bits and bytes of data. This means that there is a limit on the magnitude of a number that a computer can hold. How does our brain, so much like a computer, ones and zeroes, neurons firing or

---

Lane Pertusi graduated from Exeter in 2009 and from MIT in 2013. He has worked at Pixar Animation Studios creating the backgrounds for feature films and is currently pursuing his MBA at Harvard Business School.

not firing, store data? Can numbers as large as the number of molecules in a drop of water even fit in their full form, without compression? And all these tiny pieces of our universe interact with everything else, creating an impossibly tangled web. The best we can hope for is to understand an infinitesimal fraction of the ways our world works.

So how can any of us possibly predict that on a rainy day in June, crossing the Tappan Zee Bridge in New York, one raindrop too many will land in a puddle under our tires instead of 2 feet to the left and lift our entire 3,000-pound car off the pavement? We will reconnect with the ground in time to avoid any accident, but how can any of us, looking at the undeveloped consequence of raindrops, comprehend the multitude of possibilities that barrage us every morning as we leave our front door?

It is a universal human need to have stability — the comfort of knowing that everything is taken care of. Yet we can never have true control over the unknown events even minutes or seconds into our future. So what can we do with this discomfort? How can we live, knowing that we are all hopelessly spinning out of control — our tires never touching the pavement?

The ancient Greeks answered this question with a body (well, technically three bodies). The Moirae, as they were called, were the personification of fate. They were three sisters, spinning and weaving and cutting the thread of life. Clotho was the youngest sister and spinner of the thread, Lachesis was the middle sister and measurer of the thread, and Atropos was the oldest sister and cutter of the thread. These sisters controlled what the gods could not, the small details of our circumstance, life and death. It was they who decided where that drop of water would land.

Too bad I wasn't born back then — it would be so nice to have three sisters to blame. Lately, I can't stop thinking about fate. I can't accept that there is a predetermined path that I will follow through life. How can I deal with the inconceivable probabilities and the magnitude of the universe we exist in? How can any of us deal with this? Some of us believe in the welcoming idea and guiding force of God. It is so nice to think that someone out there has a plan for us. Yet this can't answer my questions. I cannot have faith without answers. Others give in to fate. We allow the bones to fall where they may.

Recently, I watched the movies *Magnolia* and *Slumdog Millionaire*. At the beginning of *Magnolia* the narrator tells three short stories about chance and fate. He begins the movie with the story of three men who kill a pharmacist in Greenberry Hill, London. Their names were Joseph Green, Stanley Berry and Daniel Hill. *Green, Berry, Hill.* Coincidence? He goes on to tell two more stories, each more unlikely and convoluted than the last, ending with a scuba diver stuck in a tree and a son shot by his own mother while attempting suicide by jumping. I feel like my life is often like that first scene in *Magnolia*. I feel like that narrator, trying to explain events with chance and failing because some "coincidences" are just too weird.

In *Slumdog* a boy from the slums of Bombay is destined to win the game show "Who Wants to Be a Millionaire," and his whole life he experiences things that give him the answers to all the questions. So where do I find my answers?

There is no fate in chess. On the epic eight-by-eight field of squares, I can forge my own destiny. I can bend things to my will. If I lose, it is for no reason other than my actions. If I make a bad move, it is because I wasn't paying attention or thinking hard enough. There is no luck to blame — no power other than my own mind to pray to — or at least that's what I used to tell myself. Of course, there is another factor involved: my opponent. Once I make a move, I feel helpless. I have no control over the person across from me. The only comfort I can take is that I can stop my adversary from breaking the rules — there is a set of possible moves, and he or she cannot stray from this list.

In the archaic (almost mystic) world of chess theory, there are always new terms to stumble on. For pawns alone there are innumerable classifications: wrong rook pawns, backward pawns, isolated pawns, doubled pawns, passed pawns, connected pawns, en passant pawns, pawns, pawns, pawns. In chess I know the rules. In real life, sometimes it feels like there are no rules to follow or terms to articulate our choices.

In medieval times, each of the eight pawns was given a different character. From the right side of the board to the left, they were: the Farmer, the Blacksmith, the Clerk, the Doctor, the Merchant, the Innkeeper, the City Guard, and the Gambler — because of the sinister nature of a gambler. The word sinister comes from the Latin word for "left-handedness." I am left-handed, and I often wonder what would have happened if I had been alive back then. Would I have been considered sinister for my left-handedness? More likely I would have been able to hide my sinister nature since I probably wouldn't have been able to write. Sometimes I wonder why I was born in 1990, and not in ancient Rome. I would have fit so much better there. I would have had the comfort of believing in the fates without question.

The ancient Romans had a strict code for living life, and I too have powerful moral rules I follow in my life. I, like the Romans, vainly try to impose my rules on the world. When I see a person break my moral code, and say, cheat on a girlfriend, my reaction is extreme. I want to make this person see things my way, which is really what the Romans were doing when they conquered civilization after civilization. However, I realize that had I been born then, I wouldn't be the same person at all genetically. The only way to create my genes is to have my exact two parents and their parents and their parents and their parents. This leads to the clear conclusion that all of history's sole purpose is to evolve and create me. Just kidding.

I was born to two loving kind parents in New York. The youngest of the Fates, Clotho, spools out the thread of all our lives onto her spindle, and when she spooled out mine, she decided that I would be special. Or maybe lucky. That's the thing about fate; it's discriminating. Why is any one human more deserving of good or special or lucky things than another?

When I was in elementary school and we did group projects, I used to do all the work. I didn't mind at all because it was easy and it meant that we got an A. The other kids didn't mind either, for the same reasons. I often wondered why I could do all the work with less effort and in less time and come out with a better product. The reason, I was told by parents and teachers, was because I was special — my genes said so. My grandfather was a chemist who invented flat-screen TVs, LCDs and computer monitors. My aunt is an amazing portrait artist. My father is a math professor, and my mother is a graphic design genius. The list goes on for every member of my family tree. And yet, I share half my DNA with my sister, and our talents are incredibly different. She can type 100 words per minute and has prodigious social skills, and I can write an entire software application in a night. Why am I doing college-level math while my sister struggles with precalculus? Does my destiny need numbers more than hers?

The problem with calling someone special is that, as cheesy as it sounds, everyone is special. Every person has a series of traits that sets him or her apart from others. Some people can write with their toes. Some people can blow glass. Some people can donate universal blood. Some people can get sunburned. Some people can lick their elbows, and some people can translate Russian. However, we value some characteristics more than others, and when people with smarts or looks are considered "lucky," we find ourselves blaming fate for traits that really are only "good" or "bad" because we decide they are.

Nevertheless, I often fall into the trap of looking at the world through a fate-driven lens, as if every socially accepted characteristic I have and every unlikely event in my life occurred for my benefit alone. As arrogant as it sounds, when the power went out in New Hampshire during finals this fall, it felt as if the Fates had done it all just for me. Because of the outage I got an automatic 100 on what would otherwise have been an extremely difficult genetics test, and got to work on my English final from my bed at home. Yet with 250,000 homes without heat or power, why should I benefit? What makes me so special?

Some people believe that karma evens out the discrepancies, but in my experience the Fates have no qualms about giving one person everything and taking it all from another. I have lived a blessed life to this point. The probability of my life unfolding as it has is incomprehensibly small.

Providence, Rhode Island. November 2001. We are walking. I can see my breath, and my fingers feel swollen from the cold. My parents are taking my sister and me house-shopping, despite our expressed opinion that we should not move. The sun reflects off the dirty snow and the brick, giving everything a pinkish-red color. In a couple moments I will notice something moving, and run down an alley into a parking lot to investigate. Above a snow bank, I will see a $10 bill spinning in circles caught in a draft of wind. I will catch it and be the happiest and richest boy in the world for a time. Why was I able to find that money? Because I was walking down that street at that moment in Providence, Rhode Island. Why was I in Providence? House-shopping. Why were we house shopping? Because my father had escaped 9/11 and wanted to get away from New York.

On September 11, 2001, my father had a meeting at 8:30 a.m. in the north tower of the World Trade Center on the top floor. Fortunately, he was busy that day, and decided that he couldn't afford to spare the time. He didn't go to the meeting, and at 8:45 a plane crashed into the tower. No one at the meeting survived. He walked from his building across the street to Grand Central, watching people jump from windows. I remember coming home from the bus stop and seeing my dad standing in the front door waiting for me. He was home before I was. Of course, I didn't know it then, but he had narrowly avoided death that day. His close brush was too much for him to continue working in New York, so we went house-shopping in Providence, and I found a $10 bill. Perhaps, Lachesis, the Apportioner, had measured the thread of my father with her rod and decided that he had more thread left.

Often, chess literature refers to "pawns" and then "pieces," meaning everything else. Sometimes, usually when I'm fighting with my parents, I feel more like the wrong rook pawn. I'm not sure I can win the fight, so I just guarantee a draw.

I almost never reach the end game with my queen intact. By this point I have usually traded her away for some fleeting idea of a trap that fails. Often when I fight, I do the same thing. I get fed up with the argument and try to end it in a swift coup d'etat, which typically ends up hurting me in the long run.

When I win a game of chess, there is no external reaction. I shake my opponent's hand calmly, stand, turn and walk away to wait for my next match. Internally, when I see my imminent win approaching, my insides twist into all sorts of shapes. When my opponent's finger presses into the doomed king's head and he falls face-first onto the cold, hard board, my stomach relaxes and I feel a chemical rush of pleasure.

When I was younger, I used to play competitive chess. I can still conjure the feelings of anticipation before a tournament, the dry, clean smell of the hallway outside a banquet room, the smooth feeling of the wall where it meets the rough stubble of the carpet.

On tournament day, everything goes in slow motion. I wonder if I am actually walking slowly as I make my way to my table. The board is cool and rough and smooth between my fingers. I set up the pieces on both sides without thinking about it. Mechanical. Instinctual. I don't think about winning. I don't think about losing. I think about my dad sitting in a chair in the hall, reading a math book. I think about the light that needs to be replaced above my opponent's head.

When I lose a game of chess I tell myself I did my best. I tell myself that I couldn't have won. Yet I know the mistakes I made. I know how I could have fixed them. There is no fate to blame.

In the fall of 2006, I walked out of my dorm, Wentworth, to find an ambulance in the path, in front of my neighboring dorm, Webster South. I remember laughing to myself, thinking of what could have happened in Webster to require an ambulance. I thought of my good friend Francis Patrick Logan (known as Pat), imagining in my head different things that he could have done to hurt himself. "I'm sure it's a funny story," I thought to myself and kept walking. I saw one of my other friends from Webster soon after and asked him about it. He said that he also thought that it might have to do with Pat and I had another laugh. When he said it might be serious, I stopped laughing — but I never would have guessed the truth of what had happened.

Pat was invincible to me. He was the kid who had tripped trying to jump on his skateboard off four flights of stairs, and when he hit the last step (after hitting every one before it), he stood up laughing and skated off the steps again. He was the kid who broke his arm jumping off the top bunk of a bed trying to land on someone and missing his target. When we had an emergency assembly, however, I immediately knew that he was dead. I don't know how I knew, but as I walked through those doors to the dark assembly hall, I knew without a doubt the truth. I already knew exactly what words our principal would use, and in what order he would say them. As he spoke at the podium, I mouthed his words silently with him.

"Last night Francis Patrick Logan died in his sleep."

Later we would learn that he died in his sleep of heart failure due to a congenital heart defect. The condition had existed from birth and no one had found it until it was way too late. It felt as if he was meant to die at that moment. It was predetermined. His heart was only meant to beat for 16 years. Beat 605,905,920 times. And when those heartbeats had passed, Atropos, "the inflexible," cut his thread with her "abhorred shears." The Moirae were always portrayed as cold, remorseless and emotionless. These characteristics make a lot of sense for fate. With any caring fiber in their beings, how could they take Pat Logan from this world at age 16? He was one of the happiest, nicest, funniest people I have ever known, and he died before he even finished high school.

There are few scenes in literature so poignant for me as when Hamlet speaks to Horatio before the gruesome final moments of the play. Hamlet has surrendered himself to whatever may happen. If it is his time to die, then he will die. If not, then he won't. No matter what, he tells his one true confidant, he is ready. *"There is special providence in the fall of a sparrow,"* he says, echoing the Bible's discussion of fate. I take heart from this scene. I can live with my questions when I hear these words. When Hamlet says, "Let be," I breathe a sigh of relief and stop questioning for a moment.

Sometimes, on the short walk from my room to the dining hall, I stop by the library. I walk, or sometimes take the elevator, to a random floor, find a random stack, pick a random shelf, and pull off a random book. Of course, it isn't really random, is it? I pick this book, but I pretend it wasn't my choice, and I open it to a random page. There I shove in a small index card on which I have written a few words, every time a slight variation on a theme. "I wonder who will read this," I write, or "What's your name?" or "Who are you?" or even "Can I have your number?" I feel a connection through time with a person who, days or weeks or months or years from now, will open to this page. They will see a flash of white as my card falls out of the book, and they will pick it up to read my words. Perhaps they will wonder for a moment about the person who wrote them. I feel myself grasping forward and seizing another person on the other side. Now that it is written, who will read it? I wonder if it has already been decided.

Where is my stability? Where is my comfort? I realize now that I can't know the answer. I am still in flux between demanding answers and living with uncertainty, but I feel less blind now. So, I will never return to check the book. To find out if someone wrote back.

I don't need to know now.

Recently, I watched a sparrow hop along the fence, chirping sweet reverie. I look at my faint reflection in the window. It is a ghost — an echo — a photocopy of me. The sun hits my eyes and I lose sight of it for a moment. In a couple seconds I will turn around and walk to the couch to take a nap. When I fall asleep I will dream; in the moment, in this present.

In my dream, the beach goes on forever in both directions. The boy sits in the sand. His feet are buried. The water runs over and over and over them again. He is timeless. Innocent. He has done nothing. He only sits and watches. He is forever young, yet his eyes hold the calamity of so long life. He has seen countless others walk down the sand — countless shadows walk into the sea. I want to speak to him, but I don't know how to start the conversation. So he does:

"What are you waiting for?" he asks me, and I tell him, "I don't know."

He picks up a fistful of sand, and says, "Here. Here is this moment. Hurry up — take it."

And then he drops it, letting it stream out between his fingers.

"Too late," he says.

I can't help but laugh.

"What's so funny? I'm serious!" he exclaims.

His indignation brings out the child in him. I tell him that we are all just shadows walking out to sea. He's angry now.

"You'd better get moving — wouldn't want to get stuck here," he tells me, and I tell him that I know who he is.

"You are Father Time," I say.

His eyes soften as if the sound of his name brings back memories from long ago.

"You know I don't know the Moirae, right?" he says, and I tell him that I know.

I continue my walk down the beach, and when I turn around again the boy is gone. Far out over the sea a sparrow falls into the water.

TONY DOWNER '75

Why I Say "Thank You"

October 22, 2009

Nick arrived at Langdell in September 1972. From his Long Island home, his parents — Alfred Gwynne Vanderbilt and Jean Harvey Vanderbilt — may have driven him up, or he may have flown to school, or he may have been chauffered. Alfred's great-great-grandfather, Cornelius Vanderbilt, had founded the family fortune built around shipping and the New York Central Railroad. Alfred's father — also named Alfred Gwynn — perished upon the sinking of the *Lusitania* when he heroically gave his seat in the lifeboat to a female passenger; the next day's *New York Times* front-page headline read:

LUSITANIA SUNK BY A SUBMARINE, PROBABLY 1,260 DEAD

***

FROHMAN AND VANDERBILT MISSING

As a young man, Nick's father had been named America's most eligible bachelor by *Life* magazine. He developed a passion for horse racing — acquiring Pimlico Race Course in his 20s, subsequently organizing Sea

---

John A. "Tony" Downer graduated from PEA in 1975, and has served as an Academy Trustee from 2006-2010 and from 2011 to the present; he is currently president of the Trustees. He earned his BA, JD and MBA from Harvard.

Biscuit's match race against War Admiral, and in the 1950s owning Native Dancer, the two time Horse of the Year, who won every race he entered except the Kentucky Derby, which he lost by a head, having been bumped badly out of the starting gate.

Nick's mother had her own pedigree. Her family, the Harveys, was renowned for owning a Midwest restaurant chain that served as the setting for the Judy Garland film *The Harvey Girls* (Alfred had his own Judy Garland connection, having visited the set of *The Wizard of Oz* during its filming).

St. Paul's had been the family's secondary school of choice, but Nick was drawn to Exeter's academic rigor, so there he was in Langdell, his stereo set up, his bed adorned with his comforter and pillows from home, and on his wall, the racing blanket from one of Native Dancer's victorious descendants.

***

Amy arrived at Bancroft the same day. Her parents — Bit Yui Chan and Haun Kee Chan — drove her up from their rented apartment in Stamford, Connecticut. To do so, her mother had to take time off from her job as a cleaning lady at Stamford Hospital and her father from his job as a night janitor at a local factory. Amy's parents had been born and raised in the Fujian province in southern China. Education for both of them had ended early — he had attended high school and she left after the sixth grade. Later, the Japanese occupation and then the Communist Revolution took away everything they had. Married, they fled separately to Hong Kong — Amy's mother making the harrowing trip with her two infant children in an open-air boat. Reunited in Hong Kong, the couple had two more children, including Amy, the youngest, but life never got easy. At one point, the parents and the four children lived in a two-bedroom apartment, an apartment they shared at the time with their landlord's family. In the early 1960s, an uncle had skipped ship from a Chinese merchant marine vessel when it was docked at New York, and after years of sending checks to Amy's parents in Hong Kong, he sponsored their immigration to the United States. Met when they landed in California by a distant relative, the family spent its first day in America touring Disneyland, with Amy riding bug-eyed over and over again through the "It's a Small World" attraction. Ten years old at the time, Amy enrolled in the Stamford, Connecticut, public school system with an English vocabulary numbered in the dozens of words. As a seventh-grader, her teacher introduced her to Horizons, a free-of-charge summer student-enrichment program hosted by the New Canaan Country School, established to provide local low-income children with academic bolstering (and teach them to swim as well). At the end of her summer there, the Country School headmaster informed her that the school had awarded her a full scholarship to enroll there that fall, thereby doubling the school's minority population. During ninth grade, she applied to an array of all-girls boarding schools and was awaiting their response, when her older brother, enrolled at Cooper Union, a tuition-free college, asked the question, "What about Exeter?" No one in the family had ever seen the place, but the brother had read that it was the top school in the country and it had very recently gone coed. There was a problem — the application deadline had long passed. But Amy submitted her application, and as Exeter has done again and again, the Academy took the time to review her candidacy and not only said "yes," but provided her a full scholarship.

So there she sat in Bancroft, at a school she first laid eyes on that day, far from home, removed from the familiarity of the Chinese language, culture and food of her home, alone, with only a single yellow trunk that held all her belongings. That night she cried herself to sleep.

***

Outside of his room, he was just "Nick," a somewhat shy, completely unaffected young boy who quickly befriended (and earned the respect of) schoolmates ranging from members of the briefcase gang to the rogue seniors on his hallway who would often ask if they could hide their drugs in his room because they knew that Nick, as the straightest of straight arrows, would never have his room searched by the faculty. "Wicked smart," it took Nick a semester to decode the Exeter academic formula, but once he did, look out. In an era in which B+'s were a cherished and rare accomplishment, Nick earned A's in Spanish, A's in Physics, A's in English, A's in Math — across the board, in advanced classes, not effortlessly — make no mistake, Nick worked very hard — but he was by no means a grind (later, when asked in college, why he devoted more time to solving the Sunday *New York Times* crossword puzzle than he did to most of his Harvard courses, he replied, "At Exeter, I proved to myself that I was a good student. I don't need to prove that to myself again.")

More important, at Exeter, Nick discovered two passions — creative writing and mountain climbing. Challenged by the boot camp that was the English Department, Nick responded to his teacher's critiques by finding he loved honing the craft of expressing his thoughts through the written word. He established his own voice, his own style, and at its heart was his incredible sense of humor. He possessed a wit — a blend of his extraordinary intelligence, vocabulary and an ability to conjure a smile out of everyday moments. His humor never came at someone's expense — it never possessed an edge or malicious ingredient. It simply invited you to laugh along as he pointed out one of the countless absurd aspects of life.

In a way, Nick's mountain climbing also sprang from the English Department. Not a conventional athlete, Nick opted to participate in the Outdoor Challenge program, and there, he discovered that he had a real talent for getting over or around obstacles that thwarted others. And he loved it. He loved the fresh air, the intimate contact with nature, the cerebral process of selecting the correct route and the sense of fulfillment that comes from completing something difficult. And that love drew him to Mr. Bates, the English teacher who was, on the side, one of America's legendary and most accomplished mountaineers. Bob Bates introduced Nick to the world of Alpine climbing and inspired him to see how far and how high he could go.

***

For Amy, Exeter was a journey of nonstop discovery. Having never been away from home, having never been immersed in an English-language environment, and having never lived with Caucasians, even the smallest details of everyday life there contained an ingredient of novelty. Speaking around the Harkness table and writing paper after paper after paper pressured her language skills to a degree that her American classmates, who themselves were extremely challenged by the curriculum, could not begin to imagine. Eating habits, dressing habits, establishing friendships with Wendy, or Sally, or Billy, or Freddy — all of these routine occurrences were anything but for Amy as she adapted to her new world. Two Chinese Americans quickly bonded with her, providing her the social support from which her confidence grew, and on the athletic field, her speed and her competitive determination secured her a starting varsity spot season after season. By graduation, the Chinese girl in whom Mr. Brownell and the Admissions Committee saw a seed of promise had become an Exonian who had earned a full scholarship to Princeton.

***

I reached for a coin in my pocket, and looking across the restaurant table, I said to Amy, "If it's heads, the first one will be named Nicholas."

***

Less than three years earlier, on a cool October evening, I had sat down at a vacant broker's desk at the Boston offices of Kidder Peabody and started to call the classmates assigned to me at our class's 10th-reunion PEA phonathon. After a dozen or so calls, at the top of the pile rose the solicitation card for Amy Chan. Mother Exeter was counting on her support, and my duty was to be the conveyor of that message. Amy had just stepped into her New York apartment, and this being before the days of caller ID, she answered the phone. She humored me by pretending to remember who I was. Our paths had hardly crossed at all in our three years at the Academy together — I remember a horrifically awkward dance on the second floor of the Davis Student Center, but mercifully, she did not. We quickly found ourselves in an animated conversation about the relative merits of New York (where she was working) versus Boston (where I was based). I confess that I never quite got around to asking her for a contribution, but she did sign off by saying if I was ever in New York, to look her up. To her shock, I did. And six and a half weeks from that night, I asked her to marry me. Five minutes later, having caught her breath, she said, "Yes."

***

So there we sat, in a Washington, D.C., restaurant, nervously thinking about the next day. We had received such happy news months before: "Here's a little baby," the ultrasound technician exclaimed as she shifted the wand around, "and here's another little baby."

"You can stop now," I said to myself as Amy and I absorbed the unexpected excitement of finding out that she was carrying twins. But very shortly thereafter, the doctor sat us down. The twins were monoamniotic — the one in 90,000 pregnancies in which a fertilized egg splits sufficiently late in its gestation that the identical twins share a single amniotic sack.

Unprotected from each other, and in constant contact with each other, in half of such pregnancies, one or both twins perish, as umbilical cords get knotted up or wrapped around each other's throats. From the 28th week on, the doctors advised us that, so long as their lungs had sufficiently matured, the boys would have a better chance of making it if they were out of the womb than they would by staying in it. For each of the past three weeks, Amy had undergone an amniocentesis to determine if their lungs had become viable, and that morning we received the word that they had. The next day, 32 weeks into her pregnancy, she would have a Caesarean section and our little men would take their chances out on their own.

I flipped the coin.

***

Nick and I shared a single room in Langdell my senior year, that horse blanket still over his bed, a tattered poster of the Marx brothers over mine. I studied in England the next year, and in the spring he came over to visit, and when I finished my last exam I flew straight to Denver, where he was waiting for me with his Volkswagon Dasher. It was a five-speed. I had never driven a stick, and for the next nine weeks, the two of us drove from Denver to Fairbanks, to Los Angeles, to New York and to Cambridge. Thirteen thousand miles. We were together at all times. We never came close to killing each other, even though I came close to destroying his transmission. We navigated the entire route without ever getting lost — until we arrived in Cambridge, searching for our freshman dorm. After circling Harvard Square three times with no success, we abandoned the car and hiked in for the final leg.

We then roomed all four years in college together, and in college, the passions that Nick had developed at Exeter blossomed. While his degree requirements obliged him to take courses in an array of disciplines,

Nick never missed a chance to further his skills as a humorist. In his introductory economics class, Nick came to suspect that his teacher's check marks on his homework assignments were purely perfunctory, so he decided to test that suspicion. To one question he answered, "Price gets determined when the marginal cost — your mother wears army boots — equals the marginal demand," and to another he wrote, "The supply curve shifts out whenever your mother swims after troop ships." Sure enough, the instructor uncritically checked off the army boots, but to Nick's surprise, the instructor put a question mark by the troop ships, though he provided no further comment.

Nick concentrated his love of writing into winning the annual competition for scripting the college's Hasty Pudding theatrical production. Collaborating with Caroline Franklin, Nick and Caroline won the competition in his junior year with a script entitled "Overtures in Asia Minor," a musical epitomized by the complaint of the "female" lead, "Oh, here I sit like so much cheese, and I camembert it any longer."

Nick's climbing career likewise took off. On weekends he lead rock-climbing excursions up the Quincy Quarries and the Shawangunks and during the winter, he would take on the ice of Tuckerman Ravine. His devotion to the sport, his technical skills and congenial personality earned him the presidency of the Harvard Mountaineering Club, once the domain of Bob Bates and Brad Washburn. Combining his love of climbing with his pursuit of a smile, on Halloween night, Nick would scale the exterior of Memorial Hall to hang pumpkins from the gargoyles' mouths, descending one year to discover, to his relief, that the policeman waiting for him on the ground possessed a sense of humor.

***

The coin settled in my hand. "Heads." How fitting.

After graduation, Nick and I each pursued our own paths into the world. He found Christ and journeyed down to Texas to write, while I went west to work for a bank before enrolling in grad school. But despite that divergence, our friendship remained the greatest constant and strongest relationship in our lives. We enjoyed and genuinely appreciated each other other's company. We cared deeply about each other's challenges and triumphs, listened thoughtfully to what was on each other's mind, and never lost the ability to make each other laugh.

We talked several times a week, and continuing a custom that had started several years before at Exeter, we took our vacations together. But in the summer of 1984, a summit beckoned Nick. Mt. Robson, the highest point in the Canadian Rockies, had tantalized Nick since the day we had driven past it on our way to Alaska. My suggestion of joining me on a trip to Japan could not deflect his determination, and he and a Harvard climbing buddy, Francis Gledhill, set off in August. They made great progress, ascending smoothly to the Ralph Forester Hut, situated 5,000 feet from the base. A snowstorm sealed them inside for a couple of days, but when the weather broke, they left at dawn to scale the Wishbone Ridge for the 2,000-foot climb to the summit.

***

The doctor reached in and pulled Nicholas Chan Downer into this world, his shrill cries indicating that his lungs were indeed working. Less than a minute later, his identical twin brother —Christopher Choi Downer — joined the chorus. Eighteen years later, they would replicate that sequence. With the Yale Cup they had just won perched on their seats, Nick climbed the steps to receive an Exeter diploma, with Chris right behind him — but in a move that evoked his namesake, Nick and Chris had switched places, with Nick shaking an unsuspecting Principal

Tingley's hand as he accepted Chris' sheepskin, while Chris waited straight-faced to pick up Nick's. Their younger sister, Caroline, a rising senior in the audience, detected the prank, but she would have to wait a year before collecting her own diploma on that stage.

***

In the meantime, Amy's journey had circled back to her past. The immigrant Horizon's kid returned to the program, chairing its board and, later, heading the program's national initiative. Similarly, the Country School's scholarship child served as a trustee for eight years, and in a single generation, the daughter of the maternity-ward cleaning lady commanded a seat on Stamford Hospital's board.

***

I like to think that Nick and Francis made it to the top. They were last seen on the ice face just short of the summit before a storm struck the mountaintop, wiping out all visibility and dumping several inches of fresh snow. Twenty-five years later, they are still up there, somewhere on that mountain. Just weeks shy of his 26th birthday, Nick climbed toward the heavens and did not return. Today, four young men he never met carry his name, a living tribute by their parents to Nick, our friend forever young, whose absence still leaves an empty place in our hearts, but whose memory always sparks the warmth of a loving smile.

***

Each fall, Mr. Foster tells his students the story of Nick Vanderbilt, in whose honor his classroom's Harkness table was given. One floor above, in the Academy Building, Miss Schwartz does the same for Daniel Poon Sek Chan, Amy's older brother, the family member who guided Amy to Exeter and who drowned during Amy's upper year. Two tables. Two families whose backgrounds could not have been more distant and removed from each other. One community: Exeter. The school that accepted the tycoon's heir and the janitor's daughter. Exeter. You ignited Nick's dreams, and set in motion Amy's life of service. Exeter.

***

When I reflect on that which I hold most dear — my wife, her life and our life together; our children and the shaping of their minds, bodies and character; the friendships that I have treasured then, now and always — my thoughts return to this place, to this community. To you, Exeter, I say, "Thank you."

BROOKS MORIARTY '87

January 28, 2010

February is a busy birthday month in our household, so it would not be unusual at all to find a fully frosted cake in our freezer next month. My wife's instructions for me that winter afternoon were simple: keep our three boys entertained and defrost a cake for the evening celebration. No problem, but I was restless. A stack of ungraded papers slumped on my desk, a mountain of unfolded and sure-to-be-wrinkled laundry cooled in the corner, and the subzero temperatures kept us indoors.

What mattered to my children in that moment differed greatly from what mattered to me. Our horizons, the borderlands of our worlds, framed different things. Mine edged out through the window toward the frozen pond buried in fresh snow. White pines hunched heavily on the far shore. I wondered when I would get free to slap on a pair of skates and drag a shovel out to clear a little space for future play. For my two oldest boys, the living room was world enough. Their horizon turned hard at right angles in the corners of our dorm apartment, tumbling over a makeshift fort, a rocket ship fashioned out of a cardboard box, loose Cheerios, abandoned puzzles, and stacks of wooden blocks. For the youngest, the contour of my shoulder and the arm holding him close were horizon enough. He

Brooks Moriarty P'18, P'21 graduated from Exeter in 1987 and teaches in the English Department. He is the Dorm Head of Bancroft Hall, where he resides with his wife, Genny, and their three boys, Conor, Liam and Emmet.

was fussy so I was on the move, singing snatches of "Man of Constant Sorrow," which, in one of the strange ironies of parenting, soothed him.

When Emmet fell asleep on my shoulder, his body finally giving its full weight to me, I noticed the house was unusually, unsettlingly quiet. Perhaps his brothers, Conor and Liam, had hurled themselves into the dorm to play spies or superheroes. And then I heard them: aluminum foil crinkling, furtive giggling, tiny teeth gnawing. And then I saw them: two shirtless boys, aged 3 and 5, crouching under the dining room table with faces thrashing at two bricks of frozen cake, as hard as hockey pucks. The nubby masses crumbled over their bodies and littered the carpet. When they cocked heads in my direction, I averted my eyes and resumed singing and walking. A more clever person would have changed the soundtrack to suit the moment — perhaps "Wild Thing" or "Forever Young" — but I slipped back briefly into "Man of Constant Sorrow." My horizon leading up to this moment, after all, was paradoxically more tightly delineated than that of my boys, defined by the blankness of snow and a stack of blank papers, by what was not possible that cold day.

I return to this scene often when I need to remind myself to parent more thoughtfully. For, although I did experience a brief moment of panic about losing sight of my "to-do" list and about certain animalistic tendencies in my offspring, I let my kids alone. I didn't scold or worry. I didn't let on that I had discovered them. I let them be. However briefly, I stood within the boundaries of their world.

When they emerged, faces painted with frosting, they plopped the abused cakes on the table and proudly announced that they had "de-frosted" the cakes all by themselves. How could I argue with that? The unwavering logic of their act, the verbal play of de-frosting a cake by removing the frosting with teeth, the wild pursuit of sugar, the pride in helping parents with a household task — an imaginative act with clear results: pleasure and pride. How wild, how empowering.

Staying out of their way didn't come to me as breathlessly as their wild deed, for sure. It took a bit of "work" to leave them alone, perhaps even a bit of imagination on my part. And that brings me to my topic for today: imagination as a kind of work.

Parenting finds me fascinated by daily encounters with imaginative acts, by play. My children are always stuffing sticks and gravel and wisps of I-don't-know-what into my pockets when we take walks because nearly everything is wonderful, nearly everything is a miracle, and they don't have to do the laundry. Sure, we call paintings and sculptures and songs and poems works of art and appreciate the work that goes into their creation. But what about the imaginative work we put into the more mundane, day-to-day business of living?

The thinkers who sustain me define imagination as the active assembly of what lies within our horizons into something new, fresh and original. It is the adventure of mind meeting world, according to John Dewey, who read deeply the works of Emerson, Thoreau and James. The word "adventure" makes all of this imaginative work sound so exciting. My kids read *Choose Your Own Adventure* books, and I try as hard as I can to make boring trips to the grocery store adventures of sorts. But the original meaning of the word paints a different picture. An adventure is "a thing that happens to you," something not fully in your control, not simply a ticket for free will to romp about. That meeting of mind and world can be hazardous. So, I'm curious about what happens to the adventure as we make our way.

I grew up in Illinois, about an hour's drive from Chicago. To the north and east, densely populated streets marched in tight formations toward the big city. To the south and west, factories where tractors and plows and combine harvesters were assembled spilled into the farmlands of the Midwest. I spent my childhood plumbing the landscape for its mysterious gifts — that stretch of crumpled sidewalk heaved up by winter frosts that provided the best air for leaps astride a green banana-seat Huffy dragster bike; those elm tree trunks where, after 17 years, dormant cicadas crawled out of the earth in droves, unfurled wings, and broke free from shells they left clinging to the bark. At the time I imagined the elm tree roots drove miles into the center of the earth, long enough to accommodate a 17-year march toward a brief, fantastic life swarming in my backyard. The topography of my imagination soaked in mysteries — frost heaves, insect blooms.

We lived in a neighborhood with streets that curved and had no sidewalks, a pocket of irregularity on the margins of a linear world. Across the street from our house, beyond a thin band of grass and a chain-link fence, the interstate roared on day and night. My father, who grew up in Milford, Connecticut, and watched the pond behind his home filled in to make way for I-95, wrote letters to town, county and state officials and somehow, miraculously, had the state build an earth berm topped with thick trees to buffer us even more from the highway. Along its backside, litter gathered like burrs. A mile down Harding Road brought you to a forest of low scrub trees and trails full of pheasants leaning their colorful heads onward through the brush. My friends and I sought out the pockets of quiet in those woods where the interstate vanished.

A grove of pines was our hideout from passing cars. We carved our little lives out of that forest so earnestly and fully that the insult of its clearing for more houses shattered us for a time. In a strange twist of fate, the clearing coincided with the arrest of John Wayne Gacy two towns away — a serial killer who murdered 33 young men and boys. He worked as a clown at kids' birthdays and buried his victims in the crawl space beneath his house. The confluence of those events put a strain on our play. We decided that Gacy was somehow responsible for the loss of that forest, for changing the horizon. I couldn't ride my Huffy to school any more. I could only play in the backyard for a time. Something terrible crawled out of the earth that year.

So, with a frontier spirit, I sought other landscapes to replace the one I had lost, like Crystal River, Florida, where my grandparents spent winters along a canal that looked out on miles of saw grass before spilling into the Gulf of Mexico. One time my brother stepped on a water moccasin and screamed but held it still beneath his foot until my grandfather came out with a rifle, pulled my brother away and shot the snake. A whole frog, stunned with venom, burst out of its mouth. Alligators basked in the sun on the muddy shores of the canal. The saw grass rustled on for miles, holding its mysteries. I wanted so much to explore the depths of that horizon that I concocted stories of seeing some of the wildlife I knew lived there and some of the wildlife I hoped lived there: bobcats, black bears, the elusive panther, giraffes, lions, a rhinoceros looked out at me, I just knew it. My siblings laughed at my lies, my yearning, my imagining.

One night someone set fire to the saw grass, and the neighborhood gathered nervously to stand watch and pray that the fire wouldn't leap the canal. Word passed around in the orange flickering light and smoke and heat that the arsonist had escaped from a nearby prison and taken refuge in the saw grass. A lot of the critters I had hoped lived there poured onto the banks like locusts and I felt cheated and heartbroken for the revelation coming in that way. Another landscape, another horizon wronged.

I don't remember exactly how the grown-ups aided my work of making space for these events within my horizon. I recall words like "monster" and "lunatic" and more-urgent instructions about not talking to strangers and not playing with matches. Some labels and some limits. I had to work out the rest on my own.

At some point our imagination has to go to work to make sense of this world. We figure out that it's broken and try to find our way clear to assembling the fragments into something new and meaningful. Various forces endeavor to redistrict the boundaries or serve as gatekeepers, letting in some things, keeping out others. So imagination becomes work and we're not always up to the task. But my kids, in their joy and in their messiness and in their meltdowns, remind me to keep working at it.

After 9/11 the New York State Museum in Albany set up an exhibit memorializing the valor of New York City's police and firefighters. At the center sat a fire truck burned and crushed by a steel girder from one of the towers. In an adjacent room my then-3-year-old son gawked at a separate exhibit, the history of fire trucks, and listened attentively to his grandfather tell stories about his father, and uncles, and grandfather, all firefighters in Buffalo, New York. With wide eyes he took in these stories. He took in the horse-drawn carriage with tank, the brass, the chrome, the red, red, red, and then broke free to look for his daddy, who stood in front of a very different, former fire truck. And he ran to me and jumped in my arms and looked. "What happened to that fire truck, Daddy?" How could I answer? How could I not? How could I place that in his horizon safely? How could I place it in mine? "Let's go look at the other trucks," I told him, choosing silence (how often that serves us), letting this image slip into some place without commentary for now.

That same year he had taken his imaginary friend, Bug, to preschool, and in the chaos around the finger-painting table, Bug was lost. No one but Conor could see Bug, but believe me, Bug was sitting there.

His teacher was quickly able to soothe him, but the intensity of his imaginative life threw her for a loop. She said something at pick-up that made my wife feel like there was something "wrong" with our son.

We had been living with Bug for about a year. Like any good 2-year-old, Conor whined and screamed and hit and threw his food on the floor or in our faces. When he began to understand the notion of responsibility, he did what anyone would do: He tried to pass the buck. He wasn't the one who used baby powder and flour to create snow in his bedroom; it was Bug.

My wife and I soon found ourselves saying things like, "You are responsible for whatever Bug does." Bug's antics exhausted us, but they delighted the babysitters. They kept telling us all of these funny stories about what Conor and Bug were up to on those rare occasions when we could get away for an hour or two. These teenagers seemed to have a better vision of imaginary friendship and a better sense of humor about it than Conor's teacher and parents did.

Over time Bug underwent a kind of metamorphosis. After the larval stage — "It wasn't me, it was Bug" — Conor took it upon himself to educate his imaginary friend. I have read that the parts of the caterpillar shift around and reorganize themselves at the cellular level inside the cocoon. Horns become wings, or something like that. This stage was less exasperating, and my wife and I congratulated ourselves on having a child clever enough to be sorting out the idea of responsibility in his own way. Bug learned about manners and messes with the utmost diligence. Bug became a pal, a partner in crime, for sure, but the kind of crime that makes you laugh as you try to explain why snowballs cannot be stored in dresser drawers. It was this Bug that vanished at school. This was the pal who made it easier for a shy kid who didn't like crowds to make it through some tough moments in life. Bug and Conor reassured each other. The teacher's response did not reassure anyone.

Bug eventually became a toy in our home. It happened soon after the incident at school. I think it was healthy, but I wonder if the teacher hurried up this last change from imaginary friend to plastic toy. Bug is a Playmobil figure of an angel wearing a pink frock covered in gold stars. Conor removed the wings without irony. Bug is a boy and his sister is a bearded Playmobil truck driver. When I think back on this story, I realize that the imaginary play of children can be very serious business. It is a kind of work, and that comforts me when I see them sifting and sorting through everything that lies within their ever-changing horizons.

Robert Frost once wrote that a poem "begins in delight, it inclines to the impulse, it assumes direction with the first line laid down, it runs a course of lucky events, and ends in a clarification of life — not necessarily a great clarification ... but in a momentary stay against confusion." I like to think we make little poems all the time as we reshuffle what lies within our horizons. The arrangement emerges out of impulses we half understand, makes tracks in the snow or the mud or the slush of being, requires a little bit of luck, brings delight and a bit of wisdom that puts our world in order. It serves us for a time, and then we need to bring all of our resources to bear in doing it again and again and again.

The boys now sleep and dream in beds they inherited from their great-grandparents, both of whom died last year. For 65 years they unfurled their lives together, swapping stories: about childhoods in Michigan where my grandmother worked a farm as a young girl behind the wheel of a tractor and where my grandfather earned some folding money as a teenager by running liquor from Canada during Prohibition in a rowboat across Lake St. Claire; about their shy courtship at dances and after church services; about losses and the terrors of Iwo Jima, where my grandfather fought in the Second World War; about that saw grass fire; about their three children, and the grandchildren and the great-grandchildren. After my grandfather died, my grandmother often spoke to him from one of those beds late into the night. I don't know what words passed across that divide in the darkness, but my grandmother took great comfort in those meetings. She played out the final months of her adventure by mapping out broad horizons, speaking with someone as invisible and as present as Bug. When she told her children about these conversations, no one worried and no one wondered if she had lost touch with reality. They let her be. I can only hope that the wisdom she achieved in those moments of imaginative work, in those moments of grace and clarity, rubs off through some alchemy from those beds onto my kids and onto me.

KEVIN BARTKOVICH
My Knock-Down, Drag-Out Fight with God
February 18, 2010

For those of you who don't know me, my name is Kevin Bartkovich, and I am a new member of the Math Department this year. Prior to coming to Exeter, I was a missionary living in a remote village in Uganda. My family and I were there for 10 years building a secondary school from the ground up for the children of Bundibugyo District.

This was my dream job. Was this place a paradise? Not so much, really. Much of the time it seemed we were taking one step forward, then one step back. When we first visited, in 1995, we were captivated by both the beauty and the need. Bundibugyo is in a valley nestled between the snow-peaked Rwenzori Mountains and the border with Congo. Mangoes, pineapples and bananas are abundant. The countryside is lush, the soil fertile. Yet, this was a place with no electricity, no running water, no indoor plumbing, no phone service, no paved roads and definitely no Internet. Most people lived in mud-and-wattle huts with grass roofs. This is a polygamous culture; most men have more than one wife, and women are viewed as commodities. Maternal mortality is high. Women die in childbirth so often that the typical greeting to a mother with a baby

---

Kevin Bartkovich P '16, P'18 teaches in the Mathematics Department and coaches girls soccer. He came to Exeter in 2009. He is the dorm head of Ewald, where he resides with his family.

is "*Webale kwejuna*," meaning, "Thank you for surviving." Malnutrition and disease are rampant. Malaria is endemic and often fatal. Cholera is a frequent threat. It is a place where young adults desperately want to improve themselves and their communities, but the odds against them are overwhelming.

When we arrived nobody was passing their college entrance exams. Children were eager to learn but there was a decided lack of educational infrastructure and few teachers, and even fewer who taught in English, the national language of Uganda and thus the language of the exams. Corruption in the local government was widespread, which trapped the local people in a system whereby a few families got rich while the vast majority scraped by at a subsistence level. We realized that significant and lasting change could only come from the ground up, brought about by a new generation of educated leaders. The people wanted and needed someone to come and start a school that would give them a chance at a better future. How could I refuse?

Building a school, establishing a curriculum, mentoring a faculty — all this was both a delight and a challenge, full of blessing and hardship. I made a lot of mistakes along the way, oftentimes because I thought I already knew the answers, only later realizing that I didn't even know the right questions. I remember entering into my first math lesson with high hopes. We brought over with us 200 TI graphing calculators, and I was eager to put them into the hands of my students. First, though, I created a brilliant lesson on estimation with which to kick off that first year. I marched my students outside and over to a large mango tree. "Let's estimate how many leaves are on this big tree," I said hopefully and with great enthusiasm. Silence. Blank stares at both me and the tree. Hmmm. I tried to simplify things a bit. "Let's estimate how many leaves are on this bottom branch." Still there was silence. Over the ensuing weeks, I became painfully aware of the extreme height of the mountain we would need to climb. I discovered the difficulty of teaching math to students who were unfamiliar with not only the names of but also the very concept of large numbers. In their experience, everything in the market was sold in heaps. Whether five big tomatoes or eight small ones or 14 really small ones, for them the number was the same: a heap. To everyone's surprise, through long hours of study and instruction, by the time they graduated, all of our students were passing math on their national exams.

No less steep was the humanities side of things. I learned that my students had *heard* of books. They had just never *held* one in their hands. This was a culture where stories were passed down orally, and until recently had been without a written language. Even my faculty was shell-shocked. They came from all over Uganda, arriving by public transport over the mountains, perched atop bags of produce sitting in the backs of pickup trucks. They arrived battered and weary, covered in dust from head to foot, looking around wide-eyed at this place so clearly at the end of the road. Together we worked to bring our students up to standard. After six years our first students sat for their exams. For the first time, students who went to school in Bundibugyo qualified for university.

One of my best memories was hearing the national-exam results over the radio and hopping on my mountain bike to deliver wonderful news to my best student. Here is a kid whose father was killed during the guerilla warfare of our first few years in Bundibugyo. School was his only chance. During the summer months he lived in a village far from the main road, and I just had to go and celebrate with him. He had achieved an impossibly good score on his math exam and thus had qualified for university. As I arrived, he was there greeting me with a huge smile on his face. With tears flowing freely we jumped up and down and cheered. Just last week this young man graduated from university in the capital city with a degree in finance and statistics. I couldn't be prouder.

In the midst of these success stories, we struggled to establish this institution, never sure if the school would survive from one year to the next. Our soccer team, which began with kids who had never played organized ball, was representative of the school's development as a whole. We resisted the common corrupt practice of hiring men to play for the school team, which was the normal strategy that schools used to win the district championship. Instead we relied on our own students and practiced every day, developing our boys into a team that competed year after year at the national level. Here were these boys, who at first were intimidated and afraid of playing men from the outside, learning discipline, the benefits of hard work and superior physical conditioning, and the power of believing in themselves and each other. While at first they were laughed at and ridiculed, they learned to play competitive soccer and to be such a presence on the field that they began to be feared by other districts. The high point for me came the year they played with so much heart that the corporate sponsor, Coca-Cola, gave them two complete sets of uniforms at the national tournament.

At the end of 10 years, we had 350 students and 26 faculty members. The school was ranked in the top 20 percent in the country and we were regularly sending our graduates on to university. Our soccer team was a force to be reckoned with and our focus on girls' education was turning heads as well. Getting this school established was the hardest work I had ever done, and the best work I had ever done. I had purpose, every day was focused, I felt I was making a difference. I knew I was where I was supposed to be. I was given this wonderful work to do, and I never wanted to leave.

After 10 years and four children, however, my wife, JD, was convinced that we needed to leave. She carefully considered the stage of life our family was entering as our oldest child was pushing 10, she weighed the effect of the accumulation of a decade's worth of stress and deprivation, but even more significantly, she prayed and felt the Lord telling her, "It's time to go." *I was not amused.* I couldn't imagine a scenario that would make me want to leave Uganda. Day after day we discussed and argued. She didn't back down, and I wouldn't give an inch. One night as I sat alone and prayed, surrounded by a dark cloud of anger — Why have you spoken to JD and not me? — in the midst of this darkness there appeared a small ray of light that I can best describe as bringing peace and acceptance that leaving was the right thing to do, even as I was nearly consumed by anger and resentment. Immediately, a small, quiet voice said to me, "Things are going to get a lot worse." What did that mean? When I shared this with JD, neither of us could figure out what it meant.

And so, two years ago, in February 2008, we returned to the U.S. after living in Uganda for 10 years. We immediately went out west and spent 10 weeks in a tent, one week for each year we lived in Uganda, JD and our four children and I, camping in national parks. It was a restorative time, but it did not touch what was going on deep inside of me. I knew this because when we got settled in North Carolina, every Sunday in church, week after week, I found myself weeping during the service and not knowing why. When JD and I went on a retreat to the mountains near Asheville, I finally had my knock-down, drag-out fight with God.

A friend there encouraged me that arguing with God was a legitimate thing to do, as outrageous as it sounds, so I went at Him. All the questions came pouring out as I sat by myself in a garden, shouting and sobbing as I voiced my accusations. "I followed you to Uganda and then you kicked me out. Why? Why couldn't I stay? Were you displeased with me? There was so much more to do. Why couldn't I be the one? Are you really looking out for me, or are you a capricious God who just uses people up and discards them when you've accomplished your purposes?" It was cathartic in the best sense of the word. I let it all out, I held nothing back, and I found that God is big enough to handle it. Something between me and God happened in that garden, a release and I'm not sure what else, perhaps a kind of reckoning, and afterward I was no longer weeping in church on Sundays.

The rest of the year we spent resting, recovering and looking for what was next. And I did what I always did — I exercised. After 10 years of daily soccer practice on the equator, now I was once again running the streets of Durham. Ten years previously I was a much stronger runner, able to run a 3-mile loop any day of the week. Now I was committed to regaining that form and fighting the decline in my aging body. But when I found that I was doing worse even as I worked harder and that I could no longer run even a single mile, I took to running sprints interspersed with walking. Throughout most of the school year it was my normal custom to run alone.

Then came this day last summer, June 11, 2009. I don't remember what happened that day; I only have what others have told me. I would like to share what my 11-year-old son, Joe, has written.

It can be very sad when someone you care about dies or comes close to death. Something like that happened to me. Last summer, when I was training for soccer camp, I jogged with my dad almost every day. One day we jogged to a nearby park and jogged all around it. We took a break at the water fountain. Then we ran some sets of stairs. As we jogged home, he complained that he was very tired. I was pretty tired too, so I didn't think that much of it. When we were close to our home, Dad suggested that we sprint to the corner. I sprinted to the corner. I was too caught up in the great feeling of sprinting so fast to notice that he was falling behind. When I turned around he stumbled a few feet and then just collapsed. At first I thought he was joking around, because he was making weird breathing noises. It was almost like when a horse breathes out heavily through its mouth and the lips shake. Some people came over and asked if he was OK. In a panicked voice, I said that I didn't know. Fortunately one of them had a cell phone. He dialed 911. Someone told me to go get Mom. I raced to the house. I ran in and screamed for Mom. I said that Dad fell down and was not getting up. When we got back someone was giving him CPR. He was doing the chest compressions. I saw Mom go over and help. She gave him mouth to mouth. We lived three blocks away from the fire department, so the paramedics arrived soon and then the ambulance. As the sirens blared my mom told me to go get my little brother and sister. I went back to my house. My hands numbly worked the keys to lock the door behind us. When I got back the ambulance was giving Dad shocks. Nothing was working. My mom asked if they could shock him again and asked them not to give up. They told her that they couldn't shock him anymore and that they needed to get to the hospital. A girl who lived nearby told me that he had had a heart attack. Later I learned that one of his heart valves had grown smaller and harder. This caused his heart to stop beating. They took Dad to the hospital. I went back home and e-mailed our friends in Uganda and South Sudan. I told them what had happened and asked them to pray. So many people stopped what they were doing to pray for my dad. The school in Africa, where my dad was the headmaster for 10 years, was about to riot. As they were meeting to discuss their demands, they learned what had happened to my dad. It immediately turned into a prayer meeting. Miraculously, my dad survived with no serious side effects. He had flat-lined for fifteen minutes. He was in a medically induced coma for 2 days. After his open heart surgery, his doctors told him they had never seen someone survive what he went through. A few days later I went to see him. He told me that I had been very brave. He said that I was his hero, and that I had done the exact right thing, even though I was scared. He thanked me for helping to save his life. A month or so later we all went back home. Sadly, it will be a long time before things are normal. For awhile, when I didn't know if he would be OK, I felt like a part of me was just gone, that some part of me was dying, too. Fortunately, he survived.

My fight with God was real. Did He answer? Yes.

Unbeknownst to any of us, I had been in heart failure for five years. As I lay in the cardiac intensive care unit in Duke University Hospital, it all began to come together. If I had had my way, JD would have flown home from Uganda a widow. As for the word I had received about things getting worse, there I was on our 15th wedding anniversary, flat-lined on the street, my wife giving me CPR.

There is a story that Vincent Donovan, a missionary to the Masai of Kenya, tells — a parable of faith from a tribal elder. The Masai elder told Vincent, "For a man really to believe is like a lion going after its prey. His nose and eyes and ears pick up the prey. His legs give him the speed to catch it. All the power of his body is involved in the terrible death leap and single blow to the neck with the front paw, the blow that actually kills. And as the animal goes down the lion envelops it in his arms, pulls it to himself, and makes it part of himself. This is the way a lion kills. This is the way a man believes. This is what faith is. You told us of the High God, how we must search for him ... We have not searched for him. He has searched for us. He has searched us out and found us. All the time we think we are the lion. In the end, the lion is God."

As for me, I chased God all the way to Uganda and back, and then He caught me.

JENNA COOK '10
The Nourishment of Home
March 25, 2010

This fall my sister, Sara, filled out her secondary school applications. Asked by admissions officers to describe a wonderful day in her life, she wrote about "rock climbing, cello playing, the beach, and, of course, delicious meals." She described a hand-packed lunch composed of "a granola bar, water, ice tea, kettle corn, and a scrumptious wrap." When I read her essay I wondered if it were mere coincidence that her favorite rock-climbing route is appetizingly named "The Lobster Tail." For her imaginary dinner, she writes, "Everything is delicious, and our stomachs are happily full when we leave."

An admissions officer may not understand why my sister's essay, while not solely about meals, mentions food so frequently. But I can see her love for food when she hunches down to eat (and my mother scolds, "Sara, sit up straight!"). For a moment, she heightens her posture, but then gradually her backbone rounds back out and her shoulders push forward, as her whole body cradles the meal. My parents are both women, both in their 60s, both white. One is Jewish and the other Christian. One is an elementary school teacher and the other is a cook.

Jenna Cook graduated from Exeter in 2010 and from Yale in 2014. From 2014-2015, she was a China Fulbright Scholar. Jenna is currently pursuing her Master of Arts degree at Peking University in Beijing.

In the movies, expecting parents prepare the nest by painting the walls a pastel hue, assembling a new crib, and buying diapers. My mothers followed these traditional preparations, but they did something else, too. For every children's book, my mother, Peggy, gathered about China, my godmother, Carol, purchased a cookbook. Today, our living room shelves house nearly 60 Chinese cookbooks. Some sport faded pictures, broken, floppy spines, and dated titles like, *'Oriental' Cooking: From Better Homes and Gardens.* Moving my index finger from left to right along the wooden shelf, I glide from decade to decade: The spines become thicker and glossier, as the insides showcase perfectly lit, full-page photo spreads. The recipes morph from Western concepts of Chinese cuisine like General Tsao's chicken and Peking ravoli to instructions for authentic *Mapo doufu* (a tofu dish) and *qing cai* (fresh steamed vegetables). As much as I chuckle at the dated descriptions and cringe at the portrayal of Chinese food as a heap of goopy, oily stir fry, I'm grateful for Carol's curiosity about my first home. Each stained recipe served as a tangible, tasty connection to the foreign culture of a small baby.

Through Carol's experimentation with Chinese cuisine, I learned to adore anise, five-spice, and the musty, earthy flavor of sticky rice wrapped in lotus leaves. In elementary school, I brought fish soup and marinated tofu for lunch as my classmates held their noses. "Eww! How can you eat that?" they mocked. A sea of marshmallow Fluff sandwiches, apples and juice boxes flooded the lunch table, as I savored my little island of fried rice or turnip cakes. At home I observed how tenderly my mothers handled the golden tofu, and how they savored each slurp of shimmering broth. "It's good! You should try it!" I encouraged, as the kids at school scooted their chairs farther away from me.

But when I visited China, my voracious appetite for local foods impressed hosts. Every morsel on my plate traveled directly to my tummy. Rice gruel, fried beef, sea urchin — delish! "Look! She can use chopsticks!" the local people remarked. "Wow! She even likes spicy foods!" When I lacked the vocabulary to express my thanks, I could always rely on the language of food: Eating many helpings voiced my appreciation for their cooking, but always leaving a little in the bowl confirmed that they had provided more than enough. Some of the flavors — like in the dish "thousand-year-old egg" — are so pungent that you must learn them in order to love them. "Tell me what you eat," Anthelme Brillat-Savarin famously claimed, and "I will tell you what you are." If I am what I eat, I am certainly Chinese; a trait I inherited not from my Chinese birth mother, but from Carol.

My sister and I rarely talk about both being adopted from China. She was born in Yiwu, 436 miles east of where I was born, in Wuhan. Most maps of China don't show Yiwu, which is best known for manufacturing Christmas tree ornaments. Whereas I spent four months in the orphanage before being adopted, my sister lived in the orphanage for two years.

Warm, black tea and cheap, hard candies fueled Sara's first years of life in the orphanage. A bundle of right angles, "Guigui" (meaning "precious one") scarfed dozens of dumplings and heaps of noodles her first night at the hotel in China. When my mother changed her diaper, the hip bones jutted out like thin flags, and the ridges of ribs protruded from her flesh like mountain ranges. Now, 12 years later, her knees still bow backward from the old rickets. This is how she came to cradle each morsel of food, and this is why she takes the time to smell it, to describe its texture and to flesh out each subtle flavor. She'll ask my mother some obscure question, like, "Is there cardamom in this?" or "Are you sure you didn't add capers?" Her appreciation for food is rooted in a far-away memory of hunger.

One of my friends once told me that he enjoys the light, cleansing feeling of being hungry. When he said that, my eyebrows rose in disbelief. To me, fear, anxiety, humiliation, even failure — all bow down at the feet of hunger. A raw craving, the way the stomach whines and groans, punching its fists into flesh in protest. Glazed with hunger. Dizzy. Light-headed. Irritable. I struggle to be present in the moment. How can one contemplate, create, or concentrate when one is hungry?

When my family visited the Yiwu orphanage in 2006, my sister nodded solemnly at the orphanage director, with whom years ago she was able to converse in Chinese. The director pointed to a wooden crib and said, "This is the place where you used to sleep." My sister glanced at the hard board and nodded. "This is where you liked to sit on my lap," the director said, motioning toward a concrete step. My sister never cried like I did. To me, her expression looked the same as when she is eating white rice — blank, bland, bare. Not excited about the rice, but not disgusted either. I wanted to ask her if she was more sad that she left China, or more happy that she came to America. I wanted to ask her what she thought about those orphans, who were her very same age, and still living there. But I didn't ask anything, and watched her keep her white rice mask on.

Later in the week, we traveled to Wuhan and visited my "finding site" — the place where some would say I was abandoned, the place where my birth parents waited for the police to find me and take me away. Returning to this place 14 years later, I am hungry for the nourishment only blood parents can give their blood child, for some mysterious love found only in your own mother's breast milk. The beeping and honking of cars, the black exhaust strung out behind buses, laundry hanging out of windows — for everyone else it seems an ordinary day. Who's doing the "finding" at the finding site, and who's being "found"? Years ago, the police did the finding and I was the baby being found, but now I am the one who is looking to find something. Searching the junction between the two families, the two countries, my two fates. I wait a while but my birth parents don't jump out from behind the corner, like in a dream.

What finding is there to be done here?

My sister links our elbows and holds mine close to her core, even in the scorching, humid heat. The crisp, soothing sound of her footsteps on the garbage underfoot. With a quiet strength, she lets me match my feeble steps to her guiding ones as we walk together, at the falling-apart police station, two black-haired girls with different stories but the same yellow skin and white insides. Behind a wall of tears, I glance at her face and she doesn't have the white rice mask on. She looks like she does when she's eating French onion soup — how she loves the pungent broth so much she doesn't care if the bread is burnt or if the onions were sliced too thick. Just looking at her like that — with her chin jutting out and her eyes closed and a big savory smile, even in the smelly alleyway — it makes me giggle. She is the one who finds me and nourishes me.

A finding site, like food, remains a place where things continue to be found. The layers of memories of my two mothers cooking: peeling barrels of handpicked apples, simmering them into cinnamon applesauce and canning them for the long winter. Paprika home fries on a Sunday morning with maple bacon. German chocolate cake with a thick inch of buttercream frosting for birthdays.

My favorite part of the day is from 6:40 to 6:50 in the morning when Peggy eats breakfast with me. Usually she calls up the stairs, "Jenna, it's 6:15!" A blanket of black shields the world outside my window. I groan and stumble out of bed as she cooks me breakfast —Polish perogies or scrambled eggs, French toast or smoked salmon. Sometimes it's spaghetti or a burrito or spinach pie leftovers from the dinner before.

She doesn't have to wake me up in the morning. I have an alarm. But still she does. She doesn't have to make me breakfast or prepare the place settings the night before. But she does. I like how she folds the paper napkin in half and carefully tucks it under the rim of the plate. I like how she only fills the glass halfway with juice because she knows that's exactly how much I drink each time.

I munch on the eggs and crunch the toast, while my mother reads the local daily paper. She sits in her pajamas — white ribbed cotton patterned with small blue flowers. I like hearing her shift on her chair and hearing the weight of her feet on the wooden floor. The warmth and liveliness of her body, keeping me company, while the cold, lonely wind outside whips around our house.

Sometimes she recounts a funny dream she had the night before. Something like, "I dreamt we were in China and we had those salty, thin green beans." Or maybe: "You were going on a ski trip but you wouldn't tell me who was the chaperone." Or maybe: "I was in high school again and I couldn't find my calculus class." All of her dreams, peppered with worry and anxiety — all except the dreams about food.

These breakfast moments are the best 10 minutes of my day. A secluded space of calm comfort and sleepy eyes. A sanctuary of ritual in the transition between night and day. A place where life still moves slowly and the day breathes fresh. My spirit warms up and stretches with my mother's, preparing for the big sprint of activity.

Of the four people in my family, none of us have the same blood or the same genes. Peggy's parents, Ted and Dottie, passed away. Carol's parents, Lawrence and Nonie, are also no longer alive. Sara's birth mother and father — lost somewhere in Yiwu. And my birth parents — lost somewhere in Wuhan. It is a strange act of fate how we all ended up in the same yellow house. In that house, the wok gleams freshly oiled and succulent soup simmers on the stovetop. The black tile countertop dusted with white flour, our four pairs of hands gather to knead the dough, roll it into balls, press it into circles, and place a dab of filling in the center. Then, we gather the edges of dough together at the top, what a

Chinese folktale describes as relatives finally reuniting from all corners. The flour snows onto the countertop, as laughter evaporates into the air. Balls of dough hop from hand to hand. "Who's hogging the spoons for the filling?" Sara jokes. An hour later, dozens of piping-hot, plump buns line the bamboo steamer. The fluffy dough springs back to the touch. Safe and calm, rooted. My two mothers smiling through the clouds of steam. Sara shelters a bun with her body. I take a bite. The warm faces, the warm room, the warm filling. No one hungry. Home.

AMANDA CHISHOLM '10
Motion
May 13, 2010

The gears on my borrowed bike creak and grind in protest as I throw my weight into the pedals, accelerating up the hill past the boys, pushing for the top to get the ascent over with quickly. Faintly from behind me I hear Felicien shouting something, and then Alex is laughing hysterically. I wait for them at the crest, next to a pasture full of sun and aging cows. They stop beside me, out of breath from exertion and laughter, and Alex says, "You just missed the quote of the trip." I look to Felicien questioningly and he rewards me with a vehement and heavily accented "I ATE cycling!" We laugh again until our stomachs hurt and then push onward toward our next campsite and dinner.

It is mid-August and we are three 17-year-olds on bicycles riding fast and giddily free on the rural back roads of the Normandy-Brittany coast of France. Alex and I are the Americans, sunburned and sweaty and overwhelmed by the novelty of everything around us. Felicien is fantastically French. We all carry packs full of camping gear, food and clothing, but where Alex and I have spandex, shorts, sneakers and real camping packs, Felicien cycles in Crocs, the capri pants that European

---

Amanda Chisholm traveled for two years after graduating from Exeter and is currently working toward a degree in woodworking and ceramics as part of the class of 2017 at UNH.

men seem to have such a strange affinity for, a Simpsons shirt, a conductor's cap, and, to top it all off, a giant green army pack (it towers about a foot over his head and leans constantly to the right) with a miniature American flag waving jauntily from the top.

Each morning we wake when it gets light, eat a breakfast of cereal and Cacolac (a decidedly questionable French version of chocolate milk), apply ridiculous amounts of sunscreen, and, having collapsed our tents and donned our packs, hit the road. We ride until we are tired or hungry or meet particularly interesting people or just feel like stopping, and then we break for buttery French cookies and vast amounts of water. We move fast, and most days we reach our next campsite in time for a few hours of relaxation before dark. We lie on the ground and talk about how much we hurt and how nice it is to not be cycling. We wash our faces with carefully rationed splashes from our water bottles. We admire the amount of dirt, blood and bike grease on our legs. We cook dinner (it's pasta, every time) and watch the sunset together. We set up our tents and the boys laugh at me while I try to untangle my dirty, sunscreen-filled hair, which by now is holding its ponytail shape all on its own. We brush our teeth together, spitting into the bushes, and then the boys crawl into their tent and I settle into mine, and we sleep until the sun and the morning chill tell us that it's time to get moving again.

We are together, and the country is blurring around and past us, and I have never felt this independent — this free — before. Everything we need is in our packs, strapped to our backs, and we can just go. We meet so many people, have so many conversations. Our French is stumbling and hesitant (except for Felicien's, of course), but in smiles we are fluent, and everyone we encounter seems to have all the time and patience in the world to wait for us to work out what to say and how to say it. People shout encouragement from cars and sidewalks and roadside fields and we grin and wave and shout back, and all of it, from the aches and pains to the people to the exhilaration of flying, single-file and without handlebars, down a long, straight hill, is perfect.

At night, as I fall asleep, I think back on the day — the sleepy chill of morning, tears on my cheeks from the wind, flowers in window boxes and village squares, the pure pleasure of watching a slow sunset with friends — and on how lucky I am to know the people I know and to have the opportunities I have, and I promise myself that I will not forget how to appreciate it when it is all over. And I drift off happy.

Each of us has something that keeps us happy, or at least sets us at peace in times of trouble. For me that thing seems to be motion, in whatever form it chooses to take at any given point in time. Living in a dorm on a boarding school campus, I've watched a lot of people come and go. When my sisters and I were little, we would choose a couple of lucky students every year to be our friends, and we would blissfully follow them and talk at them and reprimand them for swearing until, invariably, they disappeared at the end of the school year. The next year some would return, and others would not. We filled their places without too many qualms. That was just the way it went. We were constant, everyone else on campus was not. For a while that was fine, but for me a life completely static is not a life maintainable. Of course, I ran around and played in the mud and climbed trees with the best of my peers, but I was forever hitting boundaries, limits to my exploration in the form of brick school buildings at the bottoms of all the perfect sled runs or overzealous security guards who found our manhunt and hide-and-seek games "suspicious." Home began to feel a bit fenced in, and the older I got, the more the time between the end of one summer and the beginning of the next dragged.

Since before I was born my dad has worked as a counselor at Pasquaney. It's a boys summer camp on Newfound Lake (or Lake Pasquaney) in northern New Hampshire, built on the side of Plymouth Mountain so that, from the library (with the polar-bear-skin rug that scared me when I was little) at the top of the hill, you can look out across the water to Bear Mountain and, on clear days, the naked peak of Cardigan in the distance. We spend all our summers at Pasquaney, and it has become the counterbalance to my boarding school existence. Up there, wandering barefoot through the woods behind the funny, pyramid-shaped house the camp provides us with, looking upward underwater to watch raindrops hit the surface of the lake, I feel whole. I am free to take the time to simply appreciate the closeness between my two younger sisters and me as we watch lightning storms, huddled together on one small mattress in a dark room, the green glow of backlit leaves above the white rope hammock, the satisfaction of knowing the names of the constellations that we find with Dad on clear nights, the joy of hurling myself off the old diving raft as the sun sets between the mountains at the head of the lake — these things leave me with a happiness I can feel in my stomach, heavy in a way that centers me but does not hold me down. Certain places do this for me — lift all feelings of restraint or limit to possibility, turn me loose to move as I will.

When I was 12, Dad took a sabbatical and we went around the world — England, France, Venice, Vienna, Australia, New Zealand and Hawaii, in that order. It took exactly 365 days —we arrived back in Boston the same day we left, just a year's worth of experiences and opened eyes different. My mom stayed in America for work — she visited us once in England, once in France and once in Australia. Three times in a year. I missed her, but not as terribly as I might have.

Our almost family was constantly in motion. We hiked between double-layer rainbows and muddy sheep in the Lake District of England, spun under the vaulted arches of ancient cathedrals, inhaling the dusty, old-book scent of history. I went to school for three months in France, the only portion of the trip where Dad didn't home-school us, and working through history and math in another language, taking long walks after longer lunches on the Normandy coast, exploring the *marchét* in the rural village where we lived, and dealing with the trials of seventh grade that are present in any and all countries and languages took literally all of my waking time. We left France and hit Venice, where we wandered dirty, tourist-packed streets above murky canals and searched for something that felt real, and then went on to Vienna, where we watched the famous Lipizzaners perform on Easter morning, snowy horses moving in time like breathing clockwork over the manicured dirt of their arena.

In Australia I came into my own. We drove away from cities, as far as we could go, and camped — all of us piled into our one big tent. Dingoes yipped and raced giddy circles around our campsites, and after dark we hunted sugar gliders with our flashlights among the trees. We passed fields grazed by mixed groups of cows and kangaroos, and over it all flew birds. They were bright and bold and impossible to ignore, and so, every day, after more or less doing my schoolwork, I headed out into the bush, binoculars and camera around my neck, bird book under my arm. I saw koalas, wallabies and kangaroos inland; seals, sea lions and sharks on the coast; Tasmanian devils, wombats, platypus and spotted quolls during our brief stay in Tasmania; and more birds than I could count.

We moved on to New Zealand and the trend continued. No cities for us. We took rainy boat rides on choppy gray seas to reach the tiny offshore islands where what remains of the original fauna has taken shelter from the fast-developing world. We drove for days to reach remote mountain passes where the influence of humans has been at least somewhat thwarted by steep slopes and ever-present snow. I saw kakariki, gray New Zealand robins, kokako, tieke, pukeko, kaka, the mountain-dwelling, snow-loving, semi-carnivorous kea, takahe, kereru, weka, hihi, and paradise shelducks (also known as putangitangi). Brazen fantails flitted at my feet, picking off the insects that my passing flushed from the ground.

Tui sang for me in the top of a hastily climbed tree, the clarion whistles and bells of their calls ringing in bright-damp morning air. An albatross with a 12-foot wingspan soared level with Dad and me — it high above the sea, we perched on a cliff top. Dad almost tripped over a kiwi one night.

In Hawaii, in the water, I spun in a circle and counted 14 sea turtles. Dad and I hiked 6 miles in the rain for a 10-second glimpse of an i'ivi — a tiny flash of red that was one of the island's last native birds flitting between damp green vines.

So much, and in just a year. Thinking back, it seems like much longer. I could close my eyes and lose myself to memory for days. This stillness would not bother me. It would be unenforced, self-inflicted and simply different from the stillness that oppresses me. There is nothing wrong with stopping to appreciate, and my memories of those places and times are a part of me now — little fragments of momentum to keep me sane when all else fails. These are the memories I treasure most.

I wake to the feeling of velocity, raise my head and realize that I am no longer in my bed or even my room. I am nestled between my two sisters in a pile of blankets, and we are in the back of our minivan, moving fast and smooth through darkness. Dad, up front, must have heard me wake, because he offers a sleepy explanation — there is a meteor shower and we are going to see the shooting stars.

I am not aware of the rest of our drive. I know that I drift in and out of sleep, but I have no specific memory of the journey, only the subconscious constants of darkness and movement. At some point the car must stop, and I know that Dad carries us, in clumsy sleeping-bag bundles, to a blanket on a hill, and then we are there, huddled together, faces upturned, our backs to an old stone wall. We are cold, but it is a good cold, the warm chill of watching a Christmas parade or of cross-country skiing with Dad at night, and we have a tall, thin thermos of burning-hot cocoa. The stars, just the normal, everyday stars, are brilliant out here, and at first they are all I see, a universe of bright points turning above me. Then the first spec of dust hits our atmosphere and bursts into flame, hurtling across our little patch of sky before burning out. Its trail lingers, white fading to blue, behind my eyelids. After it comes another, and then still more, until the sky is streaked with movement. I lie there, cocooned in my sleeping bag, with the cold air on my face and star trails in my eyes, watching.

It's summer and I'm stuck in Exeter. Campus is empty and the heat and humidity press in, magnifying my boredom. I'm tired, but my sheet is sticking to my sweaty legs, my fan simply pushes the air in heavy circles, and I know there's no way I'm going to get to sleep. I lie in the dark for a while, looking at the orange glow of street lights that leaks in even around the edges of my blackout shades, then kick off my covers and get up. I feel around on my floor for my running shoes and throw on light spandex, a sports bra and a tank top, find my iPod, put on some Dave Matthews, check the back door to make sure it's unlocked, and take off. It's still too hot and now there's sweat in my eyes, but I'm happy. Instantly.

I run down Swasey, look back at Exeter from the turn in the parkway. The town is lit up, the buildings reflected perfectly in the river, their images interrupted only by a thin line of rippling V's where a great blue heron takes off at my approach and flaps slowly away, its long legs dangling, feet skimming the surface of the water. At the end of the parkway I turn left and run along the road, back toward downtown, then right up the crew hill and over the railway bridge. I slow a little as I trace the border of the triangular park, my eyes finding the turnoff to the Matlacks' street. I could run down and say hello, I have before and 11 isn't too late, but Laura's gone, off to college, a new chapter in life that, for the first time since we were 3, doesn't include me.

So I stick to the park for two legs of the triangle, then go straight, recrossing the train tracks — at street level this time — and turn right to follow Lincoln Street past Gerry's and the train station and Lincoln Street School, where, as a third-grader, I got my first detention for fighting a bunch of boys.

I head for home now but, on a whim, hook another right at the crosswalk by the church and run through southside, past Dunbar and Webster and Wentworth, all buildings I couldn't name for the first 12 years I lived here, and on past the gym and security to the dirt road that runs behind the track. I go carefully here — I've twisted my ankles in these potholes before — and slow to duck under the security bar at the bridge. If Clare were with me tonight we'd pause our run now to jump, looking up at the stars as we fall to black below, laughing and swearing as we kick through the icy water to shore, but she's home in New York and the jump isn't the same on your own, so I press on.

The fields by the observatory always scare me after dark; there's an ever-present fog that hangs over them, and I sprint the cracked cement road that leads me back to town. My second-to-last turn takes me left through downtown, past the Loaf and Ladle and the Chocolatier and the IOKA which has closed and reopened so many times I've lost count. I pass the boathouse and take one last left, sprinting up Spring Street to Will House and the bookstore.

I stop by the lion rampant flag that hangs outside the store's glass front and walk back to Will House, to flop in the relative cool of the grassy backyard. There are more streetlights now than there were when I was little — just one of the many tiny faculty kids playing outside dining hall after dark — but I can still pick out a few constellations as I listen to my heartbeat slow to normal. My cat trots across the yard to me and rubs his cheek against mine in greeting. His fur sticks to my sweat. Disgusting. I don't care. The boundaries are gone. Exeter is still small, still familiar, but something about the combination of night and motion has brought a new element to the equation. Things I have known my whole life hold new value, and I no longer feel fenced in. This is something I've discovered recently, a balance between static and movement, the ability to find motion within the confines of my everyday life, and it has made all the difference in the world for me.

I am on the end of the old diving raft on Lake Pasquaney, gripping the pebbled blue board with my toes, rising and falling with the waves under the raft, and now I have launched, and I am in the air but not long enough even to notice, and now I am deep, deep in the water, the rush of my dive fading to a slow turn, and I kick up through clear cold, grinning bubbles at the green golden rays of evening sun that slant down to meet me. Suspended in motion. My stomach fills with happiness.

KATHY BROWNBACK

September 30, 2010

Opposites attract, and they have always attracted me. I don't know how old I was when I began to sense that there was an underlying connection between contradictions. Maybe it all began with my birth — my mom used to tell the story of how, with her fifth child, she thought she had childbirth mostly figured out and wanted to spend as little time in the hospital as possible. My dad had taken my two older siblings, Missy and Jess, to his parents' house in Philadelphia, leaving Mom with my year-and-a-half-old brother, John, and a very large Polish woman named Beatrice Lummuka, who had retired from nursing to child care and ruled the place when my parents were away. She brought a combination of great cooking, a genuine enjoyment of children, and the absolute ability to inspire terror when needed, which in our case was frequent. In the very early morning of my birth on August 23, which the astrologically literate among us will recognize as the cusp of Leo and Virgo, my mom waited until the very last minute to drive herself to the Arnot Ogden hospital a few miles away, and I arrived in the emergency room a few minutes

---

Kathy Brownback has taught in the Academy's Religion Department since 1988, and has served as dean of students, clerk of the Trustees, chair of the Religion Department, chair of the Assembly Committee, and assistant school minister. She lived in Hoyt and McConnell halls with her husband, Harvey Shepard, and son Nate '08 and now resides a short walk away in Exeter. With her husband, Kathy has entered the world of dog owners, with a chocolate-brown Havanese poodle pup named Ollie.

after she walked in the door. It was not until my son Nate was born that I realized how really close I came to a chaotic landing in the middle of a deserted Hoffman Street, with the fiery and impulsive energy of Leo roaring off into the universe and the quietly pragmatic Virgo delivering her cool assessment: "This was very poorly planned." Obviously, I didn't plan this one, but it has felt pretty much that way ever since — two very different energies battling each other for my attention.

There was another side to my birth — the year before John was born, my sister, Sarah, had died of a respiratory illness that came on overnight, at the age of a year and a half. My existence as another daughter was the kind of complicated blessing and reminder that only grief can produce. I did not learn of my sister's death until I was 8 years old, but the aftermath swirled through my childhood nevertheless, and I began to sense that there are more- and less-apparent levels to our existence, and sometimes secrets we do not ever know. I don't know if my mother ever read Bertrand Russell when he said, "No one can sit by the bedside of a dying child and believe in God," but it was a sentiment with which she profoundly agreed, and I have deep compassion for one who holds it, although I eventually came to my own conclusion, and a very different understanding of God.

Another of those apparent opposites was my grandfather, my mother's father, who had played a leading role in the development of the atomic bomb during his long career at Union Carbide, which was one of the most prominent chemical companies in the world until the Bhopal disaster in 1984 forced its merger with Dow Chemical. The chief of the Manhattan Project, Leslie Groves, wrote to my grandfather in December of 1945, "No one outside the project can ever appreciate how much we depended on you and how well you performed your well-nigh impossible task." Grandfather was described in Stephane Groueff's book about the project as "a sturdy two-fisted Irishman" with a comic sense of humor (causing my brother to ask how many fists most Irishmen had) — a driving force behind the company who was so productive and had such energy that his Society of Chemical Industry award citation read "it seemed there must be over 100 men named James A. Rafferty who worked for Union Carbide and its many units." I was named after him, with my middle name James, since he died the year before I was born. My dad used to joke that I could apply to Yale — then still all-male — as K. James Brownback, and if I played my cards right they'd probably never know I was a girl until I got there. Exactly how that was to work out in practice once I did get there was left to be determined. I was my grandfather's proud namesake until as a high school student I saw the film *Hiroshima* and watched peoples' irradiated skin being peeled from their bodies, and first heard the expression "The living will envy the dead." Having always heard that the bomb was necessary to end the war, I uneasily read the debates about its use in the Truman administration, and began to wonder how necessary. But my grandfather's life was in chemistry and business, not in politics, and he was also instrumental in the development of synthetic rubber, which during the war freed the U.S. from dependence on the rubber plantations of the Philippines. "Synthetic" to him meant an improvement and it meant independence from the vagaries of the natural world. There was nothing approaching an environmental movement back then, and no question for him that there would be better living through chemistry. Only much later did "man-made" begin to suggest something artificial and inorganic, with environmental dangers attached. If he ever doubted the accomplishments of his life he didn't speak widely of it, and it is understandable to me why he believed so strongly in what he did. But he became a complicated hero for me, and remains so now.

My own father, who was part of the dairy industry, was a true conservative in most ways but was also one of the first natural-foods people I ever knew.

He was easily able to identify additives and chemical agents by taste, and never allowed them in his own products. Margarine might as well have been made out of rubber, to hear him talk about it. Just as well that his father-in-law, my grandfather the chemist, had been dead 10 years before the artificial chemistry of food began to surface as a major issue. But my father, dealing with state and federal environmental regulations at his manufacturing plants, never identified with environmentalism or anything close to it. I listened to intense and fractious debates about Goldwater between my increasingly liberal mother and my conservative father and uncle, the only benefit of which was to make the subject of whether or not I had eaten my asparagus less and less significant as the meal wore on. "May I please be excused?" became more a plea than a polite question during that political season. We hadn't even gotten to the Vietnam war yet, which took another round of heads off the table, and when I began to weigh in regularly on environmental issues my head was among them.

But it was not just at home that there were these moments of stark opposition: I gazed dumbfounded at a close friend from South Carolina who, upon hearing the news of Martin Luther King's assassination, said forcefully: "That's good. I'm glad someone finally got him." She was expressing a sentiment that our Southern friends will remind us did not belong to the South alone. But in the weeks thereafter I had to figure out what to do with the friendship, which did not survive, and the confusion of feelings, which did. From many other moments like this, I grew up feeling as though life was an endless log-rolling contest, in which whatever truth you thought you were standing on soon twisted out from under you and dumped you screaming into the river. Good and bad were terms that intertwined and at times seemed inseparable.

I would be surprised if you don't have many of the same kinds of stories, some comical and some intensely painful and some a strange combination of both. We are born with these — what Zen teacher Diane Hamilton calls the koans of our lives. A koan is a kind of contradiction or puzzle that cannot be resolved with the rational mind except in the most superficial way, as if I were to resolve mine by saying, "Well, people are different" or "Sometimes people are misguided." And at times they are, but this gives us little to go on when the people who are so different are the people you most love in the world, and you have to learn what it means to love them anyway.

Last winter my husband, Harvey, and I traveled to Israel and Palestine for the first time, and of course contradictions were on every street corner there. For the first time I truly understood why such a small sliver of land is so desperately fought over — it is intensely beautiful in its natural features and in the culture and the architecture of its many centuries of human habitation. Along with our visits to sites holy to Jews, Christians and Muslims, we set about visiting everyone we could find on all sides of the Israeli-Palestinian crisis. Though I was familiar going in with the issues and the political and religious history and the agreements and the broken agreements and the tragic betrayals all around, it was not until I was there that I really understood the geography of East Jerusalem and the Old City and the West Bank and the security wall and settlements and the various levels of occupied zones. We had dinner with Boaz, a beloved alumnus serving in the Israeli Defense Forces, who was stationed in Hebron, where the IDF tries to keep the peace between that Arab city and a small group of right-wing settlers whom most of the Jewish Israelis we talked with strongly agreed should not be there. And we walked through that same Hebron a few days later with the father of Tamer, an equally beloved Palestinian alumnus. We saw the chicken wire that Palestinians have strung up over the main street to protect themselves from debris raining down on them by the settlers, who have bought or rented apartments above the street and hope to force out the

Palestinians one way or another. But in West Jerusalem the next night we came across a circle of Jewish students singing folk songs and hanging out at the base of Ben Yehuda Street, and I was glad that Israel is where Jewish kids can live their lives without being marginalized, as the Jews have so often been — or far worse — at the hands of so many countries, centuries before the Holocaust cemented the deal. But it was not at the hands of the Palestinians that they have mainly been threatened, and it is with the Palestinians that they must find a way to share this land.

In February I went to India by myself. Harvey decided to stash his traveling shoes for this part of my winter term leave, and so I joined a tour with the Buddhist teacher and pilgrimage leader Shantum Seth, who is here today and will speak in assembly tomorrow. We started in Delhi and went eventually to Rishikesh and north along the Ganges, where the river is clear and deep and rushes over rapids between high peaks of the Himalayas. As some of you will remember, I carelessly picked up a common parasite called giardia. Luckily I wasn't sick there, but after I got home I lost 15 pounds in two weeks before it was slowly diagnosed and I recovered. In the meantime, I began to look more and more as though I were auditioning for the role of Yorick, the dead court jester about whom Hamlet reminisces when the grave-digger proffers up his skull. Alarmed friends like Susan Keeble were looking up my doctor's phone number and threatening to have me committed. I intoned miserably that giardia was code for "Gee, aren't you dead yet?" and that the name Flagyl, the drug of choice, was the short form of the verb "to flagellate." All this served to establish India in Exeter's mind as the weight-loss capital of the world.

But in all seriousness, India, like Israel, was a life-changing experience. As a teacher of mine said of my travels, "These were not two randomly chosen civilizations." Both Israel and India have been centers for spiritual seekers for millennia and both are wracked to this day by strife that in part has to do with religion. Both have deep religious texts that one would hope would have long since carried the day toward peace and understanding. Both are surprisingly beautiful. Both exude an extraordinary energy of both masculine and feminine dimension. North of Rishikesh, Shantum and I stood at the confluence of the two rivers that form the Ganges River, usually called the goddess Ganga, a place called Devprayag, where Brahmin priests hold the flame ceremony of *aarti* every night at sunset and offer prayers to the goddess for the worshippers who gather. In another hundred or so miles the river will come crashing out of the Himalaya to begin its long course westward across the country to the sea. It will become deeply polluted, testimony to India's, and to some extent every country's, inability to manage its material affairs on Earth. The river will also sustain millions, both as a water source and as a spiritual connection unmatched in India. There was something about being there — the hint of impermanence, or perhaps of eternal creation, that was undeniable as two rivers came together to form a new and more powerful one. Is it impermanence? Or is it eternity? Creation? Or destruction? To mark the power of a confluence as India so often does gave me a deep sense of a level of reality that we do not always value or even notice — the coming together of difference and the endless work of creation, out of apparent opposites — opposites that attract because they are part of a larger whole. It seemed to me that Israel and Palestine and India are countries that hold in tension the streams of our varied understandings of the world, at times forming a new bond and at times magnifying the ways in which people desperately hold onto separate truths.

For a while, in recent human history, it began to seem that all of this would fade away — science would explain everything to us and the strife of religion would take its place with other antiquities. But even science can't solve the human condition. There is a fragility to our world, and we are always aware of it. Duncan Holcomb sent me a poem he found, in which Linda Pastan speaks of "the strict contract between love and grief." We all know that contract. Everything we do is characterized by impermanence — to call attention to it seems rude and abrupt. We know it, quietly — that good things don't last forever, that love risks heartbreak and that death comes for all. So there is this anxiety that lurks, for any reasonably observant person, and even the best of science can't take it away. Science can often help clean the rivers and feed the people and cure diseases, but science by its own admission can't do much in depth with the subject of love, or the human heart. It can tell us what our brains look like when we feel love, but what is observable on a computer screen is still on the outside. We live our lives from the inside. The question of why we go on loving, which most of us do despite excellent reasons not to — that is a question that lives inside us. A teenager near and dear to me recently said to a rabbi friend, "I've made it a summer project not to have a heart." And the rabbi laughed and said, "That's a good summer project. Not much longer than that, though." Who hasn't tried it, at least from time to time? But something draws us on, and it always seems that the deeper pleasure of life has to do with knowing how to love.

In every religious tradition — in the Atman/Brahman linking of yoga, the meditation practices of Buddhism, the chants and sacred dance of Sufis and Hindus, the grounding of tai chi or qigong, the Christian path of genuine service to others, the *ayin* practice of Judaism, the shamanic connection to the Earth as a part of our being — all these are about connecting with the deep reservoir of the heart, the real source of love and creativity, what Christians might call their great koan, how we can understand the consciousness of one who is fully human and fully divine.

In most traditions the breath unites what is within with what is without, with a steady internal awareness that everything is connected. Not the same, but connected. A koan can be resolved only in that way — moving beyond apparent opposites to a deeper awareness that unites them. The poet Kabir: "Between the conscious and the unconscious, the mind has put up a swing." Or Rumi: "Out beyond ideas of rightdoing and wrongdoing there is a field. I'll meet you there." The challenge is to fit this understanding into the shape of a human life, and it is a path that goes through the heart. It also goes through the mind, but it goes through the heart, and in the end they are not separate. "Eventually," as Norman Maclean wrote, "all things merge into one, and a river runs through it." When the religions are not descending into the pit, into division and separation and absurd claims of superiority, they know of this path.

I think often about Exeter, and the ways so many people here are seeking more understanding, in the company of others or quietly on their own with other teachers and paths. The Mind/Body group is one of them. It's a challenge for us as an academic institution, one in which we want to be at the top, but want not to become heartless and emotionally drained and exhausted in the process, atop a devastated Earth. That's a big challenge, but we can't escape it. It requires an admission of vulnerability and a kind of humility, the best kind of humility. One part of it is to tap into a sense of gratitude that we often have here, for each other, for the many moments of love and depth that occur between people, for the generosity and the energy that underlie our lives here — and to know that it is far older than we are, far deeper than any of us are individually. There is much less here, at times, but so often there is this great love. The heart stretches and breaks, but is not destroyed. And in it the vast energy of the world and the particular unique paths of our own hearts are no longer opposing. They are joined. The Indian poet Rabindranath Tagore said, "The same stream of life that runs through my veins night and day runs through the world and dances in rhythmic measures." Listen now in closing to an invocation of that stream, with a drum poem of John de Kadt, about the big self that flows through us and, if we can tolerate its vastness, brings us home to ourselves, to the sound of all hearts beating, to the infinite backdrop for the unique sound of every human life.

THIS RHYTHM IS NOT MINE*

this rhythm is not mine

it comes from all hearts beating

all things opening and closing

it comes from the silent movement

of fishtails in the ocean

and from the swinging of waves and tides

it comes from the woodpecker

and from the way the ants

parade across the ground

it comes from the circling sun

and swaying leaf

that falls every autumn

no this rhythm is not mine,

but none of these

can claim it either, not even the spinning moon

in her waning and waxing

can boast its creation

this rhythm is old

and as constant as our sure death

and as sure as the way morning

appears again and again

on the horizon

nothing does not dance to this rhythm

it is heard in every speck of all the worlds

even the gods are forced to step in time

it's been around so long

it never began

*The piece may be heard at https://www.youtube.com/watch?v=cPURRzPYOnE.
Used by permission of the composer.

TODD HEARON
January 27, 2011

Good morning, Exeter. I hadn't planned on giving another meditation — I gave one back in the fall term and usually have to wait a year or so for the meditative juices, as it were, to bubble to the surface. There's not been much bubbling under this recent slew of ice and snow. But there was an opening in the schedule, and I saw something a couple of weeks ago that set me thinking. I wanted to take this opportunity to try to parse and share some of those thoughts in this forum, in this way. You can see what you can make of them.

The other day, I was walking down by the Squamscott River, our tidal river that flows through town down by the mill, that the crew members know so intimately in the spring. It's frozen now, with the 4-or-so-feet-thick ice that draws the fishermen out each year to its center to drill their meager holes and sit all night in the bone-numbing, blood-curdling cold, angling for smelt. It's something I would never want to do, and it must take a certain breed of sportsman to muster the hell-bent, godforsaken gall to drag his materials out there against all common sense — the wood and canvas and pipes that make up his little ice-fishing shanty with its propane stove — and spend all night in near-zero temperatures with just his thoughts and the whine of the wind and the powdery drift of snow

---

Todd Hearon has taught English at Exeter since 2003. He served as dorm head of Dunbar Hall and now lives in Cilley House with his wife, Maggie Dietz, and their twins, Lionel and Kempie.

that slips and curls in ghostly tendrils around the seagulls sitting around the shack, hunkered down into their lonely seagull selves, thinking their seagull thoughts. It's the picture to me of loneliness — or maybe rather, to use an Irish phrase, *ciúineas gan uaigneas,* solitude without loneliness — and since I moved here and first witnessed it, I have been fascinated and drawn to the sight. Though again, never so much as to want to attempt it myself. Exeter lost one English teacher, Jim Valhouli, on the icy river some years ago, and though he was here before my time and I didn't know him, I always think of him whenever I imagine myself walking out there on the frozen river, tempting fate with an act of faith.

But I was walking down there two Mondays ago; it was snowing, very cold; all was white. I turned the corner by the boathouse and made my way down to the water when I stopped, stunned by a little square of color pulsing way out there in all that white, a red fluttering patch, and couldn't believe my eyes. Strapped to a pole, hoisted over one of the ice fishermen's shacks, there flew, of all things, the Confederate flag, old Stars and Bars, streaming broad and defiant in the snow-laden wind. Not a soul anywhere to be seen, just that. The frozen river under snow, snow falling slantways in the wind, the white bank on the other side, snowy pines, the white shack, and this — something I, a Southerner, never in my life expected to see in Exeter, New Hampshire. On the river's other side, I could make out the old brick Powder House from the American Revolution with poor Old Glory sputtering vaguely out in front. And this. Weirdly juxtaposed: two flags. One on the river, the frozen tidal river, a kind of no-man's land, a liminal zone, a threshold space impossible to tread come spring when the crew boats would be cutting it up and down with their calls and the folks on Swasey Parkway walking by forgetful in shorts and sneakers and the trees unfolding their first, tentative green. This: what winter had made possible. My old friend, the Confederate flag, staking its claim. Then I remembered the day: Monday, the 17th of

January, our country's official commemoration of the life and legacy of Martin Luther King. And the whole scene suddenly darkened.

Christine Robinson — another English teacher now no longer with us — spoke recently to the school during an MLK Day assembly about the Ku Klux Klan marching through Exeter. That, too, was before my time — though not, astonishingly enough, outside the living memory of some of us still here (20, 25 years ago, maybe?). I've never personally witnessed the Klan, in all of its ghoulish, dunce-capped glory. Not to say I've never seen a Klansman face to face, without the mask; who knows? If I have seen one, or spoken to one, it's never been revealed to me that I was addressing a Grand Wizard of the Empire or Cyclops of the Den or whatever the crazy nomenclature. Thankfully in my life I've been spared the full-frontal ugly face of racism, spared having it spouted in *my* face, I mean. The skinheads that I've known and hung around have been pretty lamblike compared to their neo-Nazi counterparts, more interested in music and skateboarding and getting high than in cross-burning and people-bashing. But that certainly doesn't blind me to the fact that racist ideas and attitudes are out there, out here, everywhere and prevalent. Let me give you one recent example. A few nights ago I went to my local convenience store, Gerry's, down by the railroad tracks. I'll preface this story by telling you that whenever I go into Gerry's I am barraged by some of the most vulgar and irreverent and gut-splittingly funny jokes I have ever heard in my life, laid on by Larry, who's worked the cash register there for 27 years. Larry has an encyclopedic mind for these things and a stand-up comedian's snappy delivery. He was born in Exeter, and has lived here all his life. I know more about him than any casual customer should know: his multiple marriages, why they failed, his present love life (love lives, rather), his children, new grandchild, his arrests, the log-cutting business he works on the side, his hard times financially, the deaths in his family, his black Lab just diagnosed with tumors (his new yellow Lab named Listen). Every time I walk in, if Larry's working, I'm met with his hearty New Hampshire accent, thick as buttah, and a smile stretched the full length of his handlebar mustache, where it dips and ascends to the chops that themselves rise to a dishwater mullet, circa 1981. "Say, Tahd, how many Irishmen does it take to screw in a lightbulb? One ... and a fifth! [beat] How many mice does it take to screw in a lightbulb? Just two. [head-scratch] But how'd they get in theah?" And about a hundred more about nuns and Jesus and policemen and moose, things I couldn't possibly repeat in this sacred space. Many of his jokes are awful. Many are misogynist and lewd. Some are blasphemous. Sometimes I laugh; they're so bad, but I can't help it; sometimes I laugh against my better nature and judgment; sometimes I tell him that's horrible and a person shouldn't be able to get away with saying such things in our modern world. And Larry smiles and says, "I know, I'm goin' to hell. But hey, pal, I'll look ya up when I get theah."

So a few nights ago, I come in and he's standing at the cash register, and he must have MLK on the mind because as I walk up with my six-pack he gives me the joke that I will not now repeat to you, concerning King's assassination and the effect it's had on African-American sleep patterns. A racist joke. And it is crude. And what was my response? Righteous indignation? A profound, heart-weary sigh and the liberal's taking up, once again, the burden of redneck enlightenment? Even a soft-spoken, "That's not funny, Larry"? Nope. I smirked, shook my head in apparent disapproval, which I'm sure Larry did not for an instant buy, took my six-pack off the counter and drove home to Dunbar Hall and told my wife.

When I had told Larry earlier in the week about the flag on the river I was taken aback at his response. I asked him if he knew any of those ice fishermen out there, and he said yeah and began to name some names. When I asked if he could guess which one had stuck up a Confederate flag, he looked at me in disbelief. "What? Someone *did* that?" On MLK

Day, I replied. He thought for a second and then said, "I bet it was that son of a bitch who cut up my deer two nights ago. Jim [he gave a last name I won't repeat]. That's who it was. Jesus Christ, what an asshole. He did *that?*" In all the years I've known Larry, I have never seen him act with anything approaching moral indignation. But in that moment, he approached it. It was ire unhitched from any sense of irony. And it was shame, I think; I think he was ashamed of his town and one of its citizens. I'll never forget it.

***

Laughter dispels unease and can defuse the potentially explosive. Context is everything, right? I was reminded of that again when watching the comedian Michael Fowlin's performance here during our most recent MLK Day program. Racist jokes, racial slurs, ethnic pigeonholes and stereotypes, these were staples in the fare that he dished up piping hot to a full Assembly Hall. But coming from him, a black comedian, an actor juggling multiple ethnic masks and personae, it didn't explode. Its blunt force was deflected by its performative element; it was difficult to tell when he himself was speaking and when it was just another mask. The joke about the Indian employee at the 7-Eleven, the quips on gays and Asians, Jews and blacks: He made us laugh at our unexamined insensitivity and ingrained bigotry — ours personally and ours as a society — in an attempt to show us how far we still need to go. And he could say such things because of the context: because of who he is and what his program was and because we had come there to laugh at such things. And it was moving, in the end, because he showed us how openhearted laughter could lead to healing, and how self-reflection can lead to creative action. Still, why did something in me bristle when he said "the N-word"? I don't mean he said the N-word; he didn't say what it stands for, he said [quote] "the N-word." Why, I asked, did even he shrink from confronting that word head-on, the way he had confronted so many other vulgarities and unpleasantries, and, in confronting, had exposed them for the ugly boils they are? It felt to me that by avoiding that word, by evading the speaking of it freely and clearly, he had kept it enshrined in a mist of taboo, instead of revealing it in all of its explosive, historical actuality. It *is* explosive, as the F-bomb is explosive, still, to some. But here's another thing, let's be honest: not to say it is not to avoid it. To neuter it in euphemism, to clip it in contraction, is to make it audible in another way: to the imagination. The N-word; the F-bomb: what's left out resonates. You all know what I'm talking about.

In his essay "Civility and Its Discontents," Leslie Epstein makes a statement that I read some 25 years ago and have never forgotten: " ... behind the word nigger hangs the noose, just as the ovens burn and smoke hovers behind the word kike." These words have histories, have lives and deaths behind them, and we are doing those lives and deaths a disservice when we avoid or sanitize their historical realities — the nooses, the smoking ovens — still present in those words. I am not advocating their use casually or gratuitously — of course I'm not — but rather as part of a dialogue that seeks to look honestly at where we are and where we're going. Which is all wrapped in where we've been. I wish we *could* forget that these words had ever existed. But do those who lived and suffered and died, and who still live and suffer and die under their shadows, wish that? Do *they* wish we could forget?

It's hard to get at something when you're enmeshed in it, tangled up inside, like a fish in a net trying to comprehend the force pulling it to the surface and, eventually, to the frying pan. I'm trying in all this to understand something much larger than myself, something I'm immersed in, with others: racism. Other prejudices, too, of course, but for the time being just this one. I grew up with bigoted uncles and bigoted friends. When I was young I had a Confederate flag of my own hanging in my room. ("Heritage Not Hate," I liked to delude myself.) I'm a white male of an enlightened, educated sort, who now teaches at this enlightened educational institution, who grew up in the South but has now lived more than half his life in New England, lovely New England, white under snow where this year on Martin Luther King Day I watched the Stars and Bars defiantly blow in the breeze and went to Gerry's Variety Store on Lincoln Street and bought my six-pack of beer and got to hear, from my redneck buddy, Larry, why it is black people are afraid to go to sleep at night. "You're the reason, Larry," I said (no joke). "People like you." And he pulled a long, hangdog face and bagged my beer and delivered up the punch line: "Ya know what happened to the last one who had a dream."

I know what happened to Martin Luther King. He was shot in the year that I was born. I have lived my life in the shadow of his and other dreamers' absences and assassinations. The dwindlings of visions. The witherings of heights and hopes. And their resurgence: there's a black man in the White House (you should hear Larry riff on *that*). Gay couples can get married! I remember our friends Jill and Josey weeping as we watched Obama's inauguration on television together in our living room in Exeter, New Hampshire, where *they* could not at the time have gotten married. I remember their wedding in a sunny backyard in Swampscott, Massachusetts ...

Sunny times, those were. And yet — what do I do with the knowledge that these recent felicities and cultural evolutions would constitute my ancestors' worst dream? That's a historical fact. Here's another.

A few years ago, my cousin was doing genealogical research on the Hearons. Where did they come from before they came to this country, and, once here, where did they go and what did they become? I told him I'd already researched that: Hearon was Irish — O hEachtigherana, later Anglicized to O'Hagherin, then Aherne and Herne — from County

Clare; my great-great-great-grandfather (or something like that) had purportedly been a Dublin merchant. Not so simple, my cousin informed me. There's a Hearon Mountain in Germany, spelled our way. Well, I said, I've always heard we were Scotch-Irish, and ended up in Virginia. Well, maybe so, he said; that's probably the case: The Hearons apparently entered this country via Virginia in the 18th century. Then there's some migration into Carolina; some loss of fortune, some falling on hard times. My cousin had discovered a legal document pertaining to one of our less fortunate progenitors, a small landowner, who had gotten into debt or some legal dispute and had to sell off his property. And listed there on the document along with his fiscal and actual possessions, the house and cattle and poultry, was [quote]: "one slave." One slave. What do I do with this knowledge?

I've often, since that time, wondered about that slave, that human being. What was *his* name? Where did *he* come from? What was his fortune, or misfortune, in the service, under the ownership, of my family? What was his life after he was sold? Did he remain in Carolina? Was he sold farther south? Was he married? With children? If so, how did they fare? How did he die? Did he live to see emancipation, become a free man? Was he better or worse off for it?

There's a story in there — his story — a narrative for me to take up one day, to face into as part of my own, if I dare. That I never knew him personally, never saw his face, is entirely beside the point. He is implicated in my standing here today, as I am implicated in his absence, a nameless, faceless blank in the lists of history. And here's a mystery to ponder: *This would be the case whatever my ancestry, whatever my identity, ethnicity, by virtue — and by vice — of my being, or claiming to be, an American.* He is one with all of those we've bought and sold, profiteered from, villainized, debased, dehumanized, encamped, encased — he comes with the package of our brightest national dream. He is my future, in some collective way I am still trying to imagine.

He comes to me sometimes as a shadow, a darkness I can't shrug, can't be without. He hangs around, he looks over my shoulder when I write. I step on him when I walk.

He was with me, right beside me, two Mondays ago when I stood beside the white frozen river, looking at the beautiful, sorry scene. White on white. Snowy New Hampshire. A blood-red, fluttering patch. A shadow on the snow my very shape of dark. My absence of light. A second self.

***

T.S. Eliot writes in *Four Quartets*, a poem I've been rereading with my seniors, "We must be still and still moving." That is, as I take it, we must make time for reflection, which meditation can afford, and we must look for opportunities to turn reflection into creative action. To be still *and* still moving. This mediation is far from being finished. There is still much work to be done.

JONATHAN WANG

September 15, 2011

Against one of the walls of my parents' living room sits an upright piano. It's the kind that I've seen in many houses, which is to say that it is brown, sturdy and silent. My sister began taking lessons somewhere around when she was 7 and did so through a good number of her teenage years. But at least at that time, she treated piano as a chore, never giving herself over or devoting enough time to what talent she had. Since then, the piano has gone unplayed. Neither I nor my father ever learned to play the piano formally, and my mother, who claimed that she was a somewhat accomplished pianist in her youth, never played more than something that sounded like a repetitive and somber chant, three or four chords played on a continuous and progressively depressing loop. Eventually, she, too, stopped. In the time between then and now, the piano has become something else altogether, changing gradually and almost imperceptibly in the manner that autumn's crispness becomes winter's chill. Framed family photos have always sat atop the piano, but now they are accompanied by a clock radio, perhaps to create some sort of musical illusion when it is on. The bench has become a makeshift bookshelf, the keyboard cover a place for keys and mail. The space under the piano and bench is used for storing items out of the way in an area that is otherwise unused. The piano is unplayable now, simply because

---

Jonathan Wang was an English instructor at the Academy from 2008-2012. He has since moved back to New York City.

it would take too long to turn it back into one. I've spent the past couple of years trying to convince my parents to sell it or at least give it away to a person or family who will make use of it. This would be a perfect wall for a mounted plasma television, I've told them. The living room in the house is relatively small and the television currently sits nestled in a corner obscured at some angles by a tall plant, by the staircase to the second floor and even by the piano itself. But my suggestions have gone ignored. Though my mother has been a bit more open to the idea as of late, my father is a man who resists change — especially sudden change — in a manner that is almost aggressive. Routine suits him, and though what used to be a piano has now become something else, its presence against that wall provides a comfort to him that cannot be replaced by a 42-inch plasma screen.

Such was the case in the job he worked for 17 years. He woke up at 6, was on the 6:52 bus and went to his office at the World Trade Center. He never once took a sick day and used his vacation days sparingly, only to see extended family in Taiwan. I don't remember him speaking fondly of his work as an accountant but I know now the purpose each day gave him. When his firm told him they were moving to Philadelphia and they had a position for him there, he turned them down, choosing instead to stay in New York. These were a difficult last few weeks at work for him. What would he do with his time? Could he find another job, and how long would that take? The uncertainty maddened him, though at the time, he did his best not to let us in on his frustration. His last day of work was August 31, 2001. For 10 days, this was the vacation my father never wanted. He read the paper, he listened to news radio, he watched *The Price Is Right*. But he rarely left the house, feeling confined to it by a purposelessness that was all but crippling. The 11th day put some of this into perspective. "All my co-workers and I were there just a couple weeks ago," I remember him saying to me as we watched helplessly on television and tried to make sense of what we were seeing.

There is not much more that I can remember about that day, and even the two or three that followed, with anything resembling absolute assurance. Memory has a way of hiding in my mind and becomes and reappears as something else, nebulous and constantly shifting. Vivid flashes of moments appear, not unlike the way the stark white of a car's headlights on a dark road can quickly but briefly illuminate the name and number on a mailbox or the alert eyes of a small animal. That was to be my first day of school and I do remember the excitement that always accompanies it. Remembrance and anticipation come from different families, one coming after and the other before. But they share the bond of ultimately being removed from actuality. Most accounts of that day begin by noting the clearness of the sky, the immaculateness of the view of the city from any angle. It is as if the hope that such a day provides could rescue it from its fate, or that a cloudy day would have somehow made inexplicable events easier to foresee. My anticipations for my first day of school had nothing to do with what did occur and my memories of the day and what followed are also likely altered by the natural seasonal changes of remembrance. The words "Never Forget" appeared all over the city in the months that followed, and are still present, relatively modest though they may be now. But the fading of these words' presence is certainly no indication that we no longer need the reminder. In fact, I recognize it now for what it was always meant to be: a command.

By the afternoon of that day, I began hearing from friends outside of New York. By then, most of my friends and the rest of my family in the city had been accounted for. The news seemed to hit people outside of the city in a manner that made it seem as though all 8 million of us were physically affected by what was happening downtown. Spotty cell phone service did not help. I received several emails asking that I respond when I could.

They could not reach me by phone and they had become increasingly worried. Several friends remembered that I had spent a summer working in the World Trade Center and had convinced themselves that I was still there. What had been so bizarre on television suddenly became more real than I had anticipated. I was no longer just a witness but a victim. With the subways down for the next day and a half, the area below 14th Street closed except to emergency workers, and school closed until further notice, I spent the next couple of days watching the news on every channel, even MTV. I read every article in the *Times* about it, looked at every picture. "Go watch a movie or something," I remember my mother saying. The concept of home is larger than physicality. New York City is part of every story I tell, even, or especially, the ones that don't take place there. It is an integral part of who I am and I probably wear it a little too proudly. Though every person I knew well was safe, it still felt as though a dear friend had been critically hurt. The movie theaters were open, but it didn't feel right acknowledging that I could do anything but anguish at a time like this.

That Sunday at church, I remember a number in the congregation that had surpassed any I had been a part of before. It seemed we were all searching for something. Still, I cannot recall the sermon's message, its topic, even the passage from the Bible on which it all centered. But the pastor did alter one moment of the service: Usually, after the sermon and before the congregation was dismissed, the pastor asked us to greet someone around us whom we did not know. This was always a moment that gave me a sense of uneasiness. As one who has never been good at social interaction, especially with strangers, a gentle push by a pastor to meet others has always felt unnatural. Would I really become friends with someone I met in that way? There were Sundays during which I would quickly leave my seat so as to avoid this moment. But on this day, he asked us to greet each other before the sermon. I was sitting on the aisle and so turned to my right. The woman next to me, a stranger, smiled at me and said hello. I waved awkwardly as if she in fact was not less than a foot away from me. "Hi," I said. She turned her body toward me and leaned in to hug me. Noticing that my arms were dangling at my side, I reached around her and returned the gesture. "How are you?" she asked. Reflexively, I answered, "I don't know." The great irony of living in New York City is that the lack of space in a relatively small city for such a large population has made us fiercely independent and possessive of what little space we do have. For this and other reasons, I have always lived by a strict no-touching policy. Handshakes maybe, but definitely no hugs. This woman's presumptuousness was jarring, but I remember holding on a shade longer than she did. Somehow the greatest violation of our collective space managed to bring us all closer. What healing I had that day came through intimacy I don't remember wanting.

After the service, by the coffee and mini muffins, I saw Auggie, someone I had known for about a year, but who had quickly become one of my close friends. He worked in Building 7 and did a combination of running and walking the almost 100 blocks from his office to his apartment that previous Tuesday morning. His hair was disheveled, which was odd since he always took great care with his appearance. He looked sleep-deprived, as did I, and when we saw each other, he gave me a weary look that I imagine I reciprocated.

"You made it out OK," I said, somewhere between a statement and a question.

"Well, I made it out," he responded. He reached out and held my shoulder. "Can I call you sometime this week?" he asked. I could tell that he was tired of telling his story, of putting into words what could never be expressed, and was pre-empting any questions I had about what he had been through. In fact, I did not want to talk about it either.

"Please do," I said. Though we had nowhere to go, we both turned away from each other and walked in opposite directions. Before I left, I saw that he was standing alone among the muffins. That was the last time we spoke.

The Mets played the city's first sporting game since the attacks on September 21 against the Atlanta Braves. I brought my secondhand manual camera, which I had bought just recently for a black-and-white photography class I had registered for. It was in "like new" condition, with just the frame counter broken. These photos would be among my first submissions to the class, I decided: a stirring, emotional and patriotic tribute to the — to my — city. Except, when I returned home from the game, I realized that I had improperly loaded the film. I'd pressed the shutter button many times but I had not actually taken any pictures. The only images I would retain from that game would rest in my memory. I remember ushers handing out small American flags at the entrance gates. I remember knowing I would keep mine forever. I lost it soon after. During the national anthem, on the Jumbotron, the camera panned across the lines of players of both teams; it paused on a teary Mike Piazza. I remember we all cheered when we saw that. The Mets won that game on a Piazza two-run home run in the bottom of the eighth. Throughout the game, the crowd broke out often in "USA" chants, simultaneously waving their souvenir flags. But these were the Atlanta Braves. We all loved our country but we still hated Chipper Jones. There was no easy return to normalcy but I remember that sense of uneasiness that comes with laughing too loudly at a funeral. Was it too early to be celebrating a Mets win — how could we have known at the time how rare they would become these 10 years later — when would we be able to enjoy a game, or anything, without mournful guilt? To be a Mets fan is to appreciate close wins and to endure late-inning, and late-season, losses. Just the previous year, we had lost to the Yankees in the World Series, only solidifying our status as New York's second-best baseball team. We are not fans who get overly excited after a win, somehow knowing that a loss is soon to follow; it always does. That each team is in the race for a championship on opening day has not seemed always to apply to us. The prevailing sentiment among Mets fans is something close to, "One day we may just win the World Series." But this evening, I remember feeling a different kind of hopefulness: We would get past this together.

Growing up in New York City, my friends and I had few places to spend time together outside of school. Most of us lived with our families in apartments that were too small to fit all of us comfortably, especially since many of these apartments already housed more than they were made for. We spent more time at the Manhattan Mall than we cared to measure. There are only so many times you can wander the aisles of the music store or eat at the McDonald's in the basement, watching as people get out of the subway station. Since we rarely ventured farther south than the Lower East Side, the Staten Island Ferry became that rare and special opportunity to get as close as any of us thought we would to a cruise.

I remember those times standing on the back deck as the ferry pulled out and away from lower Manhattan. We were leaving home to take a journey across a tiny ocean. It was those trips that informed my understanding of what the ocean smelled like: salty and a little sick-making. The winds that swirled around our heads made it difficult to hear or speak. But aside from pointing out the towering building that seemed to touch the sky that my father worked in and talking a bit about seeing the city from this perspective, I don't remember sensing that we had much more to say in those moments. There was no use in raising our voices above the wind the way we did when the subway passed between stops. We never actually spoke about these trips before or after we made them, something I only realize now. We decided we would go, and that was it.

I remember the white trail of foam that pointed the way back and how it faded toward us like cartoon trails of gunpowder. I don't remember the first time, probably because each time felt new. I couldn't believe there weren't more of us on that ferry enjoying the ride. In my mind, we were pioneers, experiencing something in a way no one else had. Still, there was safety in knowing that we weren't venturing very far. Lower Manhattan was always within view, home never out of reach, my dad always sort of in sight. For what amounted to something like half an hour, we would leave our homes and then be brought right back soon after. After all those rides on the ferry, I never set foot on Staten Island.

Some time after the attacks, I took the ferry again for the first time since high school. The South Ferry station was sleeker than I remembered, a hall of glass that reminded me of a museum or maybe an airport. But climbing the ramp to the deck of the ferry was familiar. There was that same salty sick smell. There was that same orange paint. There, in the distance, was the Statue of Liberty. We pulled away slowly, slower than I remembered. The breeze around me picked up again as it always had, fixing my gaze on lower Manhattan. I could no longer point out where my father worked, his building now only visible in my mind's eye. I was reminded of the romanticism of this trip, the escape, but also suddenly saw how things had changed. From this vantage point, downtown looked almost as it had all along. After mourning over loss, it seemed almost inappropriate to see that it had so quickly recovered in a way that made the towers' absence inconsequential. By then, the downtown area had been cleared, only a crater remaining that I could not see from the ferry. The mangled rubble of collapse that rose higher than the buildings that surrounded it was gone. So was the smell. The layers of dust that settled on the neighborhood had been wiped away. On one of my visits to lower Manhattan the week following the attack, I traced my finger over a layer of dust that coated a window of a Chase Manhattan bank. That drawing was surely gone. The collage of posters from family members looking for their lost loved ones lingered but their corners were beginning to curl and fray, the pictures of those for whom they were looking beginning to fade and become sun worn. I loaded the film into my camera properly on those days but I don't look back at those photographs; out-of-focus images in my memory have been enough.

Sometime in the late '90s I worked for one day setting up an event at Windows on the World, the restaurant at the top of the World Trade Center's north tower. The morning was overcast. But from the altitude of the 107th floor, it felt more like we were immersed in a dense fog. We were in the clouds, the windows sweating with condensation. But the sun burned through by late morning and I remember looking out at the new view. Looking about New York City from street level, we see cars slowly making their way down crowded avenues, people walking with purpose, garbage sometimes drifting in the wake of the city's motion, and incomprehensibly large buildings, all in familiar proportions to ourselves. But from this perspective, at this distance, immensity became miniscule, details obscured. My line of vision traveled all the way uptown, past the Empire State Building, past Central Park, a distance that would have taken far more time to cover from the ground. A distance that could be reached in such a short time only through ambition and perhaps what others saw as hubris. From here those who designed and built this place where I was standing managed to transform the way I saw. Standing at that vantage point gives the viewer something like hope that one day he can also affect others in such a profound way; that he might bring others out from the vastness whose shadow imposes itself over them. But the mind tries to fill in what the eye cannot quite make out. Are those people down there? Do I know any of them? I think that's the corner where I got that great slice of pizza. The distance of time has had a similar effect on my memory. The farther I get from the ground zero of my remembrances of that day, the more I must try to fill in the minute details that made those moments real — an increasingly ambitious task. We need the change that time naturally provides us; we would never have moved forward with our lives otherwise; I have come to understand if not wholly appreciate the power of resiliency. And yet I have wanted to keep those people and things we have lost with me, despite the difficulty of such a prospect. We cling to memories, cleave to them as if they were objects, like pianos or looming towers. But they resist us, fading, changing, slyly transforming without our noticing. Still, 10 years later, I make a promise to the city of my birth, the city of my upbringing: I will never forget.

ERICA PLOUFFE LAZURE
The Transit of Venus
January 18, 2012

"All things of the sea belong to Venus; pearls and shells and alchemists' gold and kelp and the riggish smell of neap tides, the inshore green, and purple further out and the joy of distances and the roar of falling masonry, all these are hers, but she doesn't come out of the sea for all of us."

—John Cheever, *The Wapshot Chronicle*

1. Mixing Memory and Desire

At first, I was glad for his getaway. I was glad, in spite of my relatives' worries and my mother's daily reports, that, at 88, my grandfather would finally take his cross-country trip. I was glad to think of him in his own John Wayne-style Western, passing grazing horses and acres of wheat, cruising toward the Pacific. I was glad to think of him finally able to override 66 years of my grandmother's bitter will that kept his travels limited to his daily postman's route, the Rotary Club and the staged adventures of cable television. He, finally, was going to live. But as with

---

Erica Plouffe Lazure is the author of two fiction chapbooks, *Heard Around Town* and *Dry Dock*. She was the 2009-10 George Bennett Fellow and teaches in the English Department.

all journeys, the trip came with both its gifts and its costs. We journey for escape, for adventure or, perhaps, for the something our daily stasis cannot provide. But the wanting is never the same as the having, and, as my grandfather soon learned, by leaving home, he did not necessarily leave with it his problems.

For one, his once-able body grows stiff from stroke. He speaks with a slur. His hearing aids, useless. My grandmother's dementia at this time is so advanced, her demeanor is that of a baby; she communicates in nonsense songs, and therefore cannot protest their westward journey, as she certainly would have otherwise. Driving them is my Aunt Michele — my father's sister, who is one more drunk drive away from a lengthy stay in jail, who has no idea how far 3,000 miles is from our hometown in central Massachusetts, or what it means to sit behind the wheel of a car, sober, for hours, instead of hiding upstairs in her childhood bedroom with her computer and her bottle. But on Columbus Day weekend she packs the car and, without a word to anyone, drives the three of them across Massachusetts and New York, through Pennsylvania and West Virginia and Kentucky, down toward San Antonio, then Albuquerque, and finally Flagstaff, stopping along the way to visit members of our extended family. Their goal is to reach the "big trees" — the sequoias — on the California coast, where my grandfather's sister lives. But Michele forgets their medicine; the GPS melts in the heat; and the view from the highway offers no wheat fields or grazing horses. Rather, as my grandfather says later, it reminds him of the Mass. Pike. At some point, Grammy stops her singsongs and instead lies huddled in a ball in the backseat. They soon discover she can no longer walk. When my aunt starts drinking again, she finds herself lost in the wrong part of Houston, unable to find her way back to the hotel. A week later, at a bar in Flagstaff, she meets a man, who invites all three of them back to his house. They go. Once inside, the man asks my grandfather to borrow his car. He takes the keys, and disappears. My aunt panics and calls her cousin Ann Marie in Indiana, claiming they've been "kidnapped," but for some reason doesn't call the police. Hours later, the man returns on foot. He's crashed the car's front end into a stretch of trees. They find it the next day and tow it to a mechanic, who replaces the busted front tires. Then, they press on to the Grand Canyon. When they arrive, they get out of the car, take photos of the stones and drive home.

As you might imagine, the phones in my family during this time are constantly abuzz. Michele — who, for reasons far more complicated than space here allows — will not voluntarily call my parents, nor will she answer when they call. But she remains in constant contact with Ann Marie, who in turn reports the latest to my mother, who then calls me. "Pepere made his choice," I tell Mom, as I always do. My mantra for their predicament is "Stupidity isn't illegal." But I, too, grow upset with my grandfather and aunt, and wonder whether my grandmother — or any of them — will survive the trip. I should explain that, over the years, as my dad's hearing fails, Mom has become my father's ears and, at times, his voice. He's inherited — as I have — my grandfather's weak ears. When my brother and I were kids, we'd fashion a fake hearing aid out of a dry sponge tethered to a string. We'd loop the string around our ears and yell at each other, pretending to be deaf. "I CAN'T HEAR YOU!" we'd yell into the sponge before we'd tuck it into our dad's shirt pocket, snug against his smokes, and he'd pretend for our benefit to be deafer than he already was.

"What?" he'd say, fine-tuning an invisible sponge knob. "Come again?"

It's true Pepere and Michele had talked for months about the trip — they even took a test run with my grandmother to see me in New Hampshire that summer — but no one thought it would actually happen. And we didn't know they'd left until Ann Marie called my parents one day to say she'd heard from them; that they were on their way to Pennsylvania, and that Michele, at least through the phone, sounded sober. But a few days later, Ann Marie reports that Michele has stopped sounding sober, and that she is letting my grandfather — who'd lost his license after his stroke — drive the car. Something, we decide, has to be done. We track highway routes on maps, plotting like vigilantes how to head 'em off. At first, we decide, Dad and my uncle will fly to New Mexico and confront them, along with Pepere's sister from California, at a relative's in Albuquerque. But we realize Grammy is too weak to fly home. Then, Dad says he'll fly out alone and drive them back to Massachusetts himself. We give up when Ann Marie reports they've arrived at her father's house in Arizona. Michelle is behind the wheel and appears sober. They get a new GPS at Wal-Mart. Someone gives my grandmother a sponge bath. My dad finally talks on the phone with Pepere, who won't admit to driving, and who refuses my father's help. We simply have to let them be. "The best thing that could happen," my brother says, "is if they get pulled over. If he's driving, they're done. If she's drunk, they're done."

But they do not get pulled over. And they do not lend out their car to any more strangers. And while my optimism for their journey wanes with each new report, I understand what this trip means to my grandfather. My grandmother, who never wanted to go anywhere, has always been the limiting factor in my grandfather's life. But he made the most of it, attending mass daily in a three-piece suit and feathered fedora, or walking through the woods with my great-uncle, recalling his military days of sleeping in a hammock on a ship bound for Karachi. My grandmother was a housewife, a clipper of unused coupons, who'd measured her life in juice glasses of pantry Gallo. She loved her Hummel figurines and magazines. She'd spend Sundays picking apart a roast chicken. She loved nastily correcting my grandfather's French-Canadian-laced English. My first memory of her is the same as my last: she, curled on her lumpy green loveseat in a blue robe, surrounded by stacks of decades-old magazines, the television on and muted and glowing. My grandparents married in the '40s, during World War II, at an austere February Lenten service, no flowers or music, the beneficiaries of the priest's reluctant blessing, thanks to my grandfather's short-lived furlough from the Merchant Marines. In their wedding photo, Pepere wore his sailor suit; Grammy, a long white dress and an unsteady gaze. She could have gone on to college like her sister the nun, she used to tell us, but instead raised three boys and a girl. She hardly left the house after she retired from her secretarial job. Back then, there were no names for social-anxiety disorders; all we knew is that she missed most weddings and family gatherings; she never set foot in a store or had kind words at the ready; at the sight of a camera, she'd cast her apron over her face and flee. She'd stash hundreds of dollars — runaway money, she'd call it — in her magazine stacks and later forget it existed. For a while, I thought it strange how she'd repeat, several times, the details of their wedding, every time I visited. Then, a few years later, she tucked toilet paper into the toaster, pressed the lever and returned to her sofa, unaware of the countertop flames she'd left in her wake. Somehow, both she, and the house, survived. Until the extreme happens — or until someone flat-out tells you — it can be hard to understand the unmaking of a person, especially someone you're supposed to love. For even if you see it coming, ruination never announces itself. Sometimes it seeps in steadily, like a rising tide. Other times, it swallows you whole. Given what I know of her anxiety and inhibition and anger, I believe my grandmother found her peace when she lost her mind. And as I now contemplate their cross-country journey, I cannot shake my anger as I think of her curled in a ball in the back of a smoke-filled car, silent, as a urinary tract infection rages undetected through her frail frame; as my grandfather putters down the freeway at 40 miles an hour; and as my aunt dozes in the Arizona sun, her embers burning holes into the upholstery.

2. The Unreal City

Back in late 2011, the Internet was alive with speculation about a Mayan prophecy about a rare planetary alignment on December 21 — the world could end or change as we know it. The date marks the completion of a 5,000-year-old cycle on the Mayan calendar, and the accuracy of this ancient civilization's study of the stars has led some to wonder whether the year would spell apocalypse, or enlightenment, or have no effect at all. I knew little about this so-called prophecy as I planned a journey with a friend to Cancun, Mexico, in November 2011; and even less about the site of its origination, Chichen Itza, the ruins of a Mayan pyramid and observatory, and one of the world's proclaimed seven wonders.

My plans for Mexico were simple, I believed, and twofold: first, the sunshine. Second, the ocean. Take that, winter, I think, as the jet soars over acres of salt marshes, just beyond the thin turquoise shore lined by a spine of stucco hotels. An hour later, Nancy and I sit in a cab bound for our all-inclusive resort on Kukulkan Boulevard, one among the dozens of hotels I'd seen from the airplane. Its gleaming tower of stucco shines in the afternoon light, and we happily accept fresh mango juice as we wait in the atrium to check in. Later that day, we discover that the tower shields much of the sun from the hotel's scant stretch of beach, and, as it happens, the Yucatán Peninsula that week is mostly overcast. The main activity here is poolside drinking, and as we tend to avoid alcohol, conga lines and chlorine — except for an overpriced massage — there isn't much to do. Nancy, a discharged army lieutenant, just returned from a tour in Afghanistan; she'd spent October at a yoga retreat in the Berkshires. Before coming to teach at Exeter, I lived for six months in Indonesia, riding my bike through the dusty streets, groceries and a laptop stuffed into my backpack, doing yoga daily and working on a novel. The seemingly shopping mall façade of this all-inclusive hotel simply is not *us*, and we soon realize that we have not, in fact, traveled to Mexico, but rather to a place by the ocean that just happens to be *in* Mexico. A Mexico that pretends to know nothing of the drug lords seizing its inland cities and people, or of the squalor in its alleys between Senior Frog's and the Four Seasons.

And yet, six floors up, beyond the free piña coladas and water conga, there is refuge. Our hotel room's deck overlooks the sea, and the dark wooden spires of a dilapidated dock perforating the blue calm. Here you can see how the water shifts its liquid crests, how the tan sand soon cedes to the palest turquoise, and then bleeds to navy, offsetting the shimmers that collapse to their last on the pale, packed sand. One morning, an old man in a blue Speedo and white hat stretches on the beach, back arched, arms and torso flailing as in a whirlpool-for-one, a vigorous greeting to the sea. He pauses only to allow his wife to apply sun block. Then he bounds out to the ocean, flexible and free and alive.

The next day, Nancy and I join the fleets of Chichen Itza-bound buses barreling through the Mexican countryside, past thatched roof huts and dingy doorless homes and armed guards on the highway. Our Mayan tour guide, Toni Canto, tells us of the great empire of his ancestors, of their sacred pyramids and lethal athletics competitions and human sacrifices, of their complex calendars and their alphabet, of the precision in which their observatories tracked celestial patterns — particularly the transit of Venus. Nearly all their records were ruined, Toni Canto tells us, after the arrival of the Spanish Conquistador Hernán Cortés, who in the 16th century destroyed both the Aztec and Mayan civilizations. At one point, the bus passes a prison, a large stucco building with tall walls lined in barbed wire. "This is the first all-inclusive hotel," Toni Canto announces over the loudspeaker to a wave of good-natured chuckles. "When you check in, they give you a free, five-minute massage."

At Chichen Itza, we walk along the dirt-packed path toward the great stone pyramid, accosted by vendors who insist we buy their carvings of the Mayan calendar, their T-shirts, their embroidered handkerchiefs. Amid the clusters of tourists taking photos, Toni stands before the great pyramid and tells us about the feathered serpent God, Kukulkan, for whom the temple was built, and who, according to legend, inhabits the planet Venus. On the first day of spring, the sun positions across the temple and the shadow cast from its 91 steps depicts a snake — a symbol of death — descending the length of the pyramid. "Three days before the equinox," Toni Canto says, "the priests would gather a crowd, and everyone would clap their hands to call to Kukulkan. And three days later, the serpent would appear." At the pyramid's northerly face, Toni Canto demonstrates how the Mayans brought to life the temple of stone. He claps loudly in rhythms of three. "Join me," he says. As we clap, the stones' echo squawks back at us, like the caw of the Mayan quetzal bird. "Can you hear what the stones say?" Toni asks, as we clap. "Ku-kul-kan." He emphasizes each syllable with a clap, and as we summon the Mayan god from the sky, we strain to hear in our cupped hands the sacred name contained in the chirping echo.

The next afternoon, on a solo stroll by the pool, notebook in hand, I see a man supine on the patio, surrounded by a group of people. The glimpse of an unwieldy plastic tube among them assembles the words "keg stand" in my mind. But I am wrong. And I discover I am wrong just as the blond lady hovering over the man screams in Spanish, just as I see the men are wearing red medic vests, and that they are, in fact, pumping the man's massive barrel chest. His body moves from the rhythmic force of their palms, but otherwise he lies still. Everyone stops to watch the men fail and fail again to restart his heart. His wife's wails echo through the resort. I offer a silent prayer before I turn away to find a quiet spot. My hope for the man's survival, as the men pump his chest, is soon lost in my ocean of thought as I settle in with my notebook, drawing the scavenging grackles, and contemplating with dis-ease the presence of death in this supposed paradise, our summoning of Kukulkan the day before, and the unforeseen madness of my grandparents' journey.

3. Rock and No Water

In mid-November, when my grandparents return to Southbridge — safe, or, at least, alive — my grandmother's skin has turned ashen. "We need to take her to a hospital," my father tells my aunt. But she replies, "She's just tired." And they let her be. A few days later, my grandmother falls out of bed. They cannot find her. They never bother to look on the floor between the bed and the dresser, which is where the visiting nurse finds her, three hours later. My aunt goes out "for cigarettes," as she likes to call the package store, and then, drunk, drives my grandmother to the hospital. It was then they discover the urinary tract infection, which, the doctor tells my aunt, had likely developed during their road trip. My father drives my grandfather to the hospital to visit with Grammy each day. My aunt spends the week drowning in gin.

When my grandmother returns home, my father tells my grandfather that he can no longer help out as long as Michele is allowed to remain drunk in the house. He asks my grandfather to make a choice, and my grandfather, as he always has, chooses Michele. In support of my father, I write my grandfather a letter in early December, conveying the same. But I never sent the letter. And in the end, my grandmother did die, at home, in bed, within a month of her return to Southbridge. The road trip killed her, the doctor tells my aunt, giving voice to what everyone knows but would not say. I am writing this essay, three days before Christmas, when my mother calls with the news. To my surprise, I feel no grief. Later, I *write* no grief. My memories of my grandmother are thin, and I feel no loss at what I can remember; instead, I feel relief she's no longer suffering. Later, at the wake, my response to relatives who suggest that I, the writer, say something about her is this: "May she be an inspiration to each of us, to live lives ruled by engagement and love, and not by avoidance and fear." Toward the end of the evening, I say goodbye to my grandfather. He asks me to come by the house and pick out one of Grammy's Hummels. I am about to say yes when he continues, claiming that my mother had "taken the best of them but there were still a few left." The truth is that, sometime this summer, Mom had asked him for one figurine, for me, and Pepere had insisted she take more for my brother's children. Given all I could say to him in this moment, even with this false claim against my mother, I find myself paralyzed by silence. I turn away and do not say goodbye. The next day, at the funeral, the irony of my avoidance of him is not lost upon me. A week later, toward the end of my parents' New Year's Day party, Pepere asks if I'd drive him home. In the car, he mentions the Hummel again. "Come in and pick one out," he says. I consider all I've heard about refusing to inherit the ills of your family dynamics. So I take a deep breath and say, as loud as I can, that I was upset by what he'd said about my mother. "Your unkindness toward her makes it hard for me right now to be your granddaughter," I yell. I want to yell more, louder, but I don't. Not yet. Because I want him to hear me. Because I want conversation. But in the dark of his driveway, in his slow monotone, his response is, "Well, you don't have to come in if you don't want to." Then he gets out of the car. I help him to his door. He doesn't say goodbye. And when I return to my car, the words hang there, unheard. I'll probably never know if he understood what I actually said. But perhaps the reverberation in the tone of my voice is enough. Maybe no words — only echoed sounds in the car — were enough for him to know the disappointment and anger in my heart.

4. Prison and Palace and Reverberation

Last year, at a writing workshop here at Exeter, my co-facilitator invited our group to contemplate the theme of inheritance. The memory I failed to write in that session is one I offer now. A few years ago, I came across a photo of my grandmother in high school, a portrait, and in seeing it, for a moment, I saw myself: same eyes, dark hair, complacent smile for the camera. "I don't remember taking this picture," I said. But even as I said it, I knew this wasn't me. My grandfather replied, "That's your grandmother." For some reason, I'd never considered until then how much we resemble each other, how much of her DNA resides in me. Even in her last days, she'd regard me with an expression of familiarity, as though a younger version of herself had entered the room. "You're a good person," she once said, looking beyond me, to no one. The thing is, my aunt also shares our features, and it's an open secret that even before her drinking got out of control, before she fled her abusive marriage, that she'd given up a child while still in her teens, three months after I was born. My mother told me the story when I was young, and growing up I'd tried to imagine this unknown cousin. At times, I've been gripped by fear that I am, in fact, that cousin, that I am my aunt's child. And yet, I know I am too much of my mother's daughter to be anyone else's. But still, I wonder: What of her lineage, or my grandmother's, resides in me? Because I fear these genes: I fear their volatility. Their darkness. Their ruin. And I think back to the demise of the Mayans, of their once flourishing civilization, now pillars of photographed stone, and of the prophecy that our own civilization could have inherited yet another cycle of demise. But folklorist Joseph Robert Jochmans approached the implications of that prophecy in a different way: that December 2011 could have marked a time of transition, not destruction. He said, "Our moving through with either resistance or acceptance will determine whether the transition will happen with cataclysmic changes or gradual peace and tranquility." December 21 came and left, and the Earth did not flood. We saw no cataclysm. No earthquakes in the months that followed. And yet, the speculation about the possible "end of an era" captured the imagination of many: What does transformation look like? Perhaps the end of an era — or even the death of a relative — affords us the opportunity to transform — frees us from choosing the *was* that so often tends to dictate the *is*. Perhaps the possibility of transformation reminds us that choice is possible. We have a choice to resist. A choice to accept. A choice to love unconditionally, or not. We have a choice to transform. It's an idea I return to as I speak meaningless words to my grandfather in a dark car, or watch helplessly as a barrel-chested man on vacation breathes his last. For sometimes, at least in my mind, I choose to huddle in the backseat of a smoke-filled car, longing for a lumpy sofa and a stack of magazines. Sometimes, I choose to flail my arms, free before the sea, before I bound in, fearless. And sometimes I choose to stand before the ruins of *my* ancient pyramid *far* removed from the jungle of the Yucatán Peninsula, and I clap in threes, and I wait for my ancestral stones to hear me, and reply, understanding that, like my grandfather, they probably never will.

CLAUDIA PUTNAM '81
Border Patrol
January 25, 2012

Now I lay me down to sleep. I pray the lord my soul to keep. If I should die before I wake, I pray the lord my soul to take. Traditions die hard. Parents like their children to pray as they did, and as their parents prayed. As a child I got down on my knees every night. Hands clasped at the edge of a bed, I would name friends and relatives and ask God to help them out. I wish I still did this — it's akin to the Buddhist practice of *metta*, or Loving Kindness. But then came that terrifying prayer about dying in my sleep. My parents' parents, facing a higher likelihood of early death, may have found it soothing. I hardly ever slept.

Well into adulthood, when people would, kindly, I think, mention that they were praying for me, I would wonder what that meant to them. I pictured them bent over a table or a bedside, listing my name. I myself haven't prayed too often. Except when, say, trapped above tree line at 12,000 feet in a lightning storm. I knew this was cheesy of me, to call on God in emergencies only. Earlier this term, English Instructor Todd Hearon said that he struggled with petitionary prayer because he couldn't help but think that God, in all of God's vastness, must have

Claudia Putnam '81 lives in Western Colorado and was the 2011-12 George Bennett Fellow. Her work appears in dozens of literary journals.

better things to do. Intellectually, this rings true. Culturally, asking for help is uncomfortable.

There's what you *think* and what you *experience*. I went on to get profoundly lost a few times. Some years ago I read a book called *Deep Survival*, which is about how people survive in extreme situations like being lost in the wilderness after a plane crash. For one thing, they all pray. It seems that recognizing you're lost — which is what praying is — gets you found faster. Wilderness, God, lightning, pick your metaphor. When it comes down to it, we're little; that stuff is big. We make it through the night or we don't. Whatever accounts for that is as mysterious as grace.

***

In graduate school I was taught to step back from the question of God and the matter of doctrine, to look at the question of *how* people pray, the daily practice of religion. I was interested in urban Indians practicing in the Lakota traditions. I sat in cave-black sweat lodges in Denver backyards listening to men and women beg the spirits for help. The challenges they faced are shared by communities anywhere in America. Children shipping out to foreign wars. People dying of alcoholism and other diseases. Jobs that can feel meaningless, whether cleaning houses or writing code for a high-tech startup. But here there was an added layer of poignancy.

Sometimes a ceremony couldn't take place because certain songs had to be sung in Lakota. If no one had the knowledge, there could be no ceremony. In this community, as in ours, people were disinclined to ask each other directly for help. But if they petitioned the spirits during a lodge ceremony, the rest of the group would hear. Then, perhaps, someone would send a care package to a son stationed in Bosnia. Or organize a ride to your cancer scan. Canceling the ceremony meant undermining all this. I heard them making the phone calls as they searched for the guy who knew the lost song, as they sought direction on whether it might be all right to use beef liver if they couldn't get buffalo. Sometimes I could hear in their prayers a kind of weeping that sounded a lot like what goes on in *hanblechaya,* the Lakota "vision quest" rite. Help us, they would cry to the spirits, we're lost.

It's not over for the Indians. Here they are, still praying for the way back from genocide.

***

There are a lot of definitions of religion, but I have always liked Paul Tillich's broad brush. Some of you may have run across it studying here: Your faith is that with which you are ultimately concerned. Everyone has an ultimate concern. If you don't think you have one, get out from under the city lights, and lie beneath the sky for a night, alone, confronting infinity.

I had heard of the idea of "vision quest" even before graduate school, but I didn't know, then, that Indians called it *crying* for a vision. When I was around 20 I had a weird sequence of dreams. I thought I'd go sit on these hills in the middle of the Plains, to see if I had more dreams that explained what the first ones meant. Later I found out that Native Americans train for months for this. They tell themselves stories to underline the seriousness of this undertaking: So and So went up on Bear Butte, they'll say, and he came down three days later with his hair *all white.* I just thought: Dream with talking animals. Go do a vision quest.

Sacrilegiously, I climbed up on this ridge in northwest Nebraska just south of the Black Hills. I had no idea how big it was out there. I was fine for a while. I looked out at the horizon. Give me a fast horse, I thought. I want a spear. Three fighter jets ripped overhead. A big moon came up. Coyotes, supposed to have been eradicated locally, but like the Indians still hanging in, yipped and howled. I waited for my answers.

I'm not sure when in the night it struck. Some kind of terror such as you might read about in Stephen King. That's when I learned, without being told, that it's called crying for a vision. Maybe a minute ago you were full of yourself, thinking of fighter planes. Maybe you were just now imagining horses and spears. I'll bet even Jesus wept when he went out into the desert to pray.

I was sobbing, keening, begging. I was on my knees, I was curled over them, I was forehead on the ground. I am nothing nothing nothing, I am no one I know nothing, look at me, no don't look me, go away, whatever you do turn your terrible eyes away, no please, *do* look, I am just a little one, I need your help I don't even know what I need you for, I just need you because I'm small, look how big this place is, it's huge, it's HUGE, it's HUGE, I'm small, can you even *imagine* how small I am, won't you help me, please help me I'm scared, I'm so scared. I'm so scared.

If you're waiting to hear about the vision, so am I. I'd meant to stay three nights and I came down after the first. This was a lesson in petitionary prayer, in coming face-to-face with the ultimate concern, which was panic.

The spirits were teaching me how to pray.

***

Here is a legend, passed down by students at a small experiential high school in Boulder. I heard it from a parent with kids the same age as my son. Her kids went to this school, and heard it from the kids older than them. Each year, the seniors do a big hands-on project. One year, the students were down near the Mexican-American border — I didn't hear what the original project was — when they decided to rent a van, cross the border to Mexico, put on some packs and sneak back into America. They followed a route known to be used by illegal migrants, because they wanted to see what this was like. What it was like to be lost in this particular way in this particular kind of wilderness.

In the dark, they are walking in the desert. They hear voices that echo strangely. Scraps of English and Spanish that sound like neither. Metal on rock. Engines in the distance. They are thirsty. Some of them are out of shape and not ready for this. They aren't sure how far they have to go. When the lights of the border patrol truck appear, some of them are relieved and some are terrified. You shouldn't mess with Homeland Security these days — you never know how that's gonna go. You can't count on being privileged and white, especially if you're from a liberal, privileged town, to get you out of something like this.

You're doing a high school project? Border Patrol asks. What kind of high school is that?

The best kind, I thought, when I was the one hearing the story.

Well, they were lucky, and privileged, and they did get out of it. But they walked under the stars in a strange landscape and thought hard about what it might be like to be someone else, what it might feel like to be seriously lost between one place and another. For a moment they weren't so lucky. They were praying, then, with and for others who were lost.

**

Around this time I was getting to know some other travelers, people who had moved through an overwhelming landscape to come to America. When I was trying to bring some light into a dark house on the dark side of a dark canyon, I hired a Tibetan refugee in his 20s named Namgyal Tsering. The first thing he did was ask for a key to my house. He said when neighbors had seen him looking for the keys other clients had left outside their houses, they'd called the police; he had brown skin and often wore a black skull cap. But even on the first interview, I didn't hesitate to give him a key. Just my gut feeling.

Over about four years, I heard bits of his story. He mentioned how scary it had been to engage the bureaucracy here in order to get his paperwork going. In Tibet and Nepal, he said, the police were small men, armed with sticks. "But they do so much damage," he said, clasping his head, hunching.

He'd climbed the Himalaya to escape Tibet. Over a 19,000-foot pass in sneakers, just as in the stories you hear. Shortly after he'd arrived in Nepal, authorities had rounded up refugees like him. Nepal was then, as now, struggling with Marxist rebels. Fearful of angering China, it was sending back asylum-seekers. Namgyal thought it was over for him. He was beaten and thrown into an unheated, high-altitude cell in winter, packed so full that he stood all day and night. He said there were no bathroom breaks; people simply relieved themselves where they stood. He was released only because of a bribe. He'd had no reason to assume, initially, that things worked any differently here.

The story of how he got here is complex — he said it involved some help from the U.S. consulate on the Nepali end that was not met on the American side — but when he did reach America, he had no money, he spoke no English, and when he saw our customs officials and police officers, with their much greater stature and all the gear around their waists, he was terrified.

Around the time of the 2008 Beijing Olympics, there were demonstrations worldwide for a free Tibet. The Chinese reprisals in Tibet seemed harsh; Namgyal was beside himself with worry for his parents; he said the relatives of known escapees like him were often tormented especially.

He didn't have any way of finding out what was happening to them. I remember I was standing in my bathroom for some reason; perhaps he was fixing the plumbing. He looked up and said, "Tibet is gone, we will never get it back."

I heard the same deep loss in his voice, a star-shot sky arching over open plains, that I'd heard in those Native American sweat lodges. I thought of a book I'd read by a woman who'd spent 27 years in Tibetan labor camps. It reached back to her childhood before the Chinese army came, before the lush forests were destroyed, before the nomadic tribes were scattered, before the discipline of prayer was broken, before she was forced to tear ancient Buddhist scriptures, written in silver and gold ink, from their bindings and mix them with straw to plaster the walls of latrines.

A couple of years after he started working for me, Namgyal finally mustered the courage to approach U.S. customs authorities. He applied for asylum as a political refugee. Homeland Security arrested him immediately.

Namgyal hadn't told me all of the details of his journey from Tibet to Nepal and America. I had friends who'd climbed and trekked in Tibet and Nepal; I wasn't ignorant of world events; I thought I had a reasonable idea. However, as I was talking with Namgyal's lawyer, he mentioned some footage of a shooting incident on the Nangpa La, a Himalayan pass between Tibet and Nepal. This was the same route Namgyal had taken, the lawyer said, under virtually the same conditions. "You can get it off YouTube," he said. "You should watch it."

When a person goes through something difficult, many people in our culture consider it polite to say, "I can't imagine." What's more accurate is that we cannot *know*. Of course we can imagine. We should imagine. If only for a moment, let's try to be like those Boulder high school kids journeying into the wilderness to see how it might feel to be small, and exposed. I'll ask you now to watch the video Namgyal's lawyer asked me to look for on YouTube. It was shot by filmmakers who happened to making a documentary of a climbing expedition at the same time that a group of refugees attempted to cross into Nepal. The refugees were fired upon by Chinese border guards. This is not an easy video to watch, but I believe it is something we in the West must witness.

(Those reading this meditation might choose to lift their eyes now from the page: http://www.youtube.com/watch?v=LYN-mzRLABg, though Googling "Tibet Murder in the Snow Video" will probably be faster.)

The person who died before your eyes was a girl the age of many on this campus. Her name was Kelsang Namtso. She was 17. Perhaps one day you will travel to the high valleys of Tibet or Nepal, or perhaps you have done so already, and perhaps you will see or have already seen the purple kelsang flower blooming in the meadows there. How often it is that we name our daughters after flowers.

Nearly half the group who appear as specks in that wilderness were under age 20; some were as young as 7, traveling without their parents. In their homeland, their language, native dress, and religion are forbidden, as was the case until recently on Native American reservations. But traditions die hard, and so their parents continue to send them to the Dalai Lama, who in exile represents the cultural heritage of Tibet. Some of those people were only going to pray; they would have returned, facing many of the same hardships along the way.

We sent letters to Homeland Security and the Denver immigration judge, attesting to Namgyal's character as the archetypal immigrant, pleading that it was a form of national character assassination to deport him. I reached out to the media. We set up a fund for Namgyal's son and for the lawyer fees. The judge in Denver ruled that because of the risk to his life, Namgyal could not be repatriated to Tibet. ICE — the division of

Homeland Security known as Immigration and Customs Enforcement — decided it would send him back to Nepal. I called Amnesty International, which, by the way, was more helpful than I expected — I'd sort of thought they might be jaded. Someone called the American consulate in Nepal; someone else alerted the Western climbing community in Kathmandu. A hearing was set to determine if, since sending him to Tibet was not allowed, ICE could remove Namgyal to a country that would deport him straight to Tibet. Namgyal's hearing was scheduled for a Thursday. At midnight on Wednesday, ICE yanked him from his cell and put him on a plane. No coat. No money. No farewells. Not even any shoelaces in his shoes.

***

I know that the very worst can happen in life. One hundred sixty-nine of my neighbors' houses recently burned to the ground, including the homes of a Czech refugee and a Holocaust survivor. Over this past break, I hiked up Storm King Mountain in Colorado, where another fire burned 16 years ago. I found the 14 markers for the men and women who died trying to escape flames taller than the ceiling in this room, burning at 1,800 degrees. Clearly, God does seem to have a lot to do when it comes to listening to petitionary prayer.

Yet, when there was no longer anything left to *do* for Namgyal, I sat down to pray. It didn't matter whether I thought there was anything to be gained from it. We'd reached that point in the wilderness. The Himalaya loomed. I would just place myself in a chair and try to make that into an airplane seat for the last leg of Namgyal's flight. Praying *with*, even if he didn't know I was doing it.

There's never anything easy about meditation. That's one of the reasons I don't like doing it. It's not just that it's hard to still your mind and your body. It's so hard to still your heart. So much pain pours in.

After a while I pictured Tara, a Tibetan Buddhist figure. Around Boulder, she's usually sold as a green statue in lotus position. I saw her straddling a range of mountains, a white cloak over her shoulders, long, dark hair tumbling down. I begged her. "Please," I said, "he's one of yours." I felt racy, as if I'd been drinking coffee for hours, which I never do. I realized Namgyal might have been, coffee or soda on the plane. He wouldn't have had money for food. Plus, he'd been sitting for months in his cell, with nothing to think about but everything. *I* thought about everything. The mistakes made in the asylum application. That terrible journey from Tibet to America. The parents left behind, whom he still probably would not see, because he probably would be shot. His wife had told me she believed he would be shot. The American child, Namkha, who had been fat and happy until his father vanished. Maybe he'd grow up to join a gang now. I thought about the pointlessness of existence.

I looked at my watch. Ten minutes had passed. I didn't think that I had done Namgyal much good by thinking of everything for him.

I sat my mind back down in the airplane seat and reopened my heart to the *feelings*. I was there to be present, in whatever way I could be. I thought: Well, God, Tara, let me be like a battery. If he has feelings that are too much, let them spill over on me. If he needs some energy or anything I have, let him take it. I drifted in and out. My attention wasn't perfect. Waves of sorrow and rage would hit me. There was a surge, about an hour and a half in, of raw terror. Sweat all over my body, my hair wet. I thought the plane was probably landing.

Then, suddenly, this calm. I got this from a corny Hallmark card sent to me after a great loss, but I felt as though what love could do, was done.

I seemed to step out of it, to see the 747, just a small and silver thing, after all, beneath the glory of the mountains.

In the morning I learned that in response to emails from Boulder, a couple hundred illegal Tibetans in Kathmandu had risked their own exposure to demonstrate with signs outside the airport. This was completely unexpected. The American consulate, unable to interfere, nevertheless sent someone to stand as an observer while Namgyal was interrogated and deplaned, which took five hours. The consulate, more familiar with the refugee situation in Nepal than Homeland Security was perhaps willing to become, seemed much more sympathetic to what we were trying to communicate about Namgyal. When one Tibetan woman learned that the Nepali officials wanted several thousand dollars in "bond" before they deported him, she went door-to-door in her neighborhood to raise the money. She didn't know Namgyal, and neither did any of the people who contributed.

At any moment the Nepali officials could pocket these funds and still deport Namgyal immediately, so another unknown person made the 48-hour trip from India to guide him over the border to that country. I can't get over that. Namgyal was, by some cultural measures, a "nobody," a peasant from the middle of nowhere. And yet all these people who knew nothing about him went to great lengths to help. To me it was an example of a culture both oriented to the collective and truly valuing the individual, and I realized I'd never seen anything like that.

Amnesty International tracked Namgyal to the Dalai Lama's settlement in Dharamsala, while we in Boulder gathered money to repay those who had covered the bribes in Kathmandu, and that was the last I ever heard.

***

On break, as I hiked through the burn zone where all those firefighters died, I thought about how much my concept of praying had evolved. The little girl, earnest as she was, bent at the bedside, is no more. She moved too fast, was too eager to get on to the next thing, moving from Narnia at 6 to *The Lord of the Flies* at 10. The last thing she wanted was to be lost. It doesn't escape me, though, that I began this piece talking about a tradition that had outlived itself for many of my generation, then went on to accounts of people suffering because their prayers have been ripped away from them. And here I am, crying for something to fill the void I myself tore by choice.

All of Storm King Mountain is a memorial, and hiking it is an immersion in prayer. Thousands of people pray that way every year, struggling up the rough trail on loose soil much like the firefighters did, searching for the 14 markers in much the same way the rescuers looked for the bodies. Each marker is draped in memorabilia so vivid you feel as though the person might sit up and start talking to you. Levi's favorite skis. A bottle of whiskey for Jim, left unmolested by teens. A medicine shield for Terri, member of the Onondaga tribe. Many of them were college kids working a summer job. Bureaucratic incompetency killed them, blind arrogance that makes you want to spit so hard you could probably put out a whole wildfire by yourself. But in the final moments they died because they didn't put down their packs, their heavy tools, and just run. They were trained to hold onto their gear.

Traditions die hard. Most of the time, we need to cling to what we know. That's exactly what saves us, it's what keeps us *us*. We must pray in Lakota, we must use buffalo liver to do it right, we must, if we can, preserve those beautiful scriptures written in silver and gold and send our children to study with the Dalai Lama. We should know where the USA stops and where Mexico begins. We should not put down our axes and our chainsaws; they are the best tools for fighting fire.

Except, it seems, when we're trying to outrun, uphill, 200-foot flames. What's protected and what's endangered by our sense that that there are exact rules, that there's a letter of the law? That we don't need to ask for help, that there is no God, that God is too busy, that he or she is too big for us, or too important to care? That we know the way home and can find it on our own. That we always know where the borders are.

I pray the lord our souls to wake.

Notes

Deep Survival is by Laurence Gonzales.

The book about surviving the Tibetan gulag is *The Voice That Remembers*, by Ama Adhe.

A much larger part of Kelsang Namtso's story is examined in journalist Jonathan Green's *Murder in the High Himalaya*. Perhaps of additional interest to Exeter readers is this book's exploration of the conundrum in which the filmmakers found themselves as they tried to take the story public. Almost none of the other hundred or so witnesses wanted the story told for fear that their permits to climb in the region would be revoked by the Chinese. A great case study for *non sibi*, not to mention goodness and knowledge.

A necessarily incomplete account of Namgyal Tsering's "removal" can be found online in the Boulder *Daily Camera* of June 4, 2008, and the Broomfield, Colorado, *Enterprise* of June 4, 2008. Stories also appeared in print in the *Denver Post*.

In *Fire on the Mountain*, John Maclean explores many dimensions of the Storm King disaster — now officially known as the South Canyon Fire — carrying on the tradition begun by his father, Norman, with *Young Men and Fire*.

MATT MILLER
Ordeal by Water
February 29, 2012

"Drowning is not so pitiful

As the attempt to rise"

— Emily Dickinson

I

Maybe 4 when my father threw me

into a Miami pool, said *now swim to the side*

and talked me how not to drown.

So the first time I drowned I was 7,

a rubber raft, my cousin pulling me out

into New Hampshire's slate Atlantic,

Matt W. Miller teaches English at Exeter and is dorm head of Main Street North. He has received poetry fellowships from Stanford University and the Sewanee Writers' Conference and is the author of three collections of poetry: *Club Icarus*, *Cameo Diner* and *The Wounded for the Water*. He lives with his family in Exeter and surfs the frigid Atlantic all year round.

the wave as it curled into a fist, pitched

me and I fell backward forever into a palm

of sea until I was the greenhead whose crush

was what the world wished for and I

twirled the underwater in the black

of my own shut eyes because to open

my eyes would have been to lung

the Atlantic, but in the dark I could hold

and hold my breath and never drown.

And then I found my legs and stood

in the shallows of what had swallowed.

A wig of mud crowned my head,

sand it seems I am still scratching out

of my scalp. I may have cried, I know I shook

walking out of the waves back up

to the blankets of my mother, refusing

the water for the rest of the day. But still

I did not know what it means to drown.

II

Most spun-out drowning in the sea was south

of San Francisco, by the Pacifica pier.

I paddled out new: to this coast, to surfing,

to that water and its slab of autumn swells.

I didn't know the break or what rocks, what reefs,

what nictitating eyes might rise

from black to Grendel me beneath the roll

and roar of foam. I took off too steep, too deep

in the wave and felt that fist again drill

then drag me over the falls and hold me,

curl me cozily, lovingly, beneath its belly,

under its teary-eyed pillow. I refused

the water again. I swam with open eyes

toward light licking pink under the foam inches

away. I opened my mouth to eat the air

when the ocean pulled me under again.

The leash. I was on a leash. I was leashed

to my board and it was being buried

by another thickgut wave, yanking me back

inside the dark. I did not know if my eyes

were open or closed, if the circles of blue

red and green were synesthesia's gleam

of mermaid song or my skull blood

turning toxic. One last rubbery stroke

toward the surface, and there it was.

Sirens slipped back into to their wreaths

as my lips crowned first and I gorged

on air and the California hills. Had another

wave risen from its haunches to strike

I would have swallowed it to death.

III

There is a night at the Gaelic Club in Lowell,

stink of old Budweiser and Camel Lights,

the sweat of hate and sadness so deep

it has tides pulled by the moon. Maybe

25, I walk in and see a high school friend,

fellow football co-captain. Once, he popped

his dislocated shoulder back into the socket

between downs when we were losing

to Methuen. "Matty, kid, how you doing?"

he says. "Let me get you a pop. How's things?

What're you doing these days? What a day I had

down at the prison. This kiddy diddler gets a knife,

right? Starts cutting himself up in his cell

and I got to go in and stop him only he has

AIDS right, he was giving AIDS to little kids

and I'm like, 'Let him kill himself.' But no, me

and another guard got to put on these dog bite

suits and save him but the only way to do that

is to subdue him by which I mean beat him

down. Only he's tweaking, keeps coming and we

keep beating on him, beating the ever-living

loving hell out of him. We pounded away

until he stopped squirming, stopped smiling,

until my hands stopped hurting and I was running

out of places to hit, until there was nothing left

of that sick prick but a purple bubbling.

You see what I'm saying? Want to do some blow?"

We slip below the surface, a smile curling

up toward tears we won't not allow, that we'll

swallow with our voices until we drown.

"But I'm good," he says. "I'm doing good.

I come down here to have a few pops,

and wait around for that pension, right?"

he laughs and I laugh. "You good?" he asks.

"Yeah, I'm OK," I lie and clinging to the art

of each other's lies we choke down beers.

IV

The summer Hurricane Bill threw waves

with 20-foot faces along New Hampshire's

coast, I paddled out with too much pride

and not enough board. When an outside set

monstered in I had to duck dive, duck dive

until I did not dive deep enough, the last

double overhead a dragon of time and space

exploding on my back. I was spun and bent,

whipped and bit, my arms a pair of severed claws.

Yet it was not the bubbles I tried to follow up

but barnacled visions of a son who'd never know

me, a daughter who would forget my voice,

a wife who'd need to hate me one day for this.

And I began to know a little bit about drowning,

the ways to drown beyond the sea.

                                We drown

as well inside the human voice that wakes us

then breaks us upon the rocks. We drown inland,

where the sea does not reach, where water becomes

mudhut of hurt and nights are hours that drag

on forever, nights that are my naked body

scraped across a field of cracked ice, playing rigged

games of football next to U-Hauls filled with

beer kegs and frat rush boys. The kind of drowning

that picks fights with mothers, lovers, cops,

and all the friends I murdered into strangers.

The kind of drowning that folds me

into a cabinet of sleepwalking knives,

that holds a blade to my wrist in the dim lit tile

of my kitchen moonlight. Drowning where

I don't know I am drowning because so dry,

parched in fact, my scales falling into the sun

as I cross the desert on my belly defaced,

deflowered, and now to death devote

as worms gnaw into that constipated place

inside my spine. And when I do reach water

it is all thick silt and shorebreak, rolling me

back in, chalked in alluvium, drowning in sun,

beached, cooking in my own fat, my own blood,

the once rich oil of my skullbone rotting before

it ever lick a candlewick. I have been

one drowning like this. I'd once wished to keep

drowning. But what did I know of drowning?

V

My daughter was born drowning, choking

on blood and amniotic fluid caught in her throat

as I stood dumb. In my hand, the scissors

that never got to cut the purple gray rope

coiled slippery between child and mother.

She did not come crying onto her stage

but rather hacking, scratching at air,

laid out on a pan, mute as a fish, by doctors

yelling for help now, no now, yes now.

How many times must you say now in a hospital?

They took our child nameless into the NICU.

My wife was a web of torn tissue and tears

as a doctor digs rubber gloves back into her.

More bleeding down here than I like to see, he says.

Scissors, needle, thread now old hands snip

winces rip her face. *See if she's OK, make her*

be OK, she says and I run down a hall

as if hip deep in mud, watching walls implode,

doors blow open into a pool of blue swimmers

too small for March and I won't feel bad hoping

my baby isn't one of them. *Now this way, Daddy,*

someone says and then her eyes open, pools

staring, and we are right there terrified, beautiful,

drowning in what the world can take,

what it will take from us breath by breath,

rubied, from systole to diastole, each pulse

a fading out of glassy offshore tomorrows.

VI

I read that the drowning are unable to call out

for help. The respiratory system was designed

for breathing. Speech is the overlaid function.

I see this also away from water. In the pitch

and swirl of day on day we watch each other

drown because drowning does not look

like drowning. It is silent. But there are signs:

head tilted back, mouth open, eyes glassy and

empty, no use of legs, gasping, trying to swim

but not making headway, appearing to climb

an invisible ladder. We've all seen this lie

of climbing: friends, lovers, children not swimming

just thrashing in place. We watch in our homes

on sidewalks, in offices, and classrooms

eyes staring out at nothing. A friend,

she's playing, tumbling in a turquoise surf,

eyes full on love's pinks and soft blue

coral and then she is pounded into the reef,

torn across its razored skeleton, spun in threads

of her own blood, her body shredding,

shredding into all the beautiful colors and I

watch, not understanding the signs when birds

begin to flee, when the sea suddenly sucks away

from her Malaysian coast. Or not understanding

the Katrinas swallowing a mother's bones,

or my wife locked in a winter tower sleepless,

hungry, and a cold lump of coal growing

in her breast as she tries to rock a screaming

cradle where our son's hurt drowns day

into night. I spin words not knowing that

I cannot see the wounded for the water.

There are bodies drowning all around me,

my mother in the dark water of an empty

home where the stench of Dad's dead man's

chest, of his bile-leaking gut, still swims

as she lights scented candles in the soaked air.

Brothers, sisters, sons and daughters,

all the swollen tongues of a scorched earth,

all asking for mercy of unruly sea gods

while my hands seem too slow to let go

of the ship's brass railing, let loose the line —

because what do I know of drowning

but that I drown dumbly in their thousand

furlongs of tears, of blood, of bile—quiet

as a breath that will not come.

VII

There is a reason why their drowning

is my own, why I waken from the dream where

again and again my son is falling off a pier

into a bottomless black and I dive in

but cannot find him for the water is too deep,

too dark. And waking I have to run

to him, terrified as I am by those trips

taken to the emergency room when asthma

sinks a stone onto his wheezing lungs.

There is a reason why their drowning

is my own, why in winter stripped maples

I see my father drowning for 30 hours,

unhooked from the ventilator because

he was tired of swimming against the mad

currents and sick rips of his failing flesh.

There is a reason why I drown, why at night

I wonder what my mother does to fall asleep,

to brush his bloody bandages from her eyes.

When the slope of waves becomes too great,

when all of our inertias hit the shoals,

breaking's as inevitable as a frothy twirl.

There is a reason I want to drown in them

why when I reach the NICU and see

my daughter's dark doll eyes wet, alive,

and smiling under the lights I become

liquid,

        I become water.

                  And how can water

drown? How native unto that element

and fear the muddy pull?

                Born of spirit,

I know also my cells are made of water

so l will not let water be my cell.

VIII

Because there must be other ways to drown,

ways of drowning where you do not die

or you die only to rise from the waters

baptized, washed, witness to a purged

earth. There needs a taking back of drowning,

a wash of drowning in new definitions,

the drowning in another's eyes and arms, drowning

in a smile, peacefully letting go in the waters

of someone else. The drowning that saves,

heals, that allows you to keep company

with hope, makes you start swimming.

My wife, water-eyed, would have dreams

of drowning in giant waves. She tells

me this in her Brookline apartment, when we

first start dating, when I am falling in love.

So what did you do? I asked a childhood ago.

I taught myself to breathe in underwater dreams,

she said. This is how she saves me

from my own drowning, not by reaching

out to pull me from my rip currents,

but by showing me that if you don't want

to drown, if you're worried about the rising

water, teach yourself, demand of yourself,

a new way to breathe. Drowning in that light

of morning, still drowning in that silt

of soft touched lips, in those sweet waters

I took first breaths against my dry cage of ribs.

The intellectual is always showing off, writes

the Sufi poet. *The lover is always getting lost.*

The intellectual runs away, afraid of drowning.

I shall take back "drowning." I'll drench it

in my own colors, my own algebras,

semantics, permutations of pulse and swell.

My drowning is not to be a suffocation,

but an absorption into the fickle sea,

gliding in its physics, cross-stepping its gravity,

slipping its long leash of push and pull, breathing

and sharing breath beyond the limited lining

of my lungs as I carve oxygen from a spray

of foam thrown up orange and violet

in the singing out of a sailor's evening sun.

And now I dive for the cool depths

of all my others. Adrift in the flood of her,

of our children, of you, of every you and the blue

of this deluge, I cannot have too much

of water. My sea as you are my blood,

you let me breathe in underwater dreams.

The water in which I wish to drown,

the depths where I respire, you whisper

me to swim. You take November from me

and you are why there is any June at all.

PETER GREER '58
This Childish Act
October 10, 2012

First, I want to thank Bob Squires for providing the musical prelude to this meditation. And in advance I want to thank Lod Crofoot, who will provide the musical postlude. The meditation itself I'd like to dedicate to Charlie Pratt, who was an inspiring colleague in the English Department, a successful orchardist at Apple Annie, a great friend, and a superb poet. Indeed, one of Charlie's poems provides the foundation for these reflections this morning. It is entitled:

APPROACH

The golfer settles his grip, adjusts his feet;
The iron hovers — flashes and wheels around,
And the ball's gone, the golfer's poised like a bow.
We lean to watch — then suddenly, "Look! There!"
A new world is hanging in the air,
While the green like an empty heaven waits below.
Still no one moves, till at last the ball comes down,
And the green rises, or seems to rise, and they meet.
Why should we applaud this childish act?
This hero can't redeem our riddled state,
Nor chip a missile to the moon and back.

Peter Greer taught for many years in the English Department at Exeter.

Say that we're aesthetes, then, and celebrate
The craft that unifies intent and fact,
Usurps the awful accuracy of fate.

When I was young, I played a lot of golf. My parents belonged to the country club in Nashua, New Hampshire, where I grew up, so I was able to play regularly, though only during certain hours of the afternoon; the adult male members of the club didn't want me or other junior players getting in the way during prime golfing time. In fact, and this tells you something about the gender climate in which I grew up, the hours that curtailed the junior players also curtailed the female players: The men didn't want *them* getting in the way, either.

Anyway, I played a lot of golf, initially with my best friend, Lewis Coronis. Lew and I were maybe 12 when we started. And we had a rule that allowed us to test our generosity. When one of us hit a bad shot, he would ask the other if he could have a "take-over." The decision of the other usually depended on the ugliness of the shot in question; if it was *really* ugly, the player got his take-over, but if it was only *pretty* ugly, he didn't. Thus, each of us had a chance to feel generous but still allow the other's *pretty* ugly shots to stand, which gave the take-over granter a competitive advantage. And so it went: Afternoon after summer afternoon, Lew and I played 18 holes, and in a year or two we were joined by Dickie Dion and David Pope, and the four of us competed often and hard. Slowly we all improved, and ultimately we came to be pretty good, in particular Dickie, who went on to play on a satellite tour for a couple of years.

My own first significant achievement was to win the sixth division of the 1956 New Hampshire Amateur Championship. I was then 15, and head to head I beat one man after another who couldn't imagine losing to a little kid who was unable to hit the ball more than 200 yards. But typically I was steady and they were erratic, so I won all five of my matches. As ocular proof, I offer the silver bowl down in front of me. It represents the achievement, and its small size represents the dimension of the achievement; it was the sixth division, after all. But it was a beginning.

My next achievement came the following summer, in the qualifying round for the New Hampshire entry in the national Jaycees Tournament, limited to golfers under the age of 18. All who entered played 27 holes, and on one nine I shot a 32, which will ever stand as my best score for nine holes, a score that would satisfy any pro currently on the tour. So I qualified as one of four from Nashua, then went on to play in the statewide qualification tourney, in which I didn't qualify. If I had, I would have gone to Columbus, Ohio, to compete in the national tournament, which that year was won by a golfer just my age. His name: Jack Nicklaus.

By that time I was a student at Exeter, and in my senior year I finally outgrew my seat as coxswain on the varsity crew and tried out for and made the golf team. There my biggest achievement was winning the J. Eric Shellabarger Memorial Golf Trophy. If upon entering Love Gym you look to the right on the wall, you can find the photo of the golf team of 1958, a copy of which is also in front of me, and in it you will see this little fellow sitting in the middle of the first row, golf clubs crisscrossed in front of him. That little fellow then went to Yale, when Yale was still willing to accept two or three dozen applicants from Exeter, even one who was the absolutely average student that I was. There I played on the freshman team, then made the varsity my junior year. The memorable event from that varsity season, the spring of 1961, was our match against Harvard, played at The Country Club, in Brookline, Massachusetts, one of the most elite courses in this country and the site two years later of the U.S. Open won by Julius Boros in a playoff against Arnold Palmer. Here's the story:

In Florida two months earlier, where the team had assembled for preseason practice, my golf coach had inexplicably fixed me up with an astonishingly beautiful girl named Dawn Payne, who was enough taken with me, or really with Yale, to accept my invitation to come north for a long weekend that included my match against my Harvard opponent. My mother drove down from Nashua and, with Dawn at her side, watched the match for 14 holes. I was playing well and leading comfortably and seemingly on my way to a victory, so my mother left for home to prepare dinner for us, and — predictably, I'm afraid — all my attention turned to the nubile Dawn. I was, how shall I say, energized by her presence, and my game more or less fell apart, which in turn energized my opponent. My lead evaporated and I teed off on the 18th hole needing at least to tie my opponent to win the match. I hit a poor drive, he hit a good drive. I hit a poor second shot, he hit a good second shot, but, fortunately for me, it caught a sand trap at the edge of the green. My third shot I hit well, much too well, really, and with the wrong club, and it flew high over and beyond the green, destined to land in a place that would guarantee my losing the hole and our going into a playoff. Dawn was watching all of this, of course, and I was trying, clearly unsuccessfully, not to watch Dawn watching. But here the golf gods intervened. Behind and above the 18th green at The Country Club there is, or at least there was then, a large and ancient tree, and my ball more or less disappeared into it. There followed the predictable knocking sounds of ball hitting branch, and suddenly the ball reappeared, kicked down and back and onto the green not far from the cup. My opponent was as stunned as I was, with different emotions, of course, but he managed nonetheless to hit a good third shot out of the trap and onto the green. We both now had reasonable putts for four, but the pressure was on him, for he needed to sink his and then hope that I missed mine, whereas I needed only to match whatever he did. As it turned out, each of us missed his putt, so we both made fives, and in anticlimactic fashion I won the match, earning me a sweet hug from the glowing Dawn, who was essentially clueless about golf but eager to learn more about the ways of Yale men. I should add that she was sadly disappointed when it came to this Yale man, but that's another story. Anyhow, here's how *The Boston Globe* summarized the great Harvard-Yale golf match of 1961:

> Yale Sophomore [sic] Pete Greer defeated Dave Rudnick of Harvard 1 up in the seventh and deciding match as Yale's golf team beat Harvard, 4-3, yesterday at The Country Club, Brookline.

No mention of my collapse. No mention of the generous tree. No mention, of course, of Dawn Payne. So I was the hero of the hour. But I knew the truth. And so did my teammates.

That year, while I was busy helping Yale beat Harvard, Jack Nicklaus was busy winning the U.S. Open. My golf career clearly had quite a way to go. But where it went was south, as we say. I lifted weights during that summer, determined to hit the ball farther and maybe also to lure Dawn back up north, and I gained muscle but lost muscle memory, thereby producing a wildness in my game that cost me a place on the varsity in my senior year and that has plagued me ever since. For the five years after graduation, I was so discouraged that I hardly set foot on a golf course; I had come to take little pleasure from a game that I had at one time played with great control and that I had come to play with little control. Furthermore, and this was much more than just rationalization, I had come to see the game for what it was: sexist and elitist, a game of the country club set, from which I was trying to distance myself even though I was partially a product of it. In addition, golf courses turned a blind eye to environmental concerns, which were growing increasingly important to me. So in the decade of the '60s I played rarely.

However, in the 1970s, my first decade as a teacher at PEA, I was lured back to the game by, among others, my good friend Michael Drummey. Mike and I joined the Portsmouth Country Club and in the summer months played regularly, often in the late afternoon when the course was not crowded and at its most beautiful, the light of the sinking sun sculpting the landscape. Mike is an excellent athlete and picked up quickly a game relatively new to him, and I began to regain some of my skills, so our matches were competitive, but the real pleasure was not in the scores but in the beauty of the experience, and in the friendship that the experience deepened. But I did indeed get better, good enough, in fact, to win, in 1976, the first incarnation of the faculty golf tournament, shooting a 76, which is the best score I have posted in the past 50 years. More ocular proof rests here before me. But while I improved some as a player, I never became what I had been and I never really regained my love of the game, so I let my membership at the Portsmouth Country Club lapse, played less and less, and slowly lost those few skills I had regained.

In the decade of the '90s the popularity of golf surged. I lived in Kensington, some 7 miles south of Exeter, and watched as a modest nearby course that had previously been grazing land for cows became popular with golfers of myriad stripes. At 5 in the afternoon, the trucks that filled the parking lot indicated that many blue-collar workers, during those happier economic times, were taking up golf. The game thus felt less elitist. And there was evidence that, at many if not most courses, men and women played more as equals, even playing sometimes in mixed groups. The game thus felt less sexist. And a certain few courses, though far too few, showed signs of an environmental consciousness in the way they treated wetlands and trees and fertilizers. So my distaste for the culture of the game of golf was tempered to some degree. But at the same time my interest in the game, and in my game in particular, did not return. Whatever my thoughts about the culture of golf, that disinterest stemmed from one primary reason: I just hated playing poorly when I had at one time played well.

There was certainly a defensiveness in that attitude, abetted by my belief that, if I were willing to commit myself to playing more and practicing more, I could become again what I once was. Well, I was wrong: What I resisted reckoning with was that, in addition to getting rusty in those years, I had been getting older, my body no longer as flexible as it had been, my timing less instinctive and precise, my mind not as bold, my focus much broader. So when I sliced a ghastly drive far into the woods to the right of the fairway or hooked a nightmarish drive into a pond on the left, the anger at myself and the pure embarrassment I experienced were based on the erroneous conviction that I should be able to play just as I had when I was in my teens.

So why all this background? Well, background leads to foreground, which in this case means the last two or three years. In these recent years, I have discovered that I once again enjoy playing golf, however poorly I play, however high my scores. To explain, at least in part, this evolution, I want to return to the second quatrain of Charlie Pratt's sonnet:

> A new world is hanging in the air,
> While the green like an empty heaven waits below.
> Still no one moves, till at last the ball comes down,
> And the green rises, or seems to rise, and they meet.

Now in every round I play, even those rounds when my score is over 100, as it usually is, some few times all the intricacies in my golf swing integrate themselves in lovely if inexplicable fashion and I hit the ball high and straight and toward the target. And as it comes down, the green does seem to rise to meet it. It is a beautiful thing, really, and I smile, and my fellow players congratulate me on a good shot. Usually one of them, often the same Michael Drummey, says something like: "It's back!"

meaning that I have recaptured the game of my youth. But it's not true, and I know it. But I know also what a moment of such high delight does mean: It means that if I continue to play, I will be rewarded, at least every so often, with such a moment, a moment that is as much aesthetic as it is athletic. The final three lines of "Approach" speak directly to that way of looking at it all:

> Say that we're aesthetes, then, and celebrate
> The craft that unifies intent and fact,
> Usurps the awful accuracy of fate.

The unification of intent and fact: That moment when what I *want* to do with the shot is what I *do* with the shot. For that moment, my control has returned. And one of the reasons I now play the game is for such moments.

But I now play the game for another and more important reason, a very simple one: I play because I can play. I learned a few years ago that I now can't water-ski; I don't have the strength in my hands and arms to hold onto the tow rope when, boat accelerating, I try to rise from the water. For the same reason I can't climb the PEA Boulder in Pawtuckaway Park that I scrambled up when I was leading groups in Outdoor Challenge. Once years ago I walked blithely across the famously narrow Knife Edge on Mt. Katahdin; now my confidence in my balance is such that I grip the banister of any staircase I descend. And when, a few months ago, my playful stepson asked me to do a pull-up from the frame above a doorway, I couldn't get my feet off the ground. And on and on in what is a growing list of cant's. But I still can play golf. There is a Latin word, *vitalitas*, which means the "life force" and it gives us our English word "vitality," whose meaning of physical vigor is what I intend in this context. Well, my playing golf now is much about *vitalitas*. It would be ridiculous for me to say: I golf, therefore I am (*Golfito, ergo sum*, I guess it would be), but I will say that playing the game is a way for me to feel the life force even in my deteriorated muscles and my stiff joints. But here is the key point: To be willing and even eager to play golf in the frantic and flailing way I do now, I had to recognize that physical deterioration and reckon with it positively rather than defensively and negatively. I had to *continue* to try to play instead of *refusing* to try to play. In a word, I had to accept a part of myself that I didn't want to accept.

When I wrote the preceding sentence, I had an uneasy sense that I was simply joining the legion of self-help-book authors, which led me to an even more uneasy sense that what I was offering as analysis was essentially a cliché. And really it is that. But a cliché spoken out of a different mouth to different ears in a different context can take on new life, if it has a truth to it, as I believe "accept yourself" does, so I wrote on. Which, perhaps surprisingly, takes me back to the song that Bobby sang so well. The Lennon-McCartney lyrics offer the voice of a man who is worried about getting older, losing his hair and so on, and is wondering if his romantic partner will still love him when he is 64. Well, I am now older by a few years than 64, and I might be wondering what the singer is wondering were it not for the reliable love given me by my personal romantic partner, but I chose that song for another reason, and it is this: Like all of us, I have a relationship with myself, and as I have aged, I have found my one self asking my other self, in one way or another: "Will you still need me, will you still feed me when I'm 64?" I am not exactly "wasting away," as the song has it, but I am aware all the time that I am not as physically capable as I used to be. No surprise, of course, but the challenge is to accept myself as that and take that compromised self on a vacation to some metaphorical Isle of Wight, to show me that I still need me and am willing to feed me.

And now I can get back to golf, for in a way the golf course is that Isle of Wight. For years, as I have said, I didn't take myself on that vacation.

But then, for some reason I can't honestly quite identify, I started again going to that cottage with the 18-hole golf course on its doorstep. And by so doing, I stopped depriving myself not only of the occasional delight granted me by a successful shot, but more importantly of a regular feeling of *vitalitas*, of vitality, of physical vigor. And let it not go unsaid: I gained the camaraderie of the half dozen friends who make up my golfing group.

So here, finally, is my version of the words of Descartes, my Cartesian coordinate if you will: *I try, therefore I am.* I feel now an occasional frustration on the golf course that is strong enough to cause me to mutter an oath or even bang my club childishly on the ground, and often I wish in vain for the childhood possibility of a take-over, but the fact is: I keep trying. I have finally, in these recent years, come to understand that my playing golf will not be an exercise in self-flagellation if I recognize it as an experience of living vitally. And in my way of looking at things, there is nothing more salutary for any of us than to live a life as full of vitality, as full of physical vigor, as we can make it, and to live that kind of life for as long as we possibly can.

I have reached the end of this meditation, but I want to add a footnote. When I first held a copy of *From the Box Marked 'Some are Missing'*, Charlie Pratt's collection of new and selected poems, I looked in the table of contents, then turned to page 48, eager to read "Approach." But what to my wondering eyes did *not* appear was the second stanza, the sestet of the sonnet. I asked Charlie about the decision to remove it from the poem, and he said that it was more the publisher's decision than his. I told him that I loved the ending to that first stanza, when ball and green meet, but that I also loved the second half of the sestet, the unification of intent and fact. Charlie shrugged and smiled his modest, almost impish smile, as he sometimes did either in reconciliation or resignation or maybe bemusement, so I was left to my own conclusion that that publisher had made a mistake and left out something quite enriching. As this meditation indicates, that sestet certainly was enriching to me.

So, Charlie, I will continue to think of "Approach" as a sonnet, and continue to try to be appreciative of the aesthetics of the game of golf, and continue to try to unify fact and intent in my play, for I have found in your understanding of golf a depth and perspective that have helped me come to my own understanding of the role it has played in my life, from age 12 to age 72. In an absolutely non-trivial sense, your "Approach" has helped me in my approach to the game, and beyond that, far beyond that, really, my approach to my senior years and to my inevitable physical decline. All from one 14-line poem. It's easy to express my genuine thanks, Charlie, for that poem and its effect on me; what is harder to express, though equally genuine, is how much I miss you.

JEFF IBBOTSON

Monsters

October 31, 2012

What and who come to mind when you think about monsters? Frankenstein, the Wolfman, Dracula, sure. But what about the Hulk, Swamp Thing, Ben Grimm? Are they monsters? Or Fin Fang Foom? Or Zzutak? What exactly is a monster? Is Adolf Hitler a monster? Or George Gordon, Lord Byron?

From Merriam-Webster:

> 1*a*: an animal or plant of abnormal form or structure
>
> *b*: one who deviates from normal or acceptable behavior or character
>
> 2: a threatening force
>
> 3*a*: an animal of strange or terrifying shape
>
> *b*: one unusually large for its kind
>
> 4: something monstrous; *especially*: a person of unnatural or extreme ugliness, deformity, wickedness, or cruelty

---

Jeff Ibbotson teaches mathematics at Exeter and is dorm head in Lamont Hall. He occasionally speaks to dogs and teaches taiqiquan for the Taoist Tai Chi Society.

5: one that is highly successful

Take the Hulk, for instance. A brilliant scientist tries to save a cocky teenager and winds up exposing himself accidentally to gamma radiation. He then turns (against his will) into a raging monster, which is somehow the image of his suppressed id. The Hulk cares for nothing, delights in causing destruction and looks down on "puny humans" and his "puny" alter ego. OK, the shtick is perilously close to *The Strange Case of Dr. Jekyll and Mr. Hyde*. Nonetheless, what is the moral here? That life is fraught with peril? That our best-intentioned actions often result in the worst-case scenario? That good is rarely rewarded and the world itself will turn you into a monster against your will? As the storyline evolves, the Hulk becomes almost childlike and seeks merely to be left alone. Don't we all want to be left alone with our monstrosity?

How about vampire stories? Doesn't everyone wish to be immortal? What cost might we pay for such an experience? Or do we identify strongly with the hunger of the vampire, the craving for what is outside the range of normal behavior? Lonely and alone, Dracula bends others to his will and creates his own peer group. Pretty neat, if you can get over all the blood obsession and wooden stakes and whatnot. Of course, the Victorian audience of Bram Stoker's novel probably read it a bit differently than us. They may or may not have recognized the repressed feelings toward sex and violence. Certainly his British readers recognized the Victorian obsession with invasion scenarios. For many, the most frightening image from the book was that of the phantom ship full of dead men, the captain lashed to the mast and boxes full of Transylvanian soil being transported to England.

Inevitably, speaking of monsters makes me think about the fourth grade. Fourth grade, 1971 — a nexus of monsterhood. Note the pale-skinned kid with circles under his eyes and buck teeth. He stands out, he stood alone convinced of his singularity and always conscious of the overt differences between himself and everyone else. Fourth grade was a socially important time, after all, a time when one developed one's shtick — the special skill that was later to become the dominant force behind the nascent personality. Note the others in this class. Eric Reigert, for instance. Master of Seatball. That arcane sport in which everyone climbed on top of their large wooden desks and prepared to play for life and death using a medium-size red rubber ball. We hurled it at one another and hoped that the other would be hit and yet not catch it, thereby making them "out." If you caught the ball, the thrower was out. Eric was my friend and he got me out first every time. He would fling the ball at some distant part of my anatomy and, uncoordinated schlub that I was, I would invariably miss the ball. Mary Fallacaro — she ate crayons in kindergarten by the fistful. Crayons! By fourth grade she had made the transition to wax lips — phony Halloweenish lips that she wore and then inhaled on a moment's notice, provoking screams and giggles from those around her. The sheer preposterousness of it both scared and delighted the rest of the class. Jay Brown ... he was George Gobel on a small scale. A nice kid convinced that maintaining a low and friendly profile was the key to success. I was convinced he would eventually sell insurance door to door. Barry Smalls happily wearing a cravat. Obviously hoping to buddy up with some wealthy kid, to become the endless hanger-on, the factotum. He knew he didn't have the individual skill to stand out in anything and so the key for him was who he was friends with. Gretchen Vedder — smart girl supreme. Never cracked a smile, never really understood humans, I became convinced. No, she only associated with her own kind — Venusians, no doubt. And then there was Vince Gallo ... Vince Gallo. There he is in the lower left-hand corner. Vince Gallo — the Sammy Davis

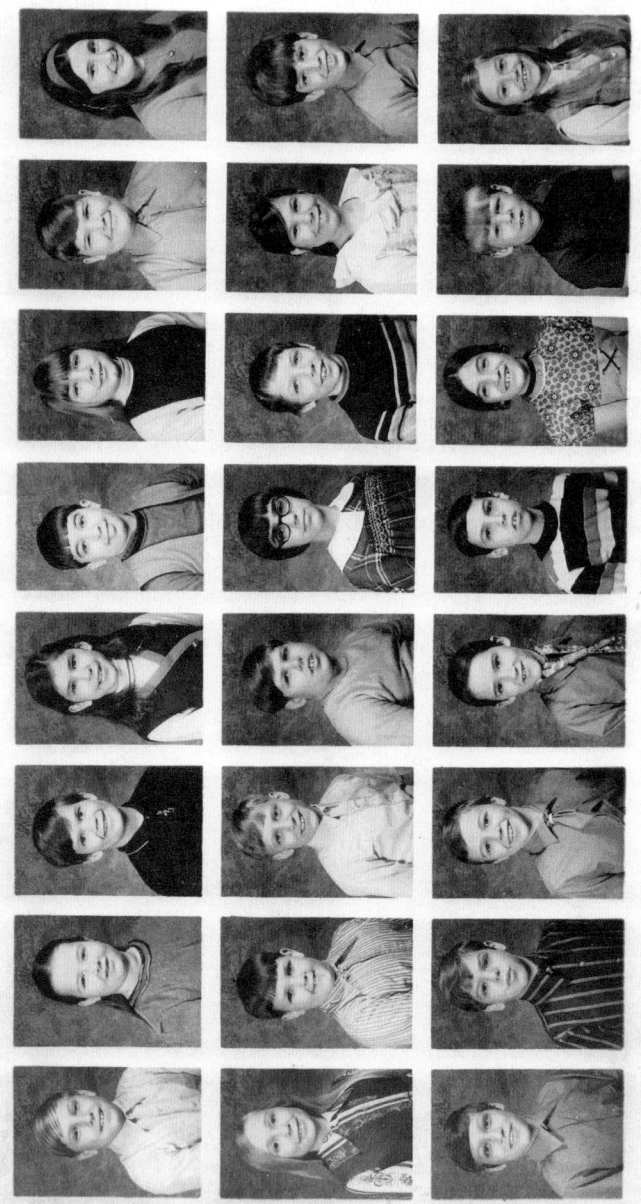

SWEET HOME ELEMENTARY - 1970-71 - MR. ZANIN - GRADE 4

Jr. of Sweet Home Elementary. He was a rogue, a charming rogue in those days. He was capable of sweet-talking his way out of any jam. He made the girls swoon, and the rumor was that he was experienced in *everything*. He once tried to involve me in an afterschool plot to shoplift stuff at a local store. I couldn't do it. Not because of the moral issues involved (although they did carry some weight, in my opinion), but rather because I knew I couldn't live the life of Gallo. I just didn't have the necessary emotional equipment and guile, the savoir faire. And I did wonder if he was just setting me up for something … Vince dropped out of high school, went to live in New York City and perfected his otherwise dubious talents. He played the guitar in an all-nude rock band and worked his way into the avant-garde crowd, eventually directing and starring in his own film, *Buffalo '66*. Somehow he talked Ben Gazzara into being in it as well as his protégée and discovery, Christina Ricci. He got a part in *Goodfellas*, became a painter and once commented: "I stopped painting in 1990 at the peak of my success just to deny people my beautiful paintings; and I did it out of spite."

Along the way he modeled for Calvin Klein and was awarded the Coppa Volpi for Best Actor at the 67th Venice International Film Festival for his performance as a wordless escaping Muslim prisoner in Jerzy Skolimowski's *Essential Killing*. Any way you slice it, Vince Gallo has been successful.

The monster in fourth-grade class, however, was me. I felt it and it drove me every day—the way in which I somehow stood out from everyone else marked me as one in their eyes, I was sure. My deep knowledge of strange facts meant that I often knew the answers to brainbusters asked by the teacher. For instance, many people are aware that the official designation of the second-tallest mountain in the world is K2. But how many know that its older and more proper name is Mt. Godwin-Austen? I was king of the Map Game, I could recognize obscure patterns quickly and I knew more of Viking mythology than anyone I knew. In the evenings I would read my father's set of encyclopedias as bedtime reading. I never knew what normal kids did. I fantasized about it in between reading about electrolytes or Kenya. And I dealt with bullies. And when I say I dealt with them, I mean I got beat up on a semiregular basis. The only way it all made sense to me was to accept that somehow I was a monster — recognizably "other," belonging to no known group or genus.

Why are monsters interesting? Why do we care about them? Because, I think, they represent the ultimate edge of individuality. Frankenstein and Dracula are both very much creations of the 19th century, a century of Romanticism and concern about the rights of individuals as they exist with larger cityscapes. To be a monster means breaking free of the normal strictures on civilized life. For most of us this is unthinkable. We all acclimate, after all. We all get jobs, wear the same clothes, vote for the same candidates. Eventually we have to accept our non-monsterhood. We become the bearers of society, the followers and promulgators of rules and rule-following behavior. We must in order to raise children, hold down a steady job, interact with a society of fellow workers. Ah, but in the dark of night, by the light of the TV screen, perhaps, come the stories of monsters to reawaken our forgotten and despised individuality. The thrill they send is illicit. Could we all still be monsters somewhere deep inside?

One of those nights, I had a dream. In this dream I was engaged to a woman and was traveling with her to Eastern Europe to meet her family and to seek their approval. The trip was long and my fiancée was nervous, but I did not understand until I arrived at the family castle shrouded among the deep, old, and dark forests of Eastern Europe. As I met the family that resided there I suddenly felt a paralyzing fear. Yes, they were monsters of the classical variety. Some were vampires, some wolfen creatures and some strongly resembled Dr. Frankenstein's creation. I gulped, the anxieties of a groom-to-be who fears that he will be killed, drained of blood or otherwise mangled should he fail this important interview. The family was courteous but removed.

In the midst of my reception a shot rang out. One of the family fell to the floor, badly wounded — perhaps killed? The offending bullet had come via one of the windows and the family quickly discerned that some person from one of the nearby human villages had fired it. The family assembled search groups and sent them out to find out the truth. I was placed in one and naturally wondered which way my allegiances would lie. Was this a test, I wondered?

As my group traveled surreptitiously about the countryside, I was able to witness the locals at their daily business. Many of them seemed to be practicing strange rituals. Garbed in bizarre costumes, flinging garlic and fennel in the air: I came to understand that this is what daily life in the shadow of the family's castle involved — strange invocations and sacrificial rites in an attempt to keep the monsters at bay. As I watched I came to feel that I had more in common with the monsters than these strange villagers. The otherness of the villagers seemed stronger to me than the monstrous family of my betrothed. If anything, the monsters were honest in their dedication to the essential elements of life (even if this meant blood had to be shed). The villagers, though, steered their lives through what they feared, what must be avoided at all costs. They lived with this fear — literally in its shadow — and yet their response was to invent nameless rites that contaminated their lives and those of their families. What lengths might they go to rather than simply move away ... their very culture was oriented to the monstrous! What kind of people could they be?

I woke with a strange feeling of calm. I felt more at home with the monsters than with those who had adapted to their existence. What was normal and what stood out as beyond normal behavior? Who, indeed, were the monsters? Who do we want them to be?

There is a quote of Rainer Maria Rilke that has always held great meaning for me, especially as I think back to that lonely boy in the fourth grade convinced of his own monstrosity: "Perhaps everything terrible is in its deepest being something helpless that wants help from us."

CHRISTINE ROBINSON
The Hashemite Kingdom of Jordan
December 5, 2012

The Hashemite Kingdom of Jordan, bordered on the north by Syria, on the east by Iraq and Saudi Arabia, on the west by Israel and the occupied West Bank, with a touch of the Sinai on the south by the Red Sea. This is tricky geography to negotiate. Jordan has the largest population of Palestinian refugees in the world, and they are not happy with King Abdullah II, and Bedouin tribes are not happy with either of them.

And 250,000 Syrian refugees pack into camps Jordan can't sustain, and a violent protest erupted in the remote tent city of Zaatari. And more than 1,000 police/army officers have defected and live in guarded desert compounds. And Al-Assad accuses Jordan of supplying arms to the rebels, the Free Syrian Army, the resistance, the terrorists. So much depends on what you call them.

And there is still tension between Israel and Gaza and the West Bank. And the protests in Jordan look like the others I had watched on Al Jazeera in my King's Academy dorm apartment: "The people want the downfall of the regime." Demonstrations have quieted a bit, but anger still shouts at the monarchy, when I had experienced Jordan as stable and safe.

A New Hampshire native and avid world traveler, **Christine Robinson** taught English at Exeter for many years from her well-worn Harkness table in the basement of Phillips Hall.

Had I been naive to assume this king, the son of a king, was a friend to the people of his country, trying his best to support the different tribes that exist in his kingdom?

And I feel some odd loyalty to, and affection for, this small country where I taught English and yoga, rode on a camel, floated in the Dead Sea, bought beautiful antique jewelry, planted trees, watched countless European soccer matches, hiked in canyons and saw stunning, dramatic desert sunsets.

And these days I worry about my friends in the Holy Land.

The ancient Biblical land of Moab and Ammon, the prophet Elijah, Jacob who wrestled with an angel whose name was changed to Israel. The River Jordan, where John baptized Jesus, and the Dead Sea, where Lot's wife turned into salt and Moses saw "the promised land of Canaan" from Mount Nebo outside the city of Madaba, and I stand one hot afternoon where he had, try to imagine what he saw in that bleak and barren landscape, try to imagine what called to him in the wind that led him down the mountain. I have often wondered why the three Abrahamic faiths emerged in this seemingly hostile land, but perhaps that's the reason. The desert is unforgiving and vast. There is a simplicity to what you need and desire: water, shelter from the fierce sun. And so the voices of prophets and the mystery of creation come together with stories of miracles, survival, judgment and forgiveness, and they build them — mosques, temples, churches — then wage war, each claiming their own truths when the desert should remind them they are all made vulnerable in this landscape.

The earliest map of Jerusalem, in mosaic, is on the floor of St. George's church in the town of Madaba, which closes down on Fridays for prayers, except for the Christian liquor store where I buy my red wine.

The tomb of Job rests in the city of Salt. King Herod the Great lived in Mukawir. I climb the steep trail to find the ruins of his palace overlooking the Dead Sea and remember the story of Salome's seductive dance and John's head brought later that evening to the son of Herod.

Petra, a city cut out from rock cliffs, is mentioned in the Bible several times and was perhaps the resting place for the Magi on their way to Bethlehem. This is, indeed, the Holy Land with its Roman ruins and the ancient fort at Karak, where Arabs defeated the Crusaders. A guide brings me deep into passageways where the soldiers lived; he shows me the kitchen, the stables, the prison. Back up to the fortifications, I stare through the slits made for archers and imagine the Christian army in disarray, bloody and retreating.

Like many countries, Jordan has its extremes of wealth and poverty. Mercedes and BMWs share the highway with rackety trucks. Mansion-top windows overlook abandoned buildings. High-end stores in fancy malls sell Gucci and Prada and gold Rolex watches while the local tailor and shoe repair shops look dusty and smoky and cramped. Vegetables in City Mall are often wrapped in plastic, but by the roadside, pyramids of fresh tomatoes, carrots, cabbage, radishes, pomegranates, strawberries and watermelon are piled high, and men or boys sit and wait in the sun or rain all day for customers. And now the people of Jordan, rich and poor, rise up in solidarity against their king.

Amman's skyscrapers, four-star hotels and five-star restaurants can remind you of any cosmopolitan city, while Madaba, an hour south, is gritty and dirty, like an "other side of the tracks" kind of town. But it's close to the school, and I go there often to shop for gifts, to wander, to hear Arabic, to find refuge.

Fifteen minutes from King's Academy, every Tuesday, I drive the same route past the camel barn and fields and gas station into snarly traffic.

Colorful banners in Arabic proclaim what I can't read but I know my way: turn down narrow alleys lined with used-clothing stores, find my parking space, sometimes up a steep hill past HJ's, as it is affectionately called. I sit at the same table that after a while becomes known as "mine." The hostess smiles, waves me to "your table," and Omar arrives with my half bottle of red wine he knows I will order, and while he twists the cork, speaks his few words of English: "It's nice to see you again." And soon he's back with my usual, every-Tuesday-night supper: basket of bread made in a brick oven, puffy and hot; and hummus with pine nuts; and fattah, a small pastry made with spinach. In the winter, a bowl of lentil soup. Otherwise, Fattoush, a Middle Eastern salad.

I reach into my backpack for a pad of paper and write letters with a pen. Here I am welcome and recognized and feel at peace. On my last Tuesday, I tell them I am going home and they tell me — the waiters, the hostess, the manager — they will miss me. And I cry, all the way back to King's Academy.

* * *

Even now, in 2012, Bedouins reside in tents. Some look sturdy; others, flimsy, made of cardboard and canvas and plastic pitched on steep, rocky hillsides or beside the highway. Their goats and sheep scrounge for food in the hot, dry months, stopping traffic on the back roads as they cross from one patch of grass to nibble on the other side. A dark-skinned young boy or two or an old lame man keeps them together with a long stick and whistles, while a wife/mother cooks *what* over a wood fire — perhaps one of those goats/sheep. Yes, there is rural poverty here and inner-city desperation, but somehow it is the Bedouins who make my heart ache. They seem so exposed to the relentless desert heat and wind. The children most likely will not go to school and their laundry strung on poles over sandy, rocky dirt looks, to my western, privileged eye, like a poem of loneliness. And yet, I sometimes see the boys on a level piece of ground, playing football, what we call soccer. And girls in heavy skirts and head scarves sometimes wave and smile at me when I drive by. They have beautiful faces, and this is a life chosen over being crammed into concrete buildings without freedom of movement, autonomy, independence: an ancient adaptation to a desert land. So I kind of admire them, too. They refuse to abandon a way of life they have known for thousands and thousands of years. Before Abraham. Before Muhammad. Before Jesus.

* * *

Jordan is also a country of contradictions and paradoxes, although perhaps just through the eyes of a foreigner: tribal and urban and modern and primitive; ruled by a king who now seems to be in crisis. Orthodox and secular Christians and Muslims defy assumptions and live together without dispute, although Sunday is a work day and Fridays are for prayers.

A land of brown stone cliffs, looking lifeless and endless until spring, when fields are plowed and green. Where some women are fully veiled and all in black; I smile into their eyes sometimes and they lift their veils to bite into a McDonald's burger at City Mall.

Where girls with head scarves wear tight, tight jeans and tops, hiding their hair but not their teenage bodies for the teenage boys who wear Adidas sneakers and name-brand jerseys and smoke on the street corners, talking on their cellphones. The sexual politics in this conservative culture are complex and sometimes ambiguous. And I wonder how those teenagers negotiate the taboos, their desires, their duty to family and to faith.

A landscape where black plastic bags float in the wind as if they were New Hampshire leaves in October, and plastic bottles and garbage line the roads, the fields, even the historic site of Jerash, where I try to see the Romans in the theater but end up kicking empty Pepsi cans. There's no place to throw them away.

Trash is as much a part of the landscape as the ancient olive groves. Families like picnics when the weather is fine; they lay out a rug in the dirt amid empty milk cartons, Coke cans, cigarette packs, bags; make a small fire, pass food around without seeing the landscape of garbage. I wonder why.

***

King's Academy is a walled compound with a security gate. Most days when you re-enter, the man who comes to know your name opens the trunk or looks in the backseat. King Abdullah, who traces his family back to the Prophet, graduated from Deerfield Academy, and he believed that such an education should be brought back to his part of the world. So he founded "Deerfield in the Desert," the only coed high school or boarding school now in the Middle East. His picture is on the wall of all administrative offices and on large posters throughout the countryside, often in his military uniform. He often visits the school in a helicopter he pilots, surrounded by many body guards. He is rather short and stout, with a gracious smile. We all stand when he walks to the stage, but the students are not afraid to ask him some tough questions about Jordan's parliament and environmental issues. I wonder which questions they will ask him now about his survival as the king of Jordan.

***

The campus looks like most boarding schools: dorms, quads, clock tower, library, dining hall, a pool and basketball court and gym with weights, treadmills, biking machines, a turf field for football, not the American game. Except for the architecture of concrete painted white, and red-tile roofs; the ancient olive trees, some thousands of years old, transplanted from Palestine; and jade plants and silly-looking hoopoe birds; and a stadium with dirt seats. The call to prayer is heard from the local mosques, and announcements at school meetings are in Arabic, like the prayer before every lunch. And the heat of a desert climate and dust storms and wild dogs barking all night and Bedouin camps just down the road and school bags left out on the lawn and an Assembly Hall with no pictures of old men, for the school is only five years new, with only three graduating classes.

All students in dress code: khaki pants, button-down shirt, blue blazer or blue sweater and a King's necktie. The boys must be clean shaven. And like all teenagers, the rebellion against it: a sweatshirt instead of the jacket. Girls wearing a colorful scarf to hide the fact that they are not wearing a tie and get scolded for it at every other school meeting. A few girls wear white hijabs, but most don't. They wear tight pants and colorful shoes.

Required tables for lunch, required waiters, lots of required meetings, required study hall, required extra help sessions and cocurriculars. Not a lot of free time. Because King's Academy is a radical idea, and it needs to assure parents that it's the right place for their sons and daughters.

The vision and reality are not in sync. There is a lot of emphasis on testing and lecturing, and there is no health course. There are common texts and common final exams. But King's has a future with the current headmaster, who believes in independent thought and tolerance and discussion-based classes. He is wise and gentle and a man I would work for ... if I could be queer, if there were an ocean to dive into, if there were maple trees in Jordan, if I could teach what I wanted to teach. Pushed back into the closet is harder than I imagined it would be. I feel, maybe idealistically, that if my sexuality is known, my homophobic students might open their hearts and minds. And I grit my teeth through their anger at Obama's support for gay marriage. Being silenced about something so crucial to my sense of self makes me wonder about other silences: those veiled women, those teenagers in the street, those Bedouin children and Palestinian refugees.

***

Students at King's are much more affectionate than Exonians. Boys often hug one another in the hallways, not the backslapping awkward gestures but authentic and affectionate embraces. And they often stand with arms thrown around one another's shoulders. Girls walk arm-in-arm to class, and they are very polite. "Thank you, Miss" after every class, and smiles from students I don't even know. Even the boy who got a D at midterm is friendly, sometimes.

Abdullah Abu Sheik admits in his self-evaluation that he was lazy. He often sits with his chair against the wall, messing with his cellphone, or asks to go to the bathroom and comes back a half hour later. He thinks Hamlet is boring and rarely has his book with him. But then, then, he begins to write his meditation.

"Five pages," he tells me one morning.

He turns it in, and I read images of young Abdullah kicking the ball against the side of his house, begging the older boys to let him play with them, hitting the back of the net in middle school, of a car accident that smashes his legs and it seems his football days are over. But he doesn't quit, learns to walk again, then run again, and he joins King's varsity football squad. Ten pages. More than he has ever written, he tells me. I go to watch one afternoon. He eludes a defender with a clever bit of footwork and sends a high pass across the field to a waiting teammate. But then, as happens so often in our year together, he says his computer broke, and he lost it. So he writes a poem for his final project.

My students call me Miss Christine, a gentle blend of formality and informality. Omar and Sharouk — Palestinians. Zein and Farrah and Mounir — Jordanians. Tarik and Mohammed — Saudi Arabians. Zarifa and Aziza, from Afghanistan. They teach me about Arab identity. I give them small slips of paper and ask them to write what Arabic words they think I should know. They write the script in Arabic, then with the English pronunciation. They think I should learn, among other things, *ma-ba'rat*, I don't know; *khalas*, enough; *keefak*, "How are you?" I try to memorize all of them to answer the teacher I share this room with in Arabic. He mostly just smiles at me. They express their cynicism of American foreign policy, their struggles with Shakespearean language, their individuality when given the chance to express it. I get in trouble a lot. Am I always an outsider? The expats and the local teachers often disagree on how or what to teach, and I am told again and again that this is not Exeter and I can't do here what I know in my heart I can. So I put the chairs in a circle and have them discuss, assign papers that ask for creativity and personal expression: Make up a constellation and the myth of how it got into the sky. How do you define yourself?

May 15, the 64th anniversary of the Nak'ba, for some known as The Catastrophe. Omar, whose grandparents lost their home and their homeland, asks me if we can observe a moment of silence, while sirens ring in Gaza and the West Bank. We will hear them in our imaginations, for outside the open windows, pigeons coo on rooftops. Omar's hands are palm up, eyes closed, head bowed, lips moving. And in this moment, I realize I am in Jordan, not so far from the West Bank, visible across the Dead Sea, and the sun sets there on poor villages and rich settlements alike. And not so far from Tel Aviv, across the King Hussein Bridge that changes its name after many Israeli checkpoints — where Boaz lives, my leftist former student friend, who joined the military as a medic, who drove me to Jerusalem and wandered in the Old City with me and waited for me when I went to the women's side of the Wailing Wall and put my wish into a small crack; who would join Omar in his quest for peace. Omar, who writes his meditation about the complexity of his Palestinian identity, for he has lived all his life in Jordan and didn't visit the land of his ancestors until he was 16. Omar teaches himself Hebrew to better understand history and occupation. A gentle boy, now studying at Columbia University. I will take many images of my time in Jordan. This one comes to me often: Omar praying on May 15.

But some people appreciate what I am trying to do and I make some good friends. My Yankee reserve melts into the desert heat and I learn how to open myself up to strangers. I even design my own birthday party and get unexpected gifts: a small water pipe, a glorious, woven rug made by local women. Steve. Patrick. Cassie. Sue. Emily. The expats teach me how to play poker and how to smoke shisha, what grilled camel meat tastes like, what a local all-male-so-sit-outside café looks like. I don't get very close to Jordanian teachers, although sometimes Hani and I talk about Arab writers and Sharifa invites me to have coffee that never happens.

And I meet two remarkable Arab women, who defy the western stereotype of meek Middle Eastern females deferring to husbands or males in general. Feisty and assertive and confident, they celebrate their Egyptian identity and claim their own. Intellectual and serious, they also embody the hospitality and graciousness of their culture.

Mona brings me soup and pickles made at home from her mother's recipe. We often go out and talk politics — her fear that Cairo will descend into violence again — or she tells stories about her Muslim father and Christian mother, her days of living in the Jewish quarter of Brooklyn and studying literature at the University of Cairo. She invites me to her homeland during the spring break, and I meet her extended family, sail down the Nile in the evening, find graffiti at Tahir Square in the camera lens, and the pyramids, and the Sphinx. I write to her about the crisis in Jordan and Egypt, and I miss our discussions at HJ's, Mona with her water pipe and me with a glass of wine at lunch.

Monica, the headmaster's wife, invites me to walk with her or stop by for tea, and she attends my yoga classes, striving each time to balance into a headstand. We talk about books we are reading, about students we are worried about, about life in the desert. During hard times, these women are alert to my loneliness in this foreign country, so far from what is familiar, and from people I love. They anchor me when homesickness roars in like the desert wind.

***

The sky is the sky, a sliver of moon become full every month, the moon signaling the beginning and end of Ramadan. In the winter, Orion is there to guide me back to my dorm apartment. I saw Orion the other night and knew that he was watching over Jordan. And the Big Dipper lets me know that 6,800 miles away from home, it is also in its place and will be seen, seven hours later, on clear New Hampshire nights. I have always looked to the stars; I have three tattooed on my right thigh. When I used to go camping in Arizona or Colorado or New Mexico, I would check the sky to orient myself. So here, in this desert kingdom, I depend on constellations to remind me that the distance from here to home can be mapped by something familiar, something steady and enduring. And my moments of loneliness translate into another language, older than civilization, a silent voice telling me that Orion watches over Exeter and the Dippers, Cassiopeia, Gemini, Leo will be there when I return.

I get a tattoo in Amman, OCEAN in Arabic calligraphy because I have, since I was a child living in Newcastle, been drawn to the tides, the smell of salt, the grit of sand, the scurry of shorebirds, catching of the curl of a wave. And I see this gesture as a way to bring my year in Jordan into some kind of permanent memory, in a script I never learn but hear every day, from the mosques, my students, the staff, in the streets of Madaba and Amman. It is a beautiful, complex, poetic language, and the few words I learn - *mahaba, suk ran, afwan, masalama, inshalla, halas, yella* — will always echo in my vocabulary.

***

Reclaim Childhood, a social service project run by students, designed for Iraqi refugees who come to King's once a month to play and laugh and forget for a while where they live. Their mothers look on in heavy dresses and head scarves, but often join in the games of tag or Duck, Duck, Goose, returning, too, to some kind of innocence and joy. I can't speak their language, don't know if they lost sons, husbands, brothers in that war I protested again and again. The refugee girls have never seen lakes and ponds, so they are a bit afraid of the water and come to the pool fully dressed. I hold Ma'an up. She seems to be about 10, with long hair and dark eyes and thin arms. She is wearing red pants and a bright-green jersey. I rest my hands under her back and legs, ask her to relax and put her head back. But she speaks Arabic and I speak English, so she panics when I let go and grabs my neck, then smiles, and we laugh, connected in a different language, what Andre Dubus might call "essential touch," Ma'an trusting me not to let her sink. "Down me," she says, so I ease her into standing up, walk with her to the side of the pool and show her how to kick. She tries, bending her knees and raising big splashes that she likes. I show her how to put her face in the water, blow hard out her nose. She tries that, too, and comes up breathless, unsure, a bit frightened. We spend 40 minutes in the King's pool, so foreign to her, so magical and distant from her life in the camp. And she teaches me by her courage to have patience, all the uncertainties of her life forgotten for a little while in that strange, clear water.

So, with some panic of my own, not knowing Arabic and uncertain about what awaits me, I wave goodbye to Mercy at JFK, cry on the hard plastic chairs before boarding and fly, through the darkness of American time into the daylight of Middle Eastern time, through six-plus hours of restless sleep, and land at Queen Alia Airport, Amman. I find my luggage, pull the heavy, black pack over my shoulders and adjust the straps, take the blue-and-white duffle bag in my right hand and take my first steps into the Hasimite Kingdom of Jordan.

I'll end with a poem:

To Become Trees

They are wrapped in black plastic I pull off,

exposing roots, thin as string.

Beetles scurry away

startled by the shock of sunlight.

Spiny branches with leaves

I can't recognize, or name.

I place them in holes already dug for these seedlings,

and pull dirt full of stones

to steady them for days to come.

I have been given a stubby axe though to hack away

at the ground.

It is hot, sweaty, hard work, gathering

up enough earth to keep these plants upright,

to keep the roots safe.

Arabic all around me now,

on my knees, using my hands,

when across the road, a waterfall

of sheep pell-mell down the hillside

to a lush garden where they don't belong.

So with whistles and shouts,

the sheep turn around and scamper

back up by twos and threes,

not as graceful as their mad descent.

I plant another, and another, and another

an act of faith that rain may come soon

to nourish the roots,

so that leaves and branches might reach for the sun.

And I return to school

with the dirt of the Holy Land

under my fingernails.

MOLLY BASHAW
December 19, 2012

When I arrived home from school that day at Cabot Farm, I walked up the long driveway, past the flock of sheep; past the two Clydesdale workhorses who looked at me in unison, one's mane falling to the right, one's mane falling to the left; past the apple orchard, heavy with fruits. A barn cat ran to greet me on the step of the farmhouse. Inside, I sat on a stool in front of the woodstove in our dining room, presenting my parents with the list of band instruments we had been shown at school: the dark wooden clarinets with their silver keys, the graceful flutes, the impossible oboe I was sure would make my head explode. "Why don't you play the trombone?" my father said, already getting the instrument down from its shelf, dusting off the fake alligator-skin case. He had played in high school and had let my brothers and me try blowing into the mouthpiece on occasion when he had taken it out to practice. Do girls play trombone, I wondered? But my dad seemed so excited by the idea of me playing his old instrument that I was quickly convinced, heading off to school the next day on the bus, carrying the big case with the golden King 3B trombone curled up inside it.

All my journeying since then seems to have sprung from that decision — as though I had also been choosing a voice, an identity, a vehicle. I later

---

Molly Bashaw is the author of *The Whole Field Moving Inside It*, a book of poetry. She was the 2012-13 George Bennett Fellow at the Academy.

learned the French name for paper clip is *trombone*. Perhaps it is a stretch, but I like to think that the trombone has been a kind of paper clip, holding the disparate pages of my life together, taking me away from my farm beginnings in Massachusetts to study and perform classical music in Europe, training me to listen to silence in the way writing poetry requires, and returning me to a place where I can begin to appreciate how all of this fits together.

At school the trombone gave me a sense of pride and a sense of belonging that didn't require much social interaction, only that I play my part well in band — a fitting remedy for me, a shy girl, at least at school, where I felt my differences as a farm kid in a community not made up of farmers. I had never dared to tell the other fourth-grade girls what went on at home on the farm, that I had often fallen asleep while riding atop the Clydesdale workhorses my father used to plow the fields or bring in hay he had cut with a scythe, or that I had assisted docking the tails of lambs, using rubber bands and a knife, in order to keep the blowflies from breeding in the tail wool. I didn't try to explain to the teacher, either, that I was tired because I had woken with my parents at 3 a.m. and dressed quickly, gone out to the barn in the light of the moon to watch and assist our sow give birth to 13 piglets in a river of blood and life, or that the sow had accidentally rolled onto one of her newborn piglets and it had died and I now knew what birth was and what death was, in fourth grade, and had stayed until sunrise in the barn, holding that piglet until my parents took it to the compost, where all the dead things on our farm went, and buried it.

I tried not to reveal these gritty realities of my life on Cabot Farm, a farm where my parents worked and were given housing, but not a farm they owned. The other kids in my class told of polo and tennis lessons at the Wenham Country Club, vacations to Europe or spending afternoons at the local beaches with their foreign au pairs. How could I explain to them at lunch, I wondered, that the ham in my huge homemade sandwich, on homemade bread I could hardly fit into my fourth-grade mouth, was from a pig I had known by name? Plumrose, our sow. Or that the cheese was from the cow I had milked some nights with my father, he on one side of her, I on the other, our heads rested against her warm body between us? Or that we sometimes felt the fetus, the calf still inside her, move across our foreheads while milking? I ate outside at recess when I could, under the big oak tree at the edge of the playground, dreaming of a white-bread sandwich with peanut butter and Fluff, and was secretly relieved when my parents were too busy or sick to make us lunches and, apologizing, sent us off to school with dollars to buy school lunch: a square of pizza, instant Jell-O, a juice box. Everything neat and tidy. Only at band practice, where I now could sit in the back row between the tubas and trumpets and wait for my big entrance, my big new brass voice, did I begin to imagine a stronger identity for myself at school.

Looking back, I am not sure why I was ashamed of being a farm girl. I don't remember being ridiculed, only that our way of life proved repeatedly not to be the norm. One Valentine's Day I told my mother I was supposed to make Valentine's cards for all of the girls and boys in my class. She brought out construction paper and scissors and glue and the latest edition of the Fedco seed catalog. We snipped heart-shaped pictures of beets, beans, lettuce, and glued them onto the cards and my mother helped me think of messages for the insides: "Don't you carrot all for me?" "I bean thinking about you." "Lettuce be friends." "My heart beets for you." We laughed doing this and I was proud of our version of Valentine love — until I arrived at school and saw the store-bought cards the others had brought, ones with Care Bears or Transformers on them, ones with candies attached. There were no vegetables. I hid my cards and told my teacher I had forgotten them. And when I went home that day with my bag full of candies, I put the cards I had made with my mother in a little shed beside the barn where my brother and I had been collecting interesting pieces of glass, bolts we'd found in the dirt, a little wooden bird that was buried in the garden.

My father invited my entire class to come out to the farm on a field trip, annually. He took us on a tour through my daily life, showing the gardens, explaining where milk comes from, that a cow has four stomachs with beautiful names, rumen, reticulum, omasum, abomasum, telling them how the compost, when turned, makes rich mulch for the gardens, and even in deepest winter is warm inside, showing them how to prune an apple tree or graft one tree onto another to get the best apples. Answering their questions. And I looked down when they held their noses and when they said, "Ewww" and when they never actually said it, but maybe thought, "You really LIVE here?" I pretended I, too, was just a visitor, and afterward would be going home somewhere else.

One day I heard some of the fourth-grade girls talk of tanning, that they were getting tan at the pool, that they needed to work more on their tan lines. I became interested in this idea, and without any investigation decided I would work on my tan as well. That afternoon, I convinced my younger brother to join me and we lay in our underwear out near the garden all afternoon, eating graham crackers and watching the pigs rooting inside their transportable pens, looking up occasionally to watch us. You have to keep turning over to get it even, I instructed Jonas, who soon grew bored and left. I stayed there, waiting for my skin to change, watching a hawk ride on the rising heat in the sky above the open field, turning over, picking and eating the laurel from the hot grass around me, finally falling asleep for several hours.

That evening at dinner our mother rubbed aloe into our sunburned faces. At bedtime she told us the story of Icarus, who had flown too close to the sun and melted his wings made of wax. My brother fell asleep, his hot face against the corduroy pillow, leaving streaks across his cheeks. "Why did he want to go away?" I asked my mother. She said Icarus wanted to get far enough away from his farm that he would not smell the compost pile or the pigs, that he would not see or hear his parents castrating animals, that he would not be reminded he was a farmer. "Why didn't he just go to the moon?" I asked her. "He could have landed there and made a dust angel on the surface with his wings. He could have returned," I said.

My mother, though she had studied biology, and seemed less the initiator of the simple farming lifestyle my dreaming idealist father had sought for us, was good at bending mythology to instruct our lives. Sisyphus, she once told me while shucking peas in a rocking chair on our back porch, was a farmer. "If you look some nights, you can see him rolling his stone still, out over the fields, massaging the aching muscles in the hills." I don't know if she had read Camus' version of the Sisyphus myth, but she always left out the part about the work having been punishment; only in college did I realize Sisyphus had been condemned to roll his stone. I had always imagined he had enjoyed it, as I guess I was supposed to have enjoyed working and living on the farm.

But like my mother's version of Icarus, I dreamed of going away. I stood in the dirt yard, doing gymnastics tricks on branches of the big maple tree, talking with imaginary reporters about how I had won my first gold medal at the Olympics. I hit an old tennis ball against the barn, speaking a language I called French. Whenever I broke a wishbone with one of my brothers and got the longer half, my wish was to live in France someday, a professional trombonist, my name circling somewhere on a marquee. After my concert I would go back to a quiet, clean apartment, I thought, in an apartment building with an elevator. I would have no animals, maybe a fish in a bowl. I would wear clean, stylish shoes and if my parents called I would never answer. I would not want to hear the rooster in the background, or the goats, singing louder than Edith Piaf, whom I would have playing almost always on my record player.

When we moved from the Cabots' farm to a farm in upstate New York my parents had been able to buy, the closing on the house was not timed exactly right with our moving date from Wenham. My father's solution was that we would stay in the barn attached to the house in New York for a month or so until the old owners moved out. I was going into the sixth grade. I was entering a new school. And I was living in the loft of a barn. But we went to sleep those early autumn nights in our sleeping bags on stacks of sweet hay, my father telling us stories in all the voices he created. He read us Robert Louis Stevenson, Laura Ingalls Wilder, he read Dickens, strange Brothers Grimm tales, stories of gold miners out West, stories that made him break down and cry, stories in which he took on the voices of women, foreigners, Southern dialects. He was Huckleberry Finn and he was Jim. My mother sang a song or played the folk music on her accordion she had learned as a young student on assignment in Newfoundland, Canada. Her music drifted up into the rafters where spiders were weaving their own tales. Below us, the animals chewed their never-ending fugue of cuds.

I realize only with a lot of hindsight that my parents were teaching us that in difficult life situations, music and stories and the imagination can be as strong as the real walls of a home. The trombone's voice could carry me through school, giving me an identity besides farm girl. My father's strong reading voice was a home for us while we lived in the barn, and when he sang to us and played his guitar, a song he often included was called "Good Times Are Bound to Come Again." Where there are stories and music, there is hope, they were saying, there is joy. And when my mother opened up her accordion and stretched it out, the huge, strong breath we heard it take was her breath, breathed back into us as song.

When I left the farm, I went to a music conservatory in a city. During my first summer break I traveled aboard a 195 foot river barge called the *Point Counterpoint II*, a floating vessel made into a performance space by architect Louis Kahn and Robert Austin Boudreau, the ship's captain and the conductor of the barge's orchestra. I was 16 and my audition for Mr. Boudreau had not been spectacular. I think he hired me only because when I told him I had come from a small farm, and was majoring in English and trombone performance at the Eastman School of Music, he recognized the promise someone had once seen in him: He had grown up the son of a Massachusetts chicken farmer and gone on a scholarship to Juilliard, later on a Fulbright to the Paris Conservatory. But I was confused by the fact that he now had chosen to have goats at his home (he occasionally left the tour to go milk them), and that he grew blueberries in his backyard, and I think even kept his own chickens. Why go back to farming once you have gotten away from that life, I wondered, once you have become something better? I still didn't get it that you could be a small farmer by choice, though it often meant a financial struggle. I still couldn't see the huge gifts my parents had given me: a childhood spent outdoors; years of healthy homegrown, home-cooked foods; a personal relationship with the flora and fauna of a particular place.

The members of Mr. Boudreau's orchestra, the American Wind Symphony Orchestra, stayed with host families all across the eastern United States during our tour. I ate dinner in at least 30 different American homes, from Pittsburgh to Lake Okeechobee, Florida, and back up the Eastern coastline. When host parents asked about my background, I found myself making up stories. I didn't want to say the word *farm* anymore. I didn't want to explain we hadn't owned the farm. I didn't want to out myself as having been, technically, "poor." Music had become my golden ticket and I was not looking back. My home was now this floating home, a magical vessel, moored each night in a different port, each passenger, each artist, equally displaced.

I finished at Eastman and went to another music school in another city, in another country. I played the trombone in England, France, Germany,

Austria, Luxembourg, Poland, Hungary, South Africa, Japan and Taiwan, with other musicians from all around the world. I had the privilege of playing beside a Japanese orchestra in Hiroshima and Nagasaki. I played Mozart's *Requiem*, Bernstein's *Chichester Psalms* and a selection of traditional Polish music with a choir comprised of German, Israeli and Polish singers; and following that concert, I walked through the sites of the WW II death camps at Auschwitz-Birkenau with that mixed group of musicians. For every intense, historically charged musical project like those, there was also a standard symphony concert, and many strange, humbling gigs to help pay the bills: at the graduation of a forestry class, or for the induction ceremony for a new exhaust pipe for BMW — backing Mike Svoboda, a trombonist who could play an exhaust pipe like a didgeridoo. For a live playback recording for television, I had to pretend to play my trombone while sitting on a straw bale, wearing a dirndl and more makeup than I ever had. I played for a wine tasting in a cool cellar in Burgundy, France, wearing mittens from a snowy Christmas-tree-cutting festival in the Black Forest. On the deck of a ferry between an island on the North Sea and the mainland I played the "Ashokan Farewell" and other American folk songs with a colleague, our sound drifting between the dark waves and a bright summer sky. Sometimes it seemed music wasn't only about the music, but also all these interesting or funny situations it got me into, the people from all strata of societies it allowed me to meet, the careful listening it made important. And my favorite moments were not the concerts themselves, but afterward: the silence, getting on a bus in the night and traveling back to a hotel somewhere, talking quietly in the dark, reading or looking out the window at the streaks of city lights, thinking of our many respective homes.

Twenty years after my wish-making on the farm, I found myself living in the heart of a foreign city, supporting myself completely by playing the instrument fate had handed me. My apartment was on the fifth floor; I had no farm animals, no garden, not even a dog. If I wanted, I could make white-bread sandwiches for every lunch. All my wishes had been granted. Why then, in the writing I began doing more and more, did the farm keep appearing? Why did I carry these "farm poems" of mine in my pockets, along with passages I had copied from other poets I admired, along with Edna St.Vincent Millay's "Counting-Out Rhyme," a poem so perfect and tight it seemed to me a recipe for everything else, a crystal, a periodic table, a bullion cube, though its one subject was simply trees? Why did I walk through the cobbled foreign streets, trying to memorize it in rhythm with my steps: *Silver bark of beech, and sallow/ Bark of yellow birch and yellow/ Twig of willow. // Stripe of green in moosewood maple,/ Colour seen in leaf of apple,/ Bark of popple.// Wood of popple pale as moonbeam,/ Wood of oak for yoke and barn-beam,/Wood of hornbeam.// Silver bark of beech, and hollow/ Stem of elder, tall and yellow/Twig of willow.* Why was my favorite book W.S. Merwin's *Migration*, and why did I lose my breath for a moment every time I read his line *but I could not let go of what I longed to be gone from?*

I thought about these things while I was playing concerts in the former East Germany in the radio wind ensemble, or riding the commuter rail home at night, by myself, our train stopped next to another commuter train. I met the glance of a passenger in the other train's window, a young woman about my age, reading in the light of the train. She reminded me of a painting by Edward Hopper and I wondered where she was going, if any of us were ever actually going anywhere, or just riding in circles on Fortuna's giant wheel, inventing stories of odyssey to comfort or amuse ourselves in the static passage of time.

When I visited home once a year I found myself playing Bach suites in the barn or in the empty grain silo, letting the sound of the trombone fill those spaces that had once been occupied by hay and grain, bringing Bach's Europe into the spaces of *my* home. I played my trombone out on the field for my father's grass-fed Scotch Highland cattle, expecting they might recognize the range of the instrument. I recorded my father singing his songs and playing guitar, something he had always done but I had never fully appreciated. Songs about farming and songs about building boats and sailing: "The Eerie Canal," "I've Been Working on the Railroad," and a song that simply goes, "You can't make a turtle come out. You can call him or coax him, or shake him or shout, but you can't make a turtle come out." I listened to these often, abroad again, after I had played a symphony by Mahler or Shostakovich in a large concert hall of a German city.

Back in this country for a longer period of time for the first time in 12 years, I feel thankful for poetry and music for reconnecting me with my roots. Presenting myself as a poet, I no longer feel embarrassed to say, "I know all the names of the cow's stomachs and I think vegetables are beautiful valentines and I once lived in the loft of a barn," because I now recognize the farm as the magical place it was, teaching me to listen and watch, teaching me to want. Teaching me the power of wishes and my own imagination. It is the farm that brought the wealth of music and stories into my life. Of course we didn't own that farm, I realize now. All those farms had always owned us.

***

Here in Exeter I help out on a small organic vegetable farm in Brentwood called Pickpocket Farm. One day in the fall, I bring home a bouquet of beautiful rainbow Swiss chard after working with Audrey in her field. The stalks are magenta, yellow, vibrant purples and greens; the leaves are laced with red veins. I make a piecrust for a quiche with eggs my mother brought me from her chickens my second week here, and while it is in the oven I work on sounding out a poem that might in some way come close to the beauty of Swiss chard. I read a few pages of the peasant poet John Clare's biography, by Jonathan Bate, in which Clare is quoted: "Everything I learned I gleaned from 'Jack and the Beanstalk.'" John

Clare, who wrote during the 19th century, in England, recounts writing poems by "kicking them from the clods of dirt" in the fields where he worked. He kicked more than 3,000 poems out of those furrows. I reread "Jack and the Beanstalk," excited to stumble on this passage about beans during the same week I am working with Audrey threshing beans in Brentwood, and excited now, during my own meditations on these themes, to have rediscovered this tale — which I think is about the magic of belief, and very literally about social climbing: up a beanstalk toward the gold of the "giants." But I want to say to Jack, and to John Clare, and to myself: Stay down here. Stay rooted. The ground is magic. All beans are magic. Take these calypso beans Audrey and I threshed. They are black and white, a black dot on the white side, a white dot on the black side: the yin-yang bean! Or the Jacob's cattle beans that look like miniature cows. You put them into the field and they come back as food. Magic!

The arts have turned my life into a treasure hunt, helping me, piece by piece, to reclaim territories of my voice, lost along the way to fear or misunderstandings. The process of creation seems to tap into the subconscious, and into the messages of the body, which, poet Anthony Piccione writes, *knows everything*. When I play my trombone now I am not running away. I am saying thank you. I am Icarus and I have landed on the moon and made my dust angels, lying on the surface, moving my wax wings back and forth, and I have decided to fly back down to the smells of the earth, to push the last of the spinach and garlic for this season into the ground, with my parents — or with whichever farmers will have me — and to sit somewhere, preferably at the edge of a field, looking out over our work. And because we are tired from this good hard work, to say thank you, thank you.

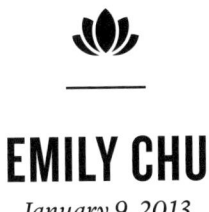

EMILY CHU
January 9, 2013

It has fallen out of fashion now to put the hyphen in between Chinese and American. The hyphen always suggested to me that there was a logical chronology to my cultural and racial identity, that I was initially Chinese and then became American somehow through that little dash. The Chinese part felt like an inheritance with which I had little current connection — it just happened to be a starting point.

I knew my Chinese heritage existed. I had a Gung-Gung and a Po-Po, a Yeh-Yeh and a Ni-Ni — all of whom spoke fluent Chinese and broken English, but I only knew vocabulary related to food in Mandarin, so fragmented English was all we had. My parents spoke Chinese when there was a secret they didn't want me to know. Every Christmas, we ate hot pot (*hǒa góa*), my favorite meal of the year, dipping our wire baskets filled with pieces of thinly cut beef, pork or rockfish into the boiling broth, pulling the baskets out and emptying their contents into our bowls, dousing them with oyster sauce (*hāo yǒ*). There was always a lot of slurping with our bowls held to our mouths, chopsticks shoveling away.

I understood this particular meal was not something non-Chinese people did. The slurping and the shoveling in particular were actions that we only

---

Emily Chu taught English at the Academy from 2010-2013. She now lives and teaches in Seattle, Washington.

engaged in around family or at the safe haven of Chinese restaurants. As my hapa cousin Jenny said at her brother's wedding when we were toward the end of a lobster dinner, "Now is when we would normally pick the thing up and suck the last bits of meat from the carcass." She stopped and gestured at her relatives on her father's side, adding, "But there are white people here."

So, I knew I was Chinese. But I grew up in Seattle, Washington, where there are plenty of Asians and most people are proud liberals, excited about their ability to accept and see past differences, and quietly careful about what they say. In addition, I was sheltered, naive and not asking the right questions. Until I came back from studying abroad in Paris during my junior year of college, I didn't recognize that my family was the only one of color in my neighborhood where I had lived since I was born. Whenever we talked about slavery or Jim Crow at school, I felt ashamed. I sensed I was at fault for the centuries of injustice and violence perpetuated upon black Americans. It was, in a way, white guilt. And I could never explain why I felt that way, but I think it has something to do with the fact that I didn't recognize I lived in an all-white neighborhood until I was 21 years old.

My middle school began its foreign language instruction in sixth grade. The options were Latin, Spanish, Chinese and French. My parents said it was my choice, and I chose French because I thought it was the most beautiful language of the four with its sophisticated sounds and the images it conjured in my head of baguettes and the Eiffel Tower. When I moved up to high school, I met my first white person who could speak fluent Mandarin, a boy named Barret, who could converse with my fluent Chinese American friends, and I felt something that was vaguely like jealousy and anger, but because I couldn't ever articulate the reasons why, I let it go. I studied French all the way through high school and double-majored in English and French in college, choosing to study abroad in Paris my junior year because I knew it was the only way I could become close to fluent.

When I first arrived in Paris, I realized it was the small phrases that I had to master if I wanted to sound like a local. "Hello" required a particular attention to the second syllable, with the first sounding almost like an afterthought: bon*jour*. When someone asked for my name, Emily was easily translated into French (Émilie), but Chu was not. I had to say it and then spell it: "Chu, c-h-u." It was the French pronunciation of a last name that marked me as Chinese with a new soft Sh sound instead of a harder Ch, and for the first time in my life, I had my mom's last name (Shu, s-h-u) — as a homonym, at least. When someone asked where I was from, I assumed they wanted my nationality, so I told them, "*Je suis Américaine. Je viens de Seattle aux États-Unis.*" But I learned that usually people weren't satisfied with that answer. They wanted to know where I was from *originally*. And even though I had been born in Seattle, Washington, in the United States, I found myself telling them, "*Chinoise. Je suis Chinoise.*" Because that's what they actually wanted to know.

Paris was beautiful. I lived there for nine months and found my favorite bakery with the best baguettes (just the right amount of crunch) and my favorite neighborhood bistro, where I learned to love eating meals alone. I found a dish called *confit de canard*, which is a duck leg cooked in its own fat until the skin is crispy, and I found a delicious hard orange cheese called *mimolette*. I only drank wine from 2005 because all the French said that was the best recent year. I loved the metro and the weekly markets and being able to go to museums for free because my program lied on our ID cards and said we were all art history students, which meant we could go to any museum as many times as we wanted without ever having to pay.

However, besides the museum trips, Paris was expensive, and I learned that one of the cheapest meals you could find was Chinese food — or, more broadly, Asian food in general. The irony was not lost on me when I would go to Chinese restaurants and order in French, using the French translations for dishes I only knew how to pronounce poorly in Mandarin. When my parents came to visit at Christmas, we ate Chinese for dinner one night. The waitress spoke Mandarin to them, and a whole conversation ensued, in which we (or rather, they) learned that she was from the same part of China where my maternal grandparents had grown up.

I lived in the 15th arrondissement, within walking distance of the Eiffel Tower, and went there often enough to sit on the grass at the Champ de Mars to become a coolly disinterested observer of the tourists there. Most notable were the Asian tourists, who showed up in packs and took what seemed like hundreds of photos. Parisians saw these groups as a running gag, and when they came up in conversation, I usually kept quiet and drank my wine. After all, I wasn't a tourist. I lived in the city. I knew some of its secrets. It became harder to keep quiet when Parisians started assigning me a specific origin and heritage. "*Japonaise! Japonaise!*" men called from the other side of the street. "*Konichiwa!*" I wasn't a Japanese girl, but I looked like one, and I started to feel a deeper kind of kinship with the groups of anonymously Asian tourists so many Parisians mocked and scorned. I might not have been a tourist, but I had been sufficiently reminded that I was also neither Parisian nor French.

At dinner once with my then-boyfriend, Tom, and one of his French friends, Cédric, the conversation shifted to Chinese Parisians. "Their French is awful!" Cédric laughed derisively. "Their vowels are so nasal." He started to imitate what the words sounded like and then stopped when he saw my face across the table. Never before had a Parisian specifically mocked the Chinese in front of me. "I don't mean to offend you," he mumbled.

Tom intervened. "Oh, it's fine. She understands," he reassured Cédric while placing a hand on the small of my back. Tom was from my study abroad program and, in hindsight, it's clear we only started and continued dating because he spoke such beautiful and fluent French.

So it was in Paris, of all places, that I realized I was Chinese. And by that I mean I realized that my Chineseness, my Asianness, was one of the first things people might see when they looked at me. It was such a simple and belated realization that shame and embarrassment ensued. I started thinking a little more carefully about my world and my past. I realized I had never had an Asian teacher until I got to college. The only Asian teachers at my schools had been in the Foreign Language Department teaching Mandarin — which I had never taken. I was hurt but not surprised when, during orientation at my first job, an older woman asked what I taught and was genuinely shocked when I told her English. She replied with a laugh, "Oh, I assumed you taught Chinese!"

I suppose my racial and cultural identity is complicated by the fact that I'm not really Chinese — I'm Chinese American. My dad has always made a distinction between the two, often saying things like, "The Chinese are bad," and insisting that I wouldn't like China because it's dirty and polluted. I have never been and don't know if what he says is true.

My one remaining grandmother, my Ni-Ni, my father's mother, keeps promising we'll go together as a family, but now she's 92, and though remarkably healthy and lucid, it's clear that our extended family won't be able to coordinate our schedules while she's still alive to visit the country she left all those decades ago, thereby literally bringing the Chus to America. Her husband, my Yeh-Yeh, worked for the Chinese embassy in Chicago, and the Chinese government was so poor at the time of their immigration that he didn't receive a salary. Quietly, without telling any of his colleagues, he got a night job as a dishwasher at a Chinese restaurant to pay the bills and support his family.

I wish I had known Yeh-Yeh. Everyone says he was very kind. He was also the love of my Ni-Ni's life. She never remarried after his death. Ni-Ni told me the story of their courtship a couple of years ago. Her family wouldn't allow them to marry until Ni-Ni finished college, so Yeh-Yeh wooed her from afar with gifts. First, he sent her a pair of beautifully engraved silver chopsticks. Then, a delicate porcelain bowl. And finally, most scandalous of all, a pink silk nightgown. I teased her about this last gift while she insisted it wasn't what it seemed, though she smiled the whole time in a way that verged on sly.

Later that day we were at the grocery store, and Ni-Ni took out her wallet to pay. There, among her credit cards, lay a photo of Yeh-Yeh when he was young, probably about the age when they first fell in love. He was handsome and slim and his smile was warm and sweet. She pointed at the photo and said, "There's your Yeh-Yeh," and I said, "I know." Ni-Ni touched his face softly with the tip of her pointer finger before closing the wallet and putting it back in her purse. This is a love I wish I could see in person. This is a love that feels central to how the Chus came to the States and why we persevered and remained. I can understand a piece of it now, but I've lost the full, live dynamic of what that kind of deep and abiding love must have been like.

It feels to me like the term "Chinese American" carries inherent within it an element of this not knowing, this forgetting, sometimes purposeful and sometimes unintentional. My extended family lives across the U.S. now: Washington, California, Utah, Illinois, New York, Virginia. We don't keep in touch. I haven't seen or talked to my two cousins on my mom's side in over five years. And as a result, we don't often revisit old family stories or history. We don't sit in someone's living room and tell each other what we remember about my three grandparents who have died.

Then again, there are some things I would rather not remember, like the smell of stale urine that followed my Po-Po everywhere when I knew her because she had Alzheimer's at that point in her life and couldn't ever get to the bathroom on time. I wish I could un-remember when I accidentally broke her favorite mug while washing it and how she mourned the loss quietly, putting the pieces back in the cupboard like they might reassemble themselves into something whole again if she was gentle and careful enough.

My mom tells me that before the Alzheimer's, my Po-Po was an amazing cook who spent hours cutting vegetables and meat into pieces that were all exactly the same size so they would cook at the same rate. My mom's older sister gave me a locket years ago, and inside is the official portrait taken when Gung-Gung and Po-Po got engaged in China. She was 15 and carries no discernable emotion on her face. He was 20 and possesses a certain confidence that seems to suggest he has won a prize. He had originally been meant for her sister, but he saw Po-Po, thought she was more beautiful, and the marriage was arranged. Eventually, they moved to the States with their three children (my mom was the only one born in America) because Gung-Gung was going to study applied mathematics at Princeton, where he once held the door open for Einstein, who said, "What a nice young man."

I want to know how Po-Po felt about the engagement. I want to know if she thought her future husband was handsome. I want to know if she was nervous or scared. I want to know what their wedding was like, who was there, what food they ate. But that story is gone, and if I get married one day, I know I'll wish I could layer those details of knowledge about Po-Po's engagement and wedding on top of my own. I'll wish I could understand how different or similar our experiences were. I want to know my Chinese Po-Po, who wore beautiful *qi pao* and was apparently stubborn and meticulous. I want to un-know or un-remember my Chinese American

Po-Po, who couldn't recognize her children and scared me with the lost look on her face and the stained shirt that she wore every day because she refused to take it off.

Her American name was Irene, which is also my mom's middle name, and a constant reminder to me that my mom buys long-term-care insurance in preparation for the same disease that took Po-Po. "Put me in a home when I start forgetting," she tells me. Though she hasn't been diagnosed, she assumes Alzheimer's is her future. Every time she misplaces her purse, every hesitation over a word becomes a sign of the inevitable. Her frustration and fear move me to a state of denial. "Your purse is probably upstairs," I reassure her. "Everyone forgets words," I say. I don't want her to give in to forgetting. I refuse to accept this disease that embodies loss. If she forgets, another gap will appear in the narrative of our Chineseness and Americanness that already feels like it will never be whole and thus can never be fully claimed as our own — as my own.

"Don't try to take care of me yourself," she says. "It's too hard." Something I know for sure about being Chinese is that we place a high priority on respecting and caring for our elders. It's a responsibility, a duty. "Don't take care of me," my mom insists. And I know I'll do as she instructs because I'm scared. I'm scared of changing her diapers, scared of fighting with her about taking a bath, scared of watching her disintegrate piece by piece, memory by memory, every day. And is this fear of my cultural and familial responsibility yet another loss as I move further toward American on the sliding scale of identity? Or is it a sensible adaptation to being both Chinese and American? Or perhaps it's just a rational decision unrelated to identity. Still, if independent of inheritance and heritage, then why do I feel so ashamed already, so sure that I've betrayed something larger than family decades before the choice will be finalized?

I never learned Mandarin when I was little because my parents had both been sent to Chinese school on the weekends in Chicago — and they had hated the experience. "We didn't want to put you through that," my dad said. I appreciate their empathy, but I somehow feel guilty every time I step into a Chinese restaurant, and the waitress asks me "How many?" in Mandarin. When I reply in English, sometimes she looks disappointed, like I've hurt her. Other times, she's just as short with me as she is with her Chinese-speaking customers, and then I long to be treated rudely in Mandarin instead of English. I guess I'm looking to reclaim a part of my Chineseness through the language —to listen and understand, to be listened to and understood.

This Christmas, when my parents wanted to know what I might like as a gift, I asked for the full set of Rosetta Stone in Chinese. From the website, it was clear that I needed only the first level or two to order food and carry on simple conversations, but I figured if I was going to learn Chinese, I might as well be thorough about it. One of the first sentences the program taught me was, "*Zhè xie nǔ rén zài zuò fàn.*" The women are cooking food. The photograph accompanying the sentence featured professional chefs in a restaurant, but I prefer to imagine my mom and my Po-Po at the kitchen counter, cutting carrots and celery into perfect, regular pieces. *Zhè xie nǔ rén zài zuò fàn.*

I clearly have trouble pronouncing the different tones that Mandarin requires — and it's those tones that make the language beautiful. When I used to listen to my parents or grandparents speak Chinese, I never heard the lyricism of their words because I was too caught up in the fact that I didn't understand what they meant. I hadn't anticipated how lovely I would find the rhythm and melody of this language when I slow down to form each word in my mouth, lingering over the sounds. It's like music.

Wǒ shì jūng gúo rén. Wǒ shì měi gúo rén.

EMILY MEEHAN
Peace of Cake
January 30, 2013

The little peaks of chocolate frosting sticking to the wall leaned toward the floor as if trying to reconnect with the rest of the cake to which they originally belonged prior to impact. Three-year-old Delaney ran down the hall, cleared the overturned dining room chair, sidestepped the shards of dinner plate, and ran into the room, eyes bulging. "Mommy! Why would you throw the chocolate cake?! Why?!"

Peals of laughter echoed right outside the kitchen as the girls in the dorm came in from dinner, and then I braced, listening for tittering whispers from others who may have ascended the stairs just minutes before.

"Mommy is tired and got very upset. I'm sorry, honey," I tell my daughter.

Hills of snow leaned against the brick building — all visible outside my third-story window. My husband was frustrated at the baby toys and dishes all over the place, and another load of laundry was starting to molder in the basement because I couldn't leave the baby for the amount of time it took to get down the four flights of stairs without him climbing up and falling off the kitchen table. Again.

Emily Meehan works for a global education technology company and lives on campus with her husband, poet and PEA English Instructor Matt Miller, and their two children, Delaney and Joseph.

That winter Delaney and I were sharing our season of temper tantrums — for very different reasons. So when she readily accepted my weak explanation with an "Oh. OK," I wondered if she was experiencing a nascent moment of empathy. But her horrified fix on the cake crime scene betrayed her composed verbal response. It was a most wrongful death of a perfectly good dessert. Working her through the outcome of my outburst would clearly take priority over explaining why I did it in the first place.

I was trapped in an Exeter winter. My closest friends were hours away in Boston, in New York, in San Francisco. I had made a few attempts to join a local mothers group in town. There was a trip to a local library, where we all gathered with our crusty burp cloths and leaky boobs trying to keep our cranky toddlers on best behavior so we would be accepted into the group. But I felt like this was the worst time in my life to strike out and make new friends — I wanted to lean on the love of my old friends, who would understand that my vocabulary recall was not up to snuff because of sleep deprivation; who would appreciate and thrill to my sarcastic and off-color remarks about the physical assaults of what many refer to as the "fourth trimester"; who would find humor and a true resourcefulness in my use of a gym sock as a burp cloth and baby bottle for measuring a 2-ounce pour for a Perfect Manhattan. Which I would then drink. While breastfeeding.

They would also know that my infant was screaming because of acid reflux and not because of my mothering style, and that I definitely did NOT want to spend any more time thinking or talking about babies or the latest bottle cleaner, or the new "hooter hider" that allowed you to publicly nurse privately. I was starving for intelligent conversation and wanted to sit at my desk and respond to time-sensitive emails, think strategically, wear nice work clothes and drink a whole cup of coffee while sitting down. I know these were supposed to be precious times, but domestically, geographically and professionally, this felt like a raw deal. Hence the guts of my daughter's chocolate cake streaking down the wall.

It was the first time in my life that I wasn't working. I wasn't on any "maternity leave" where I'd be going back to a routine and professional track. My phone wasn't ringing with companies begging me to come work for them. In truth, there was no way I could have been holding up a job — primarily because there was no sleep, and baby Joe had already been kicked out of day care because of incessant crying: "We just can't keep holding him, there are other babies here, too," the nice ladies at the day-care center told me. "We just don't think your baby's personality is a match for our center."

I felt homeless being at home. I had not even a basic set of skills or talents to bring to bear in the house. I actually received a "housecleaning for dummies" book as a wedding gift. I couldn't take offense because it was no secret that I needed help in the household department. I had previously outsourced all domestic responsibilities for years so I could focus on what really mattered — my career. Cooking? Eat out or take out. Or what could be more delicious than a Stop & Shop rotisserie chicken? House cleaning? House cleaner. Baking? Cookiesdirect. com. Making Halloween costumes? C'mon people. Who doesn't feel childhood nostalgia smelling those store-bought plastic masks and vinyl suiting. And interior design? To me, this was an exercise in, as one friend derisively described it, "pillow pickin'."

I didn't anticipate my 30s to be a period of a professional holding pattern, let alone a regression. I never envisioned that I would be a stay-at-home mom for any period of time. My mother always worked and it never occurred to me that I would or should step out. In fact, throughout my twenties I was trying to define a clear path to a VP or even C-level position (C-level meaning chief of fill-in-the-blank-important-job) by the time I was in my mid-30s. For years my self-worth was calculated by the job title multiplied by the employer's reputation in the industry. The notion of pursuing personal goals outside of work — all the years invested in playing piano, writing for pleasure, spending quality time with family, volunteering for charitable causes — I considered a wasteful pursuit. At the time, I understood the trajectory that my life needed to follow and that it entailed a marriage, children and probably a modicum of domestic responsibility. However, it took great effort for me to conjure up an image of a family, let alone feeling what I heard was the maternal longing or some biological clock ticking. I would periodically hear references to the "work/life balance" or read about the practical ways to achieve said balance in articles circulated by the HR Department. But it didn't make sense to me. I felt at my core that these personal struggles other people talked of would never be mine. What part of life was worth balancing with a great career? Clearly the latter should be prioritized at all times.

I don't know how I became so fixated on professional success or why corporate America played such a central role in my feelings of personal achievement. But it definitely started in college when I picked up an Intro to Macroeconomics course to add some diversity to the seven literary periods I was trying to navigate as an English major. While I appreciated the intellectual gifts imparted by the studies of Restoration and 18th-century literature, I was ready to apply those concepts and lessons to some real tactical operations of everyday life on the street.

I was pathetically captivated by concepts of supply and demand and the forces shaping our nation's and the world's economy. That a change in interest rates, or that an individual, deciding how much to save or spend at the household level, could lead to large-scale economic relationships, was fascinating to me. Just learning about the sequence of phases — the economic contractions, expansions and peaks that make up our business cycles — made me feel like I was gaining access, or that I'd found a key to a door that I assumed would always be closed to me. Maybe I had felt that way because of my upbringing and where my parents worked. My mom was a reading teacher in Lowell, Massachusetts, and my dad worked as a CPA for the federal government in the Department of Defense. The private sector really employed no one in my immediate or extended family, nor did anyone have large sums of money invested in the market at the time, so I simply had limited exposure to non-government-funded work opportunities. In fact, for most of my childhood, whenever stock market data was reported on the radio, I thought it was a football game where one team called the Dow Jones Industrials played against another team called the NASDAQ. The scores always seemed really high to me, but I never questioned it because I didn't know or care much about football anyway.

While I enjoyed learning about micro- and macroeconomics, I was no class talent. Sure, I would fly out of the gate with exceptional grades, but halfway through the term my head would pulse and then palsy with effort trying to shift a supply-and-demand curve when the price P of a product was determined by a balance between production at each price (supply S) and the desires of those with purchasing power at each price (demand D). "Now how can I demonstrate a positive shift in demand from D_1 to D_2, which would result in an increase in price (P) and quantity sold (Q) of the product?!" It felt like training my foot to hold a pencil and write sentences, and required my utmost concentration to follow a correct train of thought. I nearly sabotaged my GPA by taking accounting and economics electives. But I made up my mind that a career in investment banking was most definitely for me.

I showed up at interviews with Goldman Sachs, Lehman Brothers, and other quant-based consulting firms, and they would look at my résumé and look back at me with a bemused look and say, "Why are you here? YOU are an English major. Wouldn't you be better off pursuing a career in teaching?" This type of response only fueled my resolve to find gainful employment where I could wear a power suit, get a fancy business card and, if I was lucky, let symbols on a ticker tape dictate my mood swings.

The real truth was, if those prospective employers looked at my underwhelming or mediocre grades in the core courses that I thought guaranteed success in their industry vertical, they would apply their very honed analytical and risk mitigation skills to deduce that the prospective employee sitting in front of them would most definitely crash and burn.

So the job market and I agreed to compromise. I settled in a perfect cross section of my interest and capabilities — at the bottom-most rung in a publishing company as an editorial assistant for higher education financial textbooks. Just cracking the binding of one of those glossy 8-pounders set my senses afire. Really. Not really. This was not the flashy, jet-setting trade publishing industry. There were no junkets with John Irving, or the latest chick-lit author or Oprah's Book Club winner. I foolishly hoped to get a leg up on the finance world by actually studying these texts. Didn't really pan out that way.

With the next job, things started to heat up. This time I was the author, or, technically speaking, the "industry analyst," doing lots of writing about the very heady and intoxicating industry of ... (wait for it) ... telecommunications! PBXs, repeaters, hybrid fiber-coaxial cable, twisted copper pair and analog signals were my new lexicon. After I became conversant in telecommunications, I started covering the internet industry right as it was taking off and reaching levels of "tulip mania." Perky, thin, beautiful PR reps with professionally whitened smiles following call scripts would pound the phones all day hoping to book analyst meetings for their big dot-com accounts. Because if your company name was mentioned in an industry analyst report, it could mean millions of dollars in purchasing decisions by Global 1000 companies, and quite possibly an almighty initial public offering (IPO). We analysts sat in the ivory tower safely watching the flurry of activity in the world below, with front-row seats to watch companies joust in the competitive marketplace. We met with new CEOs of dot-com startups, who blew into company headquarters with dark scoops under their eyes exhausted from the analyst road show, demo-ing the same thing over and over again, honing the elevator pitch for investors. We made our bold predictions, armed with tools to size a market and chart its projected year-over-year growth.

There were live TV appearances, conference presentations to large crowds in various auditoriums, lots of press quotes, sought-after sound bites for *USA Today, The Wall Street Journal, Fortune, Forbes* and scores of industry trade rags. Lots of parties, ungodly amounts of company flare, urgent responses to news of company mergers and acquisitions, ballooned egos, little sleep and lots of fun.

When I wasn't working, the roomies and I were couching out, playing house, running errands and hitting the night scene in Boston. It was just stuff we did when we weren't working. On average, I wasn't a great roommate. I didn't sort through my mail, I kept odd hours, didn't clean the house —why should I if I barely used it?

During the holidays I would return home to Lowell and see the same people I graduated with hanging out at the same bars, working in what I thought were dead-end jobs in going-nowhere mom-and-pop or small-town businesses. To me, they were paralyzed in their comfort zones because they never pursued work or a life in a big city. I suspected they lacked ambition and intellectual curiosity and a base level of courage to at least stick a toe beyond the Greater Lowell area. I pitied those who married early, and borderline grieved for those who married their high school sweethearts. The notion of being tied to anyone romantically before age 30 seemed like personal and career suicide, and an unnecessary distraction. I made a point to pursue relationships with people to whom I felt only casually attracted, and where I had secured a controlling interest.

That said, I was starting to have some good late-night conversations with this one guy. He was a bit of a lost soul, but he had what I thought were some unharnessed skills. The way he could get his crew of friends organized for various social engagements demonstrated marked skills in efficiency and leadership, and his living-space design indicated a spatial-relationship aptitude that I could really learn from. There were some downsides. He was pursuing a life of poetry, which had a $0 billion market potential, there was a sharpness in his tone that I didn't like, and while it was usually offset by overt and frequent romantic gestures, it was going to take more than that to melt the ice queen. Plus, he had serious football weight to lose. I kept him at arms length and begrudgingly agreed to let things play out, but I was sure to set expectations accordingly. "Don't expect much from me. Figure your shit out or get lost. I don't need the headaches."

After a few years putting in late nights, weekends trying to finish consulting projects, advising countless entrepreneurs how to strategically position themselves ahead of the competition and achieve sky-high market capitalizations — everything started feel repetitive. SO many hours, and the outcome was the real money just got funneled into someone else's pocket. As I watched this script repeat itself, it started to feel empty and meaningless. Who, really, was I helping? What real impact was I having with this job? The jargon pumping out of the PR agencies for these startups was more than I could bear. Every company offered a "robust platform" that "demonstrated ROI" and "leveraged" something, or created "synergies." Almost all of them claimed to change or create a new "paradigm." I couldn't understand how the market could support so many online retailers of sock puppets. Profitless companies with shaky business models at best were scoring tens of millions of dollars in venture funding. I made a game of playing stump-the-chump with the PR girls, and asked purposefully technical questions that I knew they either didn't want to or wouldn't be able to answer. They'd bumble through the phone call and sign their follow-up emails with "cheers."

Everything started to feel untenable. What was more worrisome was that I realized I lacked a foundational knowledge that would allow me to scale because I didn't really have the tools to accurately size highly undefined and ultimately brand-new technology markets. I started thinking it might be time to go back to school.

The stock market crash from March 2000 to October 2002 caused the loss of $5 trillion in the market values of companies. The parties stopped, people left Silicon Valley in droves, warehouse after warehouse of startup dot-commers had furniture fire sales, poor employees working tirelessly — foregoing paychecks for stock options that would hopefully cash out when they went public — went back home to Mom and Dad's house with empty pockets. I have bags of business cards of companies that just evaporated sometime after Friday, March 10, 2000. There were some good ones. Anyone remember Excite.com? Or the famous merger of AOL/Time Warner? One of my personal favorites was the Enron/Blockbuster partnership to bring video to your home. Half of that party went out of business, the other half went to jail.

Business school seemed like a sensible last-ditch escape from all the uncertainty and a way to define a new path or get to the next level. Terms like "social entrepreneurship" and "double bottom line" were mentioned more frequently in MBA programs and business publications. Some enterprises were using a second bottom line to measure positive social impact. Could it be that there were ways to apply business skills to a cause for greater good? Could we help the passionate yet disorganized administrators climb out of the red, and become self-sustaining? I liked it. It was possible that I might be able to earn a living AND feel good about it!

Gradually, eventually and often reluctantly, I admitted to myself that I did indeed love that darn poet with the tone issues and overtly romantic bend. He had the audacity to distract me from work and expose me to meaningful things in life. And though I was no aficionado on the art form by any stretch, I believed in his work and figured maybe I could possibly apply my marketing and business skills to help this poor poet build his brand and get some market awareness. Last, but certainly not least, my culinary and housecleaning skills were shockingly no match to his — not that my bar was high. This relationship might have synergies!

Things may have moved a little quicker than we had planned. While sipping wine al fresco on the caldera of Santorini during our honeymoon, he mentioned, "I mean, don't get me wrong if you ARE pregnant, that's totally awesome. But if not, what do you say we wait a year or two?" But nine months almost to the day from our wedding, we were three. I was, for a while, professionally unfettered by the presence of a baby in the context of nurturing my precious career. I continued to invest in cultivating my work life with the same drive. But family stakeholders — my mother, my father, my mother-in-law — started to express concern. "Why don't you take a break? Take some time with Delaney. You never get to see her."

I was also picking up on some trending demographic and psychographic data among female friends and colleagues in executive-level positions. Those that had "made it" were either single or divorced, and if they were married they either had no children or their children were grown. When I was regularly boarding the weekday 7 a.m. airline shuttles to Philadephia,

New York and D.C. — I often found myself the lone representative of my combined gender and age bracket. Where were MY ladies? Still, I rationalized my travel experiences as convenient and necessary personal escape from the hectic life at home. These were invaluable opportunities to focus on my work, enjoy some uninterrupted thought, and eat and drink on the company dime, right? I'd return home and see that I had missed the deadline to enter my son for his favorite gymnastics class, or another week went by where I failed to make good on my promise to help Delaney with her piano after school, or the spelling test came home with too many errors because I wasn't there to practice with her. My toddler, going through the typical developmental stage of intense Mommy-need, would have to acclimate to 48-to-72-hour segments of life without me. After being gone for three days, I came back from a six-hour drive from upstate New York, and walked in the door still all suited up from the last meeting. He looked up at me and, perhaps confused or even startled to me suddenly standing there out of my standard uniform of red zippered sweatshirt, yoga pants, disheveled hair and no makeup, burst into tears.

I was losing the battle and taking my family down with me. Last summer, Ann Marie Slaughter's article in *The Atlantic* titled "Why Women Still Can't Have It All" featured a picture of a toddler peeking his head out of a woman's briefcase. It was a harsh redactment of the working mother's progress. Slaughter writes:

> Women of my generation have clung to the feminist credo we were raised with, even as our ranks have been steadily thinned by unresolvable tensions between family and career, because we are determined not to drop the flag for the next generation. But when many members of the younger generation have stopped listening, on the grounds that glibly repeating "you can have it all" is simply airbrushing reality, it is time to talk.

She goes on to say, "I still strongly believe that women can 'have it all' ... I believe that we can 'have it all at the same time.' But not today, not with the way America's economy and society are currently structured."

Well. The mama grizzlies roared out of their dens and shredded Slaughter's article in heated posts and angry editorials — how dare this woman throw her hands up in the air that way and set us back like this? There were many counterarguments offered by many women with many stories about perfectly balanced CEO/mother combinations with no traces of insanity. But we can't get more than 24 hours in a day. Someone or something is getting the short end of the stick because there are only so many ways to divide up the pie. Or, in my case, the cake.

I think back on that evening three years ago when I threw the cake and the chair because I was losing the domestics battle and depressed that I never reached my long-term career objective. But meaningful part-time work that pays well in my field is hard to find. I realize now that the time I invested in that C-level career track all through my 20s and early 30s did actually land me in an executive level role, but it was one that I defined, and one in which I could decide where and how much I worked. I have a scenario that feeds my head and doesn't eat my life, at least for most months of the year. If I hadn't invested the time and effort all those years, I would have to take the full-time load with a two-hour daily commute. The real achievement is that I can walk my kids to school rather than having to leave when they are still asleep and come home minutes before bedtime. I can go into my daughter's school to help the second grade with their writing every week. I make executive decisions to decline a more senior role at my company so my son and I can play in the yellow submarine in the Dover children's museum and race the cars that we built together in the new exhibit. I can say "no" to taking on a stimulating new role or project because I wouldn't have the opportunity for my daughter to coach me on the best technique to hit the jump and achieve maximum speed on our sledding hill.

There are still periods of compromise, tradeoffs and general bad decisions made in an effort to maintain the balance that I've been able to create for myself. I should not have preoccupied my son with a tube of diaper cream a couple of years ago so I could take a conference call (anyone at all familiar with the properties of diaper cream will understand the ramifications of said decision). Distracted with so much mental chatter of kid requests, work requests, board of director requests, family requests, I often exit the shower with only one leg shaved and hair shampooed three times because I couldn't remember if I did it in the first place. I frustrate my husband by asking him the same question over and over, because while he's answering my question I've moved on to consider whether I need to update a slide for tomorrow's presentation. I've left the house with a bag of work documents in one hand and a bag of dirty diapers in the other, and driven off in my car with the work papers in the trash and poop in my passenger seat. I have hired the iPhone, TV and Wii console as babysitters for last-minute urgent phone calls or WebEx demos.

But I can talk to my divorced single mother VP boss and tell her to hold her thought so I can help my son go potty, or get him a snack. I can decide not to travel because I have a sick child. I can spend a workday at Brigham and Women's sitting with my mom while my father undergoes heart surgery. I stay up with Joe when he has whooping cough, or take Delaney to basketball, or I can try to play the fiddle as my friend claws the banjo late on a Thursday.

It can feel like too much at times, but I think this is my version of having it all. And like the old cliché goes, you may not be able to have your cake and eat it, too, but sometimes it's better just to throw that cake and watch it explode across the wall.

KAREN INGRAHAM
Rooted
February 20, 2013

I knew trees first as the two-by-fours and thick square beams that framed my family home and as the warped hardwood floors that moaned under foot. I knew them as the sawdust my dad's circular saw spit out as he cut boards, those fine granules that settled on the hairs of my arm like snow. I knew them, too, as the cords of logs a dump truck would spill onto our gravel driveway every fall.

When I was 8, I sat in my red wheelbarrow, brushed the blond bangs from my eyes, and watched my father stand a wide log on its end. His eyes were hidden behind square-framed glasses that tinted in the sunlight, and small flecks of wood were caught, like flies, in his greasy, onyx hair. His hands, each one an atlas of scars, were gloveless as he gripped the ax handle low, and — in one big sweeping arc — raised it above his head before crashing it down upon the wood. The splitting of fibers sounded like the cracking of small bones. I watched the pits of his white T-shirt darken as fractured pieces of wood shot out from the ax's blade. Soon, a pile my small arms could manage had collected at his feet.

Karen Ingraham has worked in Exeter's Communications Department since 2008. In her own writing, she enjoys exploring how "place" impacts one's sense of identity. She lives in Exeter with her husband and two small children.

I had gloves to protect myself from the spiders and the many-legged silver bugs that hid in the bark of the split wood, unaware they had left the log yard, the forest — that home would be a cool, dark cellar before the furnace blaze claimed them all. But I liked to feel the wood's skin, so I tucked the gloves into the back pocket of my jeans and fingered the paper-thin birch bark that curled like wrapping paper ribbon when you peeled it off. I ran my hands along the petrified, dark wrinkles and the smooth, cool gray scales of other logs that had been trees with names I did not yet know. My fingers became sticky from the logs that still oozed sap, freshly severed from the stumps left behind in the forest to rot.

I liked the smell best, how it seeped into my clothes and hair, how the rows of stacked wood scented the cellar, masking cat litter, dust and laundry dryer sheets. It was not unlike the smell of those cut two-by-fours or the cyclone of sawdust piles I blew off my dad's worktable. But it was different from the way a forest smelled to me then. It wasn't the clean scent of evergreen trees mingling with the sweet gasoline smell from my parents' two matching white Polaris snowmobiles.

I rode on those snowmobiles before I could walk. Swaddled in a snowsuit and blanket, I would be tucked between dad's legs; his Sorel boots braced against the foot wells near the Polaris's engine. The motor's heat would escape out through the console, over the handlebars, and turn my cheeks rosy. My dad's left hand, covered in a black, furry mitt so large it looked like a bear's paw, would tuck me closer to his slippery one-piece snowsuit before each bump and turn on the trail.

By the time I was old enough to ride on the back of the machine, my arms clasped firmly around my father's torso, he had already taken me on most of the trails immediately surrounding Berlin, a pulp and paper mill town at the northern foot of New Hampshire's White Mountains. The trails were part of a larger snowmobile network that ran into Canada and

Maine, most of which crossed industrial forests owned by the region's paper mills. We whizzed by clearings with tree stumps buried under snow, then rows and rows of spindly trees that blurred like too-wet watercolors as our machines whined by, thumb throttles fully depressed.

I knew those trees mostly as backdrop to the smooth, packed trail that could often fit two lanes of traffic. I knew them a little better when I had to pee. When I would step off the trail, sometimes sinking in the snow past my knees, to find a tree suitable to hide behind. I always picked the larger, older ones. They were fewer in number than the pole armies of young birch and pine that looked as if they could snap in any fierce wind.

***

The Eastern white pine, *pinus strobus*, grows tall and straight. Its branches, the living ones, beginning in earnest far up the trunk, extend fists of deep-green needles toward the sun. Brittle, scaled grenades hang from these fists — brown cones that fall to the earth with a dull thud, lying there until a squirrel takes and buries the seeds and begins the combustion of life.

The white pine's bark, like our skin, changes with age. Deep furrows appear on surfaces that grow thicker and darker, defined by ridges of scaly, prehistoric plates. If left alone, a white pine might easily live to 200 years or more.

I was 13 when my dad decided to help our cousins cut down the white pine that stood near Uncle Henry's cabin on Aker's Pond. I don't know how old the tree was.

I don't know how thick or wrinkled its bark had become either. At 45, my dad's temples had begun to gray, his waist had thickened, and his hands and knuckles wore ridges of scars that shone bright against the darker skin around them.

The cabin was built on a strip of waterfront bordered by industrial forest. We brought our snowmobiles there once or twice. I remember shivering in the unheated cabin until a fire had been built in the belly of the wood stove.

In the summers, my mom, dad, older brother, Michael, and I sometimes drove the 40 minutes to the cabin for a family cookout. It was north of Berlin — off Route 26, down a washboard and pockmarked dirt road — and stood in a row of several other small, clapboard structures — many painted in too-bright greens, reds and blues. Like the houses in Berlin owned by French Canadian loggers and millworkers who worked in the forests or at the machines that churned logs into a soupy pulp mixture or pressed out paper towels, newsprint, toilet paper and copy paper.

There were several trees — tall pines that claimed the empty spaces around these cabins. The tree my dad was to cut must have stood out from the others. Maybe its roots had begun to tunnel under the cabin's foundation, or its branches loomed ominously over the shingled roof. Perhaps it was dying. Or, maybe my uncle had simply needed firewood.

It was two weeks before Thanksgiving when dad threw his ax in the truck to go help Uncle Henry, Neil and Mark cut the tree. Neil, a high school chemistry teacher and my uncle's son-in-law, was also one of dad's best friends. They often began and ended Friday or Saturday nights cracking the tabs on half a dozen each of Michelob Light and Pabst Blue Ribbon beer cans.

I never asked how many blows dad landed until he, and not the tree, fell. As if uprooted from the earth himself, he had stumbled into the cabin, collapsed onto the couch, heaving and gasping until he wasn't anymore. Neil started CPR. Mark got into his car and sped to a nearby convenience store in the one-gas station town of Errol to dial 911.

***

On Lake Umbagog, just a few miles from the cabin, loggers used to dump thousands of logs into the water, netting them together with booms — a chain of logs linked together. These flotillas would form and grow throughout the summer and fall — vast islands of floating timber frozen in place during winter, unlocked by the spring melt. When the water ran fast and high, barges would tow these log islands to the mouth of the Androscoggin, and men would feed them to the river, force them downstream for 35 miles until the logs beached on the shores of the mill yards.

Logs now travel by truck on Route 16, which leaves Errol and goes south, following the river to Berlin. The road bisects Thirteen Mile Woods, a tract of protected forest where stretches of whitewater race over smoothly polished boulders along shorelines with stands of uncut white pines.

Moose frequent the sides of this road, sinking their hooves deep into the muddy pools that form during the spring. Known as "Moose Alley," this stretch of pavement's speed limit is checked by the animals' substantial presence, and also by the frost heaves — large, ugly asphalt welts that swell and crack the surface during the colder months.

In the village of Milan, the road and the river separate for a handful of miles, interrupted by a small collection of farms, trailer homes, and the few nice houses owned by people who work somewhere else.

Near Berlin's outer limits, water and road rejoin, passing the vocational college and the bar where people used to bring coolers of beer and listen to cover bands. At the first cluster of neighborhoods, the road becomes Riverside Drive. Boom piers, miniature manmade islands of boulders encased by timber and used to separate one paper company's logs from another, appear in the middle of the river, lined up like sentries on a long march home.

This is the route my father's body traveled by ambulance.

***

The tree Dad cut down each Christmas was usually a young spruce, big enough to poke the ceiling in the family room after it was planted it in the tree stand and Mom had given it a good long drink of water. Our Christmas trees were never like ones from the tree farm — genetically engineered, nourished, and pruned to have the ideal girth, height and shape. Ours had large gaps between branches, their shapes roughly resembling those of the better-manicured trees.

We never paid for a tree. Each year, Dad simply parked the van from Reward Supply Co., the small electrical parts store he managed in town, on the side of a road just outside of Berlin. Then, he walked into the woods and found a tree to cut. The fact that he did not own the tree, or the land it was on, never seemed to bother him. Maybe he went on land owned by the pulp and paper mill, which sat in the center of town like some fat king feeding on fresh logs from the hundreds of thousands of acres of forestland that were the mill's fiefdom and our suburbs. Maybe Dad had figured that the mill bosses weren't going to miss one tree.

I accompanied him one year when I was 8 or 9, trailing behind Michael, who followed behind Dad, as we penetrated the forest. My maroon-and-gray moon boots squeaked on the dry snow, the woods otherwise still except for our shuffling feet. Mostly what I recall is feeling excited to be out there with my dad and brother. It was an adventure, and we were explorers. We bushwhacked by trees either undesirable or not the right type, my breath fogging in the air before me.

I don't know how far in we walked. It probably wasn't that long before we came upon the spruce that we all agreed was best. Dad had taken a hacksaw to its trunk and, in no time, we were retracing our steps, the tree dragging behind Dad like some prehistoric tail.

Sticky with sap after we returned home, I went to the bathroom and opened the Crisco-like tub of industrial soap that sat on the counter. The tub's white substance had the consistency of custard, and I liked to put a little bit into my palms and squeeze my hands together so it would ooze out the cracks between my fingers. The soap smelled like turpentine. Dad used it every day to remove grease and oil, or paint and plaster — whatever had discolored his hands from whichever project he had been working on.

There was strength and purpose in using that soap, and I mimicked Dad's surgeon-like approach, where he would hunch over the oval sink, lift up the faucet handle with one wrist, and scoop out a sizable chunk of soap with three fingers. Then, with patient rhythm, he worked the soap all over his hands, pumping and squeezing them before the gray, milky lather rinsed down the drain.

**

There are blights and diseases that are cankers on the surfaces of trees. Trunks suffer bulbous outgrowths or leaves turn sickly shades before infected limbs snap off in death. But it is only until a tree is bored into that its life is fully revealed. The annual growth rings lapping around the core's circumference tell a story. The number of rings reveals age; the width and density provide clues to what the tree has weathered. Were there droughts, floods, seasons that were too hot or cold? What had the tree been through? How had it survived?

It took the ambulance more than an hour to reach Dad and transport him to the hospital in Berlin. He was gone by the time doctors fed electricity back into his body, commanded the machines beeping at his bedside to fill and empty his lungs.

He had always said "See you later" to Mom, too. Dad wasn't one for goodbyes. Except that day. He must have sensed something when he picked up his tools and said, "Goodbye. I love you" to her before he left.

He had loved music, too. Country, folk and blue grass mostly. One hot day in July, Dad drove our Suburban through a mowed hay field in Stark, New Hampshire, another small town north of Berlin best known for its history as a POW camp during World War II. Dad parked alongside cars filled with other families who had come to listen to the annual fiddlers' contest. Our Suburban was not that far from the stage, and I could hear wooden bows being drawn across strings at a fever pitch.

Michael and I had come as much for the ability to run and wrestle on sweet-scented hay grass as for the music. For Dad, it was one of the few times during daylight I saw him relax.

After a game of Frisbee with Michael, I walked up to the stage to watch the fiddlers more closely. The instruments looked frail with their thin exoskeleton of wood, but their timbre resonated within me. I watched the performers as they cradled their chins against cherry veneer and strummed as if possessed: their bodies pushing and pulling at the melody; their fingers and bows a blur before me.

Kids who were probably fifth-graders like me competed in their own age group. I was jealous as my foot kept the beat, my body bobbed to the rhythm. I played the clarinet in my school's band, and I could make my fingers press the keypads and cover the drilled holes along the instrument's artificial resin body in patterns that elicited melodies. Yet, as I stood there and felt my skin cooking in the hot sun, the clarinet was no longer enough. I had to have a fiddle, I thought.

As dusk arrived and the contest ended, Dad took me back to one of the fiddler's trailers, where he purchased a child-sized fiddle. I listened in respectful awe as the fiddler showed me how to rosin the horsehair bow and turn the small knob at one end to tighten the hairs until they became taut enough to glide and bounce off the strings. I picked up the fiddle and rested my chin in the shallow black dish. Plucking the strings, I looked up at my dad. He was still wearing his straw hat, and his skin was darker from the day's sun. A man of few words, he had simply smiled at me.

I never learned to play the fiddle. There wasn't anyone in Berlin who could give me regular lessons. And yet, its magic endures. Popping open the scuffed metal latches on the worn case still elicits a sense of awe, as if the instrument inside has answers to questions that I haven't yet asked it. So, I pluck at the strings from time to time, listening to the sounds vibrate off the delicate wooden body.

***

I don't remember Dad leaving on the day he died, when I last saw him or if I said goodbye before he drove away. I didn't go behind the hospital curtain to say goodbye either. I don't think it was allowed.

Instead, under harsh fluorescent hospital lights, I became nauseous on the wicked scent of antiseptic, and watched, dry-eyed, my brother sitting slumped in a chair and crying silently.

Then, somehow, Michael and I were in my aunt's car, and I was watching the moonlight glint off the river for the few minutes before my aunt turned onto our street.

"Stop staring," my grandmother had chided me. From the car, I had arrived on a stool at the kitchen counter. My chin rested on my folded arms while I stared straight ahead, not seeing anything, really. My grandmother stroked my hair, afraid, I think, of the dry eyes.

Mom returned from the hospital and was in the family room with my aunt. I pictured her glasses fogged from tears; her brown eyes bloodshot. Her salt-and-pepper hair crimped from fingers looking to grab onto something, anything. I could hear her sobs, rising and falling; words occasionally breaking from her lips between large gulps of air. *Breathe*, I silently commanded her. "What am I going to do?" she said to my aunt.

Sliding off the kitchen stool, I crept quietly up the carpeted stairs, avoiding the places on certain steps that would groan too loudly in a house now muted by grief. The weight of my loss settled thickly on my bones, bending me forward. I felt older by the time I reached the second floor and disappeared behind my bedroom door.

That my father had fallen, been cut down by his own body, seemed unnatural. He was supposed to be sturdier than any tree. I had spent my short life watching him bend metal and wood to his will — organic matter was no match for him. And yet, he was gone. That thought formed for the first time as I slipped my nightgown on and pulled myself into bed. With my head, I nudged my cat over on the pillow and pressed my cheek into the warm spot she left behind. The cat's fur soon became damp from my tears, which she methodically licked away.

Home was a shrine to Dad's handiwork, a manifestation of his love for us, of the nurturing he never put into words. The stairs he built that lead up to the second floor. Their landing the perch on Christmas Eves where Michael and I would watch drunken relatives dance on the hardwood floors below. My bedroom's walls were knocked out, expanded because I needed more room to play. The house's sloping eaves were turned into closets and cubbies, where boxes of grown-out-of toys and holiday decorations lived. The second-floor deck off my parents' bedroom, their wide, dark-stained planks on which Michael and I camped on hot summer nights. And the two club houses underneath, framed by square wooden posts, walled in by scraps of plywood and accessed by iron-pipe ladders, connected to the house yet separate.

As a family, Michael, Mom and I never talked collectively about what it meant to lose Dad. Not in those first hours and days without him and not in the months and years that followed. Instead, we each held tightly to our own grief, as if our memories of Dad were some prize we were too selfish to share. Nobody had the courage to disrupt the daily ritual of coping, so we grasped at normalcy, however superficial.

Mom worked all day, came home, made dinner for us, and then often found temporary refuge in the TV and too many glasses of white wine. At 16, Michael had a driver's license and a truck, so he was simply gone more. Maybe that was normal for a teenage boy.

When he was home, the kitchen cabinets sometimes splintered under his fists, or the refrigerator door slammed repeatedly as he pumped it open and closed in a frenzy of anger. He blamed Mom for Dad's death. She should have known, he'd yell. She should have saved him, he meant. You killed him, he'd finish. Michael, stop, she'd sob.

I stood there silently on those nights, an audience member in an empty theater. It started simply enough — just a little overwrought mothering. His grades. He was going to stay back if he wasn't careful. His truck. Did he know how expensive new tires were? It escalated from there.

You drink too much, he would yell.

You must not love me to say such things, she would charge.

Well, you didn't love Dad. You let him die.

Words drained the room of oxygen. My chest hurt then, my breathing came fast and shallow.

I learned about photosynthesis in seventh-grade biology class. We were taught that trees trap the sun's energy in the chlorophyll that flows into their leaves. Trees are autotrophs, self-feeders, and use the energy to break down the water and carbon dioxide they've absorbed. The hydrogen and carbon they keep, but the oxygen is released.

We would all suffocate if it were it not for trees.

I walked up Eighth Street on a spring day six months after Dad died. The steepness of the hill sometimes caused our van to slide down backward in the winter when Dad drove us to school. It was a five-minute walk from our house. From the top I could see out across the river, beyond the cemetery where my dad lay — the grave that we never visited as a family. Past the hospital shrouded by trees bright in their lime-green leaves, to the uneven rise and fall of mountains that interrupted every horizon I sought. The highest peaks were still kissed by snow.

Taking a sharp right, I walked down the dead-end road and past the gate where the pavement gave way to dirt and turned on to one of the many trails that entered a forest of young trees. Desperate for sunlight, the trees stretched upward, crowding each other in their hunger. Not yet thick enough to be razed as their parents had been, they were left alone, growing and competing in the space given them, as we all must do.

As soon as I left the dirt road, I began sprinting on the trail, seeking reprieve from a house bowed under by the weight of grief masked behind tightly drawn smiles. Dodging roots and rocks and pumping my arms hard up small hills, I ran until my lungs threatened to stall, until they were burned clean by the exertion.

Sitting down against a tree and digging the heels of my sneakers into the humus beneath me, I leaned against the bark until I could breathe again.

The leaves above rippled in the wind, a tide of miniature lungs exchanging oxygen in their own rhythm of life. Somewhere nearby, birds chattered, and I imagined them to be the cardinals, yellow finches or swallows that feasted at our birdfeeders — the ones Mom always kept filled, her bird guide within easy reach of the window.

There was a stillness otherwise. No whining of dirt bikes or ATVs driven by high school boys with nothing else to do. Only the faint white noise of the pulp mill's hisses and grunts.

My husband, Pete, has been teaching me about trees, how to name each one by sight. I've never known them in this formal way, but I have come to realize the importance of it. How recognition, a naming, yields a new form of intimacy. On each hike we take into a forest or up the flank of a mountain, he asks when we have stopped, "That one over there, what is it?"

It's hardest in the winter, when the leaves have fallen, my only clues the bark and the other trees rooted nearby. We are in Pawtuckaway State Park, in Deerfield, New Hampshire, crunching through New England snow — our boots breaking the frozen crust and imprinting on the powder that lies trapped beneath. It is a loud snow and discourages conversation while we walk.

Pete has a Master of Science degree in forest ecology. He knows trees in a way different than I do, which families they belong to, which species can coexist with others. He often tells me stories of their biology, of how they compete and survive in spaces too harsh for others. How those that remain standing have adapted to what nature and humans heap upon them. The forest we are in is made up of such beings, ones that have bent to the wind, bowed to the snows, escaped the ax.

I take off my fleece glove. The palm of my hand caresses the cold, smooth surface of the tree bark. The gray skin feels thin, too thin, and the nubs that mottle its surface are like old sores, rough against my fingertips.

"It's a beech," I say with confidence.

"Why?" he replies.

"Its bark is smooth and gray, so I know it's not a maple or birch."

Brown, shriveled leaves still hang from some of the branches, too. Another clue. Beech is one of the few species in the Northeast that does not shed all of its leaves, which sound like brittle paper ornaments in a January wind. It's a sound that reminds me of waves washing over tiny pebbles on a beach, dragging them forward, pushing them back — a cacophony of applause.

"You're right," Pete says, smiling. He is always pleased when I get one right. It is proof, perhaps, that I have listened to his teachings. Or, maybe because it's something else we can share while we are outdoors.

Near him the wide, deeply furrowed bark of an old sugar maple and the silver bark of a yellow birch, etched with long, thin fissures running horizontally up its trunk. Above me on a small embankment are Eastern white pine trees. Their coniferous green needles are the initial clue they are either spruce or pine, yet I often confuse them, still blind to subtler traits.

We start walking again. Our boots shatter the stillness of the slumbering woods, drowning any possible calls from birds that forfeited a journey south this winter. Pete is telling me about ironwood. I had spied it without assistance. He tells me about how these trees thrive, the soils they like. I listen, one of my mittened hands reaching out every so often to grab a limb or press against a trunk for balance as I negotiate the trail.

JAMIE HAMILTON

December 18, 2013

What is the first sign of a heart attack?

We all look at each other.

"Out of breath," says Joe.

"Exhaustion," adds Ernie. I nod in agreement.

"Indigestion, for sure," says Maria.

Arnie is adamant: "Excruciating headache, with pain spiraling around the jaw.

"Nope, none of these," says Steve, our teacher. "The first sign of a heart attack is that you are DEAD. The first and last and only sign. You are the lucky 40 percent who have survived a heart attack. Welcome to our class."

Cardio-rehab classes. Three times a week, Monday, Wednesday, Friday, for eight weeks at Monadnock Community Hospital; three hours each day, with an "educational component" added for our enrichment. Most of July. All of August. Into September. My summer. 2013.

The Rev. **Jamie L. Hamilton** was a religion instructor at Exeter from 1995-2014. She is now Rector of All Saints' Church in Peterborough, New Hampshire.

There were nine of us in my class — my buds, my cohorts, my partners, my team, my allies, eventually even my saviors — who would joke almost every workout about taking a break to have a cigarette, or plan a fantasy escape to find a tub of ice cream, or exchange our water cooler with a keg. We called ourselves the Saltless Wonders. We met in the small cardio gym, off the wellness gym, off the emergency room. Each morning we would sign in, weigh ourselves, and then slip the base of our portable EKGs into homemade cotton pouches that we wore like necklaces. Modesty never shadowed our care, as we all helped each other find the right places on our chests to stick the four conduit wires. We were hooked in. Wired up, with each of our heart rhythms flashing on the overhead monitor. Barbara, the Boss, and her team — Steve, Caitlyn, Ebe and Donna — took our blood pressure and monitored our pulse and pace. We were ready to go. We were survivors. The nine of us.

My boys, I called them. Though there was Maria, Italian, 80, and the only other woman, who loved to share her Sicilian recipes with me; she had had her valve replaced. The boys called her Mrs. Cannoli. They called me The Baby because I was the youngest, by decades.

Joe, who was almost 90, was still married to the same woman for 65 years, had the guts and the tenacity to get through a quadruple bypass. He was hard of hearing, a knobby-knock-kneed flirt, who always made me laugh with his terribly funny sexist jokes. Arnie, a retired airline pilot, was so stubborn he almost died arguing with his wife about not going to the hospital. He was still suffering from arrhythmia. Ernie, the manager of the Market Basket in town, had a pacemaker and a bypass and needed to lose 100 pounds. Tom, with his soft Southern drawl, was so, so quiet. We worried until he let us know that he was in the middle of lowering his lovely wife of 40 years into the grave when he sank to his knees gripping his left arm. Hurting over the loss of his love, he cried often. I sometimes held his hand as we walked around the indoor track. The other Tom, with his second pacemaker, had taught seventh-grade band, but his passion was his sax. He always told us what key Bill was in when he blew his nose. Bill was a diabetic, with early-onset heart disease and high blood pressure. During his first few days on our team, he was wheel-chaired away each morning to the ER because his blood pressure spiked over 200. And then there was Marcel, tattoos stacked on his arms; he drove a big black truck and he always brought his wife with him to speak on his behalf because he choked up when asked any question about his leaky heart. He called me Darling and Hon and I called him Sweetheart. He was a great listener with lots of great-grandchildren.

I liked my exercise routine, even while all wired up. And I hated the "educational piece" of my recovery — the lectures, especially the show-and-tell part. I didn't want to see or feel any pacemakers. Nor did I ever examine the plastic tubing masquerading as veins. I closed my eyes during all the videos. As did Marcel. But strangely enough, what I hated most was the large plastic anatomical heart model, which sat from its perch in the center of our table and was a part of every class, with its base, apex, atriums, ventricles, coronary arteries and anterior diaphrymatic surfaces.

The open/shut chambers hinged so that you could see the inner workings of the heart.

When were the days that I could just trust in the inner workings of my heart? That it would just beat, all on its own without a thought or worry? The model sat in its arrogance, in its plastic virtue of perfection, as a reminder of how wounded my own heart was. Was my heart beating? Yes. Did I trust it? No longer.

Broken-heart syndrome: one of the many names of my type of heart attack. Also called Takotsubo cardiomyopathy. Very rare. About 1% of all heart attacks fall into this category. Most doctors have never heard of it. About 20 years ago a Japanese medical team discovered the syndrome and named it as such because when the heart is under its full distress, it balloons up and resembles the fishing pots (*tsubo*) used to catch octopi (*Tako*).

It's also called stress-induced heart attack. It strikes women for the most part, in their late 50s through their 60s, usually after a horrific event. Your home burns down; your spouse gambles away your life savings; there is a sudden death of a loved one. You are involved in one of life's train wrecks, and as a response to the shock, your brain sends messages to your heart to shut down. And shut down it does, as all your coronary arteries go into spasm, not because there is anything wrong with the heart muscle, but because your heart is following direct signals and messages from the central dispatch of your brain. One of my technicians told me that she hated seeing Takotsubo on the chart, because not only did the patient suffer a heart attack, but there was always some other huge indignity. "There's just so much sadness. No one wants to walk in the room."

But wait. I was playing tennis. I was happy. I was on vacation. It was the Fourth of July. The cardiologists assumed that I did not have Takotsubo because I was under no immediate stress, no calamity, no tragedy. For 15 percent of the 1 percent who have this strange heart attack, there is no known source: a massive cross-wiring of sorts. And later, when I asked the doctor "Why?" he shrugged his shoulders and said, "I have no idea."

A few days after the attack, I was discharged into cardio-rehab. While on the treadmill, I was barely walking and I needed to hold onto the side rails for balance. My speed was 1. Barbara the Boss, who was only 5-foot-2, stood on the lower rung of a stepladder in order to reach my arm and flag my blood pressure. Cuffed and wired. She asked me how I was doing.

"I don't want to talk about it, except to say, I feel like hell. And I am so tired. So very tired. And I am so tired of being so tired. I don't want to be here. But I can't not be here. Am I ever going to recover?"

Barbara sighed. "Jamie, look around you. Look at everyone in this room. Look carefully. Don't rush. What do you see?

"I see a bunch of folks who had heart attacks."

"Look good and hard. I want you to think of what happened to their hearts. You know each one of their diagnoses."

"Yes."

"Imagine their scenes ... their event." And then she waited, and I obeyed and I imagined. "OK, listen carefully," she continued, "your heart went through more than any of these other hearts here, with much greater trauma."

"Are you kidding me?"

"Your prognosis is great; you will fully recover, as if the attack never happened. But you need to absorb what happened to you. If one survives Takotsubo, which you did, then you will have a great recovery. But the 'if' was big. Your heart was stunned into a great silence. It will take time to recover. Don't live in the past or future of your wellness; be present to today and to your victory. Honor your heart. Listen to her. And give her the credit. You are lucky you are here."

Treadmill Talk. "Thank you, Barbara, I needed that clarity."

I could feel my shoulders drop, my jaw loosen and relax, and the tightness in my forehead release into a sigh and a prayer: Patience. Be the patient patient. And be thankful. I am alive.

It was a Sunday night. I had been ambulanced to the Catholic Medical Center the day before, after spending two days at home ignoring my exhaustion. Dr. Flynn, my cardiologist, came into my room. I was waiting for news about my echocardiogram. I was assuming that he would tell me that I had a simple infection, easy to fix, no problems, just as he predicted.

He cleared his throat. Not a good sign. "Jamie, the apex of your heart is not moving. Your left ventricle is barely functioning. Most healthy muscles pump about 65 to 70 percent of the volume of the blood with each heartbeat and you are pumping about 25 percent. I have no idea how much of your heart is damaged or how much we will be able to save. Tomorrow we will do an angiogram. We will insert a catheter through a vein in your wrist and then inject an iodine dye into the vessel, which will let us see where the blockages are in your coronary arteries. And how many we have to deal with."

"What do you mean when you say you don't know how much of my heart you will be able to save?"

"It looks as if parts of your heart have been significantly cut off from blood supply. When that happens, those parts die."

"This is not good news."

"I am sorry, Jamie, I am giving you really bad news. But we have tomorrow. You will be first on the morning docket and we will go in and see what we can do."

The secret attack of a heart failing undetected.

I thought of my two beautiful daughters, and knew I would not call them. I had texted them from the ambulance, telling that I was "having a heart incident" but that I was OK. Leave it at that for now. I thought of my mother, who died three years ago, and my good friends and my brother and sisters. I wanted my rosary so that I could roll one bead into the next with names of my loved ones as my prayer. I did the next best thing: I imagined my beads and rolled my index finger against my thumb, with name after name rolling off my tongue — my family, my friends, students, colleagues, parishioners, my own mentors, monks, authors and poets. I was calm. I was breathing. I was frightened.

And then I thought of all the times I failed to live out of my heart: a lack of compassion, patience, empathy and peace. A deathbed confession of sorts, I guess, though the memories didn't feel heavy or morbid. More like a "re" "collecting" of experiences — freeing, even liberating. I felt received, even held, redeemed and forgiven, just as I was.

And then, just because I always remember "THE EVENT" in time of difficulty and stress, I remembered the night Morey died.

I was 10. We lived on a 500-acre cattle ranch. Family friends had come for the weekend: Morey and his wife, Ernesta, whom we called Ernie, and their three kids, Bruce, 14, Leslie, 12, and Jann, 10. Bruce and Morey went hunting before dinner. I was in the kitchen peeling potatoes and Bruce exploded into our farmhouse. The front of his shirt was covered in blood.

"I've shot him; he's dying; I tripped; the gun went off; help me, help me."

My mother called 911 and then my parents and Ernie took off after Bruce to reach Morey. My mother asked me to direct the ambulance to the clearing.

I have told this story before, but this next part is the part I always leave out: Leslie and I waited and I could see the ambulance from the distance, sirens wailing. Leslie turned to me and said, "I want to be the one to tell them how to find my father."

"Of course."

The men jumped out of their screaming vehicle and shouted, "Where is the downed man?"

And then Leslie fainted. One of the men grabbed me by my collar, pulled me off the ground and into his face. I smelled cigarette breath. "Tell me where to go."

"Put me down and I will." He did. "You drive up the road almost a mile and when you can drive no further, look to your left. There is a path. Walk up the hill, and when it forks, go right and follow it up to a clearing. They will be there."

They ran to the lights and gunned their engine.

Leslie was still on the ground. I put her head into my lap and ran my fingers through her hair. She came to and asked me what happened. "You fainted."

"Please don't tell anyone that I didn't tell the men how to find my father."

"Of course." And I never did. Morey died on the way to the hospital.

For many years, I thought that I was calm because I was cold and uncaring. That parts of my heart had been cut off and had died and I had no feelings. That was why I could manage so well in the face of chaos and trauma. My heart had failed when Morey died. I shed no tears. I was calm. My childhood was chaotic, but I was always calm. And I could be calm, because I lived with a heart cut off. I wasn't about to change; I needed to survive. But my heart was limited.

On that July night, on the precipice of possibly my health drastically changing forever, and in the midst of so much calm, I held my 10-year-old self like I would a daughter and told her that she was brave and strong and courageous. And that she had a good heart, no matter what they were going to find when they went searching.

The next day, in the operating room, as the dye was lighting up my coronary arteries, Dr. Flynn said, "Well, will you look at that." Dr. #2 said, "Oh, what gorgeous arteries." Dr. #3 said, "I want her heart."

"Jamie, Jamie, we're done here. Unbelievable. You have Takotsubo. It will take you a couple of months to recover, but you're going to be just fine." And then Dr. Flynn lifted his hands up in victory. "You have a beautiful heart."

Kathy Brownback came out to my summer home in Jaffrey to see me during my many days of recovering and asked me how my "broken-heart syndrome" was breaking *open* my heart — and toward what? "What is your body telling you — with so much drama and potential tragedy and yet with no lasting physical harm. How perfect. What does your heart need from you?"

What great questions. I am still trying to answer them — a lifetime's work, really, but I can say this much. July and August became a time of letting my broken heart be broken and to love her just as she was, and to trust her. Maybe I had been carrying too much stress. Maybe I had asked too much from her. Maybe it was time for me to faint and to wake up and have someone else ease my brow, and not to hold onto my stance of calm. I turned to friends for food and for sleepovers and for rides to the hospital. I talked about my anxiety and fear and cried when things went bump in the night. I let myself be afraid and needy.

My workout buddies, my heart boys, taught me to awake to each day as a gift, rather than as a given. The new day is not an accident. The new day is teeming with the sign and sustenance of the spaciousness of Life and Love. As the days passed, every act became an act of gratitude. Turning off the alarm clock, and I was thankful that I could hear, that I had hand-and-eye coordination. I could arise from my bed without assistance. I was thankful for the miracle of my eyesight and that I could sit in a chair without being strapped in. I could drink a glass of clean water using my own hands. I could breathe without mechanical assistance. I laughed over the ingenuity of a teabag, the chewiness of a pecan and the perfect precision of my foot landing on each step as I walked up the stairs to the gym.

My attention to simple things felt like praying, praying without ceasing, a reminder that "This is the day that the LORD has made, let us rejoice and be glad in it."

Gratitude consecrated my life and my labor and made me feel Real, like the Velveteen Rabbit, and made my heart precious.

GENNY BECKMAN MORIARTY

January 15, 2014

Emmet, our youngest, is dressed as a frog. He is 4 months old, strapped to my chest in one of those BabyBjörn front carriers. Traveling in a pack with other "fac brats," the bigger kids rush the doorbell at each new house, reaching for coveted treats, and gleefully stashing them away. They measure success by the heft of the bag — their loot. It is late for Emmet, and getting chilly, so I wrap a quilt around his legs and hold him close, loving the weight and the warmth of him there on my chest. He is just old enough that he is starting to babble, and as the hour grows later and he grows sleepier, he starts to coo. He draws out his aaaahhhs and oooohhhs in long, breathy syllables, each time changing the notes, and at first I think he will sing himself to sleep, but he seems to be experimenting, listening intently to the sound of his voice as though it is a thing of beauty coming from outside himself. I'll never forget those stars, and his song, and the long walk home through muddy fields, slowly making our way past the pond and the warming hut, under the cold night sky.

***

In 1957, my dad, a 22-year-old choirboy with a beautiful baritone much bigger than his skinny frame, made his way from Buffalo to L.A. to

Genny Beckman Moriarty P'18, P'21 works in the Communications Department and advises a small group of students who live in Merrill Hall. She and her husband, Brooks, live in Bancroft Hall with their three sons and a dog.

work for the Santa Fe Railroad. On weekends, he sang with a country and western band, entertaining the crowds at grand openings for supermarkets and scoring gigs at Riverside Rancho, where many country stars got their start. His group was offered a recording contract, and he might have found fame and fortune if fate had not intervened in the form of a draft notice.

My parents' story begins in church, at Midnight Mass on Christmas Eve. My father, having finished active duty in Fairbanks, Alaska, is home for a visit before heading back to sunny California. He and my mother stand next to each other in the choir, and after, at a party next door, they kiss under the mistletoe. Six weeks later, they're engaged to be married.

Life, as it will, has had its way with my parents. They moved often for work, and my mother hated being far from her family. I know there were years that it was hard to call forth the current they felt when they first met, but music, love and faith have been threads that weave throughout my parents' marriage, stitching them together for over 50 years, through money struggles, job losses, ailing parents, health scares, and the challenges of shepherding six kids through their teenage years and into adulthood.

In the mornings, my mother wakes us singing, "Rise, and shine, and give God your glory glory." At bedtime, my father strums guitar and sings us to sleep, songs by Glen Campbell, Buddy Rogers and Kris Kristofferson. My father has a beautiful voice, but he is hell on lyrics, so my mother provides the words when his memory falters — or he makes them up, a song for every occasion, much sillier and saltier than the originals. I have a vision of him, a few years ago, standing in their sunny kitchen, serenading me in the early morning as I prepare my return to my menfolk, waiting for me in New Hampshire. Impishly he croons, "If you need a friend, I'm sailing right on by ... " rather than "behind," the way the song actually goes.

Though my parents handed down their love of music to my siblings and me, to our great regret, none of us received my father's singing genes. Shyness inhibits him now, but in unguarded moments, Emmet still plays with his voice, narrating his days with his own made-up melodies and funny, irreverent lyrics. I take pleasure in Emmet's gifts, knowing he inherited his unfailing ear and his sweet, clear voice from my father — along with his angelic face and the devilish sense of humor.

My siblings and I stake our claim on family heirlooms — this roll-top desk, that egg-spattered cookbook, or the shirt my dad wore on stage at the Riverside Rancho 60 years ago: a beautiful Western number in pale gold, heavy brocade with shimmery pastel threads and mother-of-pearl snap fronts. We stockpile objects and stories, laying claim to the legacy of their love and the example of their lives.

To my parents' great regret, and despite their best intentions, most of us did not hold onto our Catholic roots. I lack my parents' convictions and my uncertainty leads to fear. Heredity is a wayward thing. Sometimes genes can skip a generation.

My mother's smile, my father's eyes; I treasure my inhcritances, but there is something else that I hold onto. I clutch my worry like beads, tawdry trinkets that I share among my children.

We believe in the dangers that lurk in dark shadows and the perils that await us at every turn; we know that only constant vigilance can keep us from harm. Anxiety may be our family creed.

In parenting, I weigh and measure, agonize and second-guess. Fear clouds my vision and clutters my mind, blurring the space between the way things are and the way I fear they might become or ought to be.

My children are hoarders, indiscriminate in their passions. When they were small, their treasure boxes were full of an odd assortment of detritus: collections of used, bloodied Band-Aids, loose hardware, electrical tape, decaying plant life, and bits of old food. Conor and Liam would scoop woodchips into little piles at the playground and carry them home in their pockets, sobbing if any of them happened to fall on the ground. I used to fear *their* fear of losing things was pathological.

It is a Saturday afternoon in late spring. Southborough, Massachusetts. We are standing along one side of the pond that frames our long driveway and acts as a refuge for baby snapping turtles, a blue heron and a mama goose who guards ferociously her gaggle of goslings. Daily, my two boys make their way down the hill from our house, where they stand at the water's edge, skipping rocks and trying to catch frogs in their long-handled nets. On this day, a Saturday, Brooks is either teaching or coaching, and I am trying not to feel resentful about having the kids by myself again. They have been whining and fighting all morning. Our friend Matt, who teaches Classics (some of you might know him as Dr. Hartnett), has finished his classes and is there with his toddler son, Quinn.

Conor, my oldest, is 4. He grasps a wilting dandelion in his hand, and as a few of the seeds begin to blow away, he lets out a howl that can be heard clear across campus. I snap at him, impatient with the size of his grief.

Matt laughs, gently. "It is hard to imagine anything more inconsequential than a dandelion seed," he says. And then with a note of wonder, because it occurs to him, and because he is one of the kindest people I know — and because sometimes it is so much easier to muster up compassion for someone else's child than for your own — he offers, "But to him, it contains the whole universe."

Matt's consummate grace in that moment helped me find the compassion that in my anxiety over my child's intensity, and the embarrassment I felt at parenting in public, I had squelched.

Four years later. We are staying with friends as we wait for our new home to be ready, at another boarding school in another New England town, in New Hampshire. We're in a crowded café on the Cape. Liam, who is 6, is beside himself. I wrangled him here from the beach, where he cried for half an hour at the prospect of leaving behind the 15 pounds of rocks, sand and shells that I refused to let him bring into the car. Lunch is over, and we are getting ready to leave. In a frenzy, he scoops up ripped paper placemats, straw wrappers and dirty napkins like a madman. Stuffing them into my purse, he begs me to carry them home. He is shrieking hysterically, and I can barely speak, afraid there is something terribly wrong with my child, afraid that it's my fault, afraid I will burst into tears or strangle him.

This time, my friend Emily helps me to see. She looks at me and smiles, "It's so symbolic, isn't it?" Of course, it isn't the wrappers or the rocks or the shells that Liam really cares about. The ground beneath him is sinking. We just left the only home he remembers and he is grabbing at anything he can hold onto in his two small hands. I know this, somewhere, but am too blinded by my own worry to recognize it. It is hard to imagine anything more inconsequential than a dirty napkin, but to him, in that moment, it contains the world.

***

In the fall of my sophomore year at college, I sort of lost myself, in a long, slow slide that led to three incompletes and a leave of absence the following semester. A financial aid student from a small town at a big urban school, I had no money and little confidence. My parents had moved away and were struggling financially, and I was pining away over a boy who was definitely not worth it. I felt unmoored; I was heartsick, homesick, unsure of myself. My anxiety manifested as an inability to sleep or eat. Waiflike to begin with, I dropped pound after pound that I couldn't afford, making my psychic loss tangible — and I was as thin of skin as I was of flesh.

Twenty-three years later, I stand in our small cottage on a wheat farm in Cubbington, England, and cry on my sister's shoulder. One of my boys has descended into an ornery, irrational place — made worse by the dwindling hours of daylight, his history of anxiety and the long miles from home. I can't get him out of his darkened room, can't get him to eat or dress or leave the house without a fight, and I am tired of fighting.

I want to savor our last few weeks on this lovely isle, but instead I am wishing us home, hunkered down in our own living room, out of earshot of our gracious hosts, away from expectations that we should be making the most of every moment. This time, there are no words to calm me. Instead, my sister holds me, assures me it isn't all in my head, that what I'm dealing with is hard and real, tells me I am a good and caring mom, and that she loves me.

And later, that's what I will do with him. I will hold him in my arms, tell him what he's dealing with is hard, that he's a good, sweet boy, and that I love him.

***

Last Christmas, I wrote a letter to my brother Matthew about that long-ago night with Emmet singing, including with it a short dreamlike story I wrote 20 years ago. The story itself isn't brilliant, but something about it still makes me happy when I read it today, maybe because I was on the brink of my adult life when I wrote it, when the doubts of my sad sophomore year began to mix with a sense of wonder and possibility for the future.

I wrote all the time then, usually in a spiral-bound notebook, in an endless attempt to give shape and meaning to my life, for no other audience but myself. Those journals captured my first fledgling attempts at singing on paper, for the sheer pleasure it gave me to listen to the sound of my own voice on the page.

The letter and the story perhaps made a strange sort of gift, but sharing it was leap of faith and a nudge to both of us, as we let our youthful ambitions give way to resignation, crowded out by duty, caution and the noise of daily life.

I told him I wished for us what I wish for my kids — a kind of courage that would have each of us sending our long, clear notes (and our reedy, warbly, thin ones) out into the night, heedless of anything but our own curiosity and joy.

So, here I sit, writing at my dining room table, Pandora streaming in the background, on a Thursday afternoon in December. On the table sits a bottle of Windex, a paper towel and a paper airplane. Beside my laptop, a handmade bracelet crafted from beads in the shape of reindeer heads. A lone army guy lies facedown next to that. Across the table, a grinder full of cinnamon and sugar, a half-eaten bowl of pasta with ketchup and Parmesan cheese. Behind me, on the breezeway into the kitchen, stacks of school papers, artwork and bills perch precariously amid half-read magazines, piles of matchbox cars and the lone soldier's missing plastic platoon. At times, I feel we're swimming under the weight of so much stuff.

And yet, as I weed and I sort and I pick through the piles on my desk and the litter in my mind, let me also remember to live the lessons that my friends, my parents and my children try to teach me: to be present in my life, exactly as it is right here, in this place, at this moment, in my treasure hoard of now.

***

"Death," as my youngest will tell you, "is a screwy, screwy shit."

And it is. I agree. It is a screwy shit, indeed. We're granted such a limited number of moments in our lifetimes; it's a pity we squander so damned many of them.

Distracted, we wish them away, half-listening to our children's stories as we think about the bills we have to pay or checking Facebook and typing emails as we talk on the phone to our mothers. In our impatience, we hurry them away, yanking arms as we rush off to school. In wondering what others will think, we muffle our voices and stifle our dreams; in anxiety over how our kids will turn out and how we are to blame, we don't see how those moments slide between our fingers.

How hard we try to hold onto the minutiae, while recklessly tossing dandelion seeds and helplessly watching the years take flight.

***

About two and a half years ago, my father was diagnosed with colon cancer. Since then, he's gone through six surgeries, a couple of stays in intensive care and a course of chemo that nearly killed him, leaving him with blistering burns on his lips, in his mouth, down his throat and into his digestive tract.

Each time he enters the hospital, an ever-changing permutation of Beckman children and grandchildren surrounds him. We do not travel lightly. We are loud, we are many, we are sometimes unrefined. In his small room, crowding around his hospital bed, we come together — sometimes cheering him, more often tiring him, but always, providing testament. To his love for us. To his courage. To this sprawling, troubled, loving family he helped create.

At times, we cannot bear to watch. And yet, he shows us how: He takes each moment as it comes, singing about his IV drip, flirting with the nurses, flashing us by accident and laughing through it all. When the pain gets too great, he closes his eyes, and we wait. Between surgeries, he keeps working, as a chaplain, in this same Catholic hospital where the nurses dote on him and the attendants greet him by name. Holding hands and wiping brows, he comforts other people facing death.

This is a man who faced real losses — a beloved sister at a young age; his mother, when he was 9; and three brothers, well before their time — but never, never loss of faith or sense of humor. His courage comes from his beliefs, but also from having lived through tragedies and survived.

My father doesn't agonize about what the future will bring. When the surgeon tells him, after his last surgery, that the tumor is too close to a major artery to be removed, he sighs. "Well, I guess that's another bump along the road." He keeps putting one foot in front of the other, and he prays.

My mother, who rails at life's minor injustices with the strength of a gale-force wind, in these moments shares his strength, and lends it to her kids. She counts our many blessings and fingers them like pearls.

My faith is not as sure as my parents'. Praying with my boys, I invoke "God, the universe and nature." I don't know what happens after we die, but I do know that there are blessings here, on Earth. Maybe the nearest thing we have to being one with the flesh and spirit of whatever God there is, occurs when we enter the space between selves and allow ourselves to touch. I trust in the communion that exists in that meeting space, and I believe in these things, too, that my parents handed down: I believe in crowded hospital rooms and bearing witness. I have faith in serenades in sunny kitchens and the taste of blackberries on a fog-covered hill, under clouds that are heavy and low, close enough to touch.

Little Much Afraid, my mother used to call me, after a character in a book we read together. I am not fearless, but I remember what Ellie MacQueen '14, a wise student who traveled with us on the Stratford program, wrote: "Being brave isn't being unafraid. It's being scared straight and doing a thing anyway." That's my parents' courage, and I want so much to pass that on to my boys.

I pray that my little one, in years to come, will remember more than just those long hours spent huddled inside his bedroom in England, looking out into a yard that was dotted with pear trees, and apples, and plums, retreating from a world that was so like his own, and so different. I hope he'll remember sprinting up Helm Crag, dodging sheep and piles of dung, miles ahead of his parents and his younger brother — never thinking to stop and look down until he'd nearly reached the top.

I pray he will choose, more and more, to loosen his grip and throw his arms out wide, as he did in Dover, smirking into the wind that threatened to throw him, topple him, off of that clay white cliff.

"Grace will abound," my father preaches, on the Feast of the Holy Family. Sitting in the pew next to my mother, I wipe my eyes and nod.

***

Our kitchen floor is sticky and covered in crumbs as I pad across it for a glass of water. I have been awake since 3, my heart and mind racing in tandem. Wired as I am, I half wonder if I should stop struggling to sleep and seize these fleeting, uninterrupted moments to myself. Instead, sinking down into our sofa, I wrap my cold toes in a fuzzy black blanket, pull the other end up, and watch my better self from behind a screen — get up and write, pack lunches, do laundry, make myself a cup of strong black tea. Somehow, the idea alone brings my pulse rate down, and I close my heavy eyelids.

When the alarm on my cell phone goes off a short while later, I groan and hit snooze. Not sure who will receive it, I send up a little prayer for fortitude and manage a smile as my oldest comes in, chattering about a dream he had last night.

One by one, the younger two come trailing behind him. Flitting in like birds, resting long enough to reassure themselves I'm here. Humoring my requests for hugs, maybe even a cuddle or two, before fluttering back into the other room. I can hear their sweet morning songs, and it makes me happy.

Emmet, I had a dream that you were a ghost.

There was a tsunami and the water was flooding all over me. I had to try and hold my breath. Then I came up on top, and it was epic ... even though it was scary.

My dream had a talking bird, and SpongeBob was there.

I'm gonna live in Hawaii and go surfing every day!

Their conversation ranges from the profound to the prosaic. Their voices mingle, interspersed with giggles that give way to cackles and shrieks and shouts.

I am grateful for morning and the lifting of darkness, when the curtains draw back and the lights come on and suddenly, they are there center stage, three boys laughing and whispering, telling their dreams of the night before.

I start humming softly, murmuring the lyrics to an old Townes Van Zandt tune, one I used so often to sing my baby to sleep, before he started scolding me for singing off-key.

And the mornin's born of the lights of love . . .

You will miss the sunrise

if you close your eyes

and that would break

my heart in two.

I don't remember all of the words, but I remember enough.

If you needed me

I would come to you

I would swim the seas

for to ease your pain.

TYLER CALDWELL
January 22, 2014

In first grade, I peed my pants at the school lunch table because I was too scared to ask my teacher if I could use the restroom.

As a child, I often chose to deal with my problems boldly and silently. I didn't scream incessantly like Dakota Fanning in *War of the Worlds* or cry obsessively like Natalie Portman in every movie she has ever been in. I've never had to deal with aliens invading Earth, except for maybe in first grade when my lunch table teacher was from Australia, but I was a relatively quiet, cooperative kid. I didn't scream or cry at my Australian teacher's weird accent, I just silently peed my pants instead of asking the scary teacher with the strange voice if I could go to the bathroom. My twin sister might call me a wimp, but I like to say I was adorably shy.

Throughout my childhood, my twin sister, Alexa, would often speak for me, which is why I had my incident at the school lunch table — because Alexa was not there to ask if I could use the restroom. She would tell people important facts about me; at least, in her mind they were facts. To this day, she prides herself on knowing more about me than I do. As an adult, I can laugh about this, but as a kid, I felt somewhat paralyzed by her pronouncements. She would say things such as, "My favorite color is blue, so Tyler's favorite color is green because that is my second-favorite

---

Tyler Caldwell came to Exeter in 2011 and teaches in the English Department. He is dorm head of Soule Hall and coaches varsity boys crew.

color" or, "*We* are sad today because our soccer team, the Kickers, lost." Alexa would also make my decisions for me. "Tyler, you want Raisin Bran for breakfast." I am still not sure whether my hesitancy and indecision prompted her to speak for me, or whether my uncertainty grew from her bold assertions. Either way, the dynamic became increasingly evident. The more she spoke, the less I used my voice to navigate the world.

When we applied to a private day school in kindergarten, I am sure Alexa answered the questions for both of us and talked our way into getting accepted. The main thing I remember about our application was my parents' congratulating me on my ability to skip. Apparently, that was something in my skill set that really impressed the admissions office. However, when the registrar's office placed us in different classes, I lost my ventriloquist. Listening to conversations take place around me but rarely participating, I quietly wandered through the halls to and from my cubby. Nine years later at my eighth-grade moving-up-day ceremony, a classmate since kindergarten confronted me. "I haven't heard you speak a single word," he challenged. Not knowing how to respond, I shrugged my shoulders. Why ruin my perfect record?

Growing up as a twin, I assumed that somehow the personality traits were split between us. Alexa was bold; I was cautious. She was assertive; I was passive. On our soccer team, Alexa liked to play high attack so she could score goals and terrorize the other team's defense; I preferred to play sweeper, and I was too timid to venture past the half-field line. In our family videos, Alexa assumed center stage as I danced around the edges of the camera frame. She was definitive; I was indecisive. She got all of the speaking genes, and I had all of the listening genes.

This is not to say I never spoke. Moments after shutting the car door for our 50-minute drive home from school, my little sister and I would play 20 Questions or I-Spy. My sisters and I would create and perform our own plays in our living room, casting our Beanie Babies as characters. At home, I would sing in the shower. The sound of the rushing water and the shampoo clogging my ears hid any imperfections in my tone as I belted out top-40 hits. One evening when I was 15, my mother invited some friends in the English Department over to our house. After showering to get ready for the dinner, I left the bathroom, my towel clinging to my hips, to find my current English teacher, shell-shocked, standing on the landing. I was less embarrassed by the fact that I was half naked, and more horrified that she had listened to me singing for 15 minutes. Here is a boy, she must've thought, who is hesitant to speak much in my English class but is not afraid to belt out "Bye Bye Bye" in the shower? My voice often rang throughout my house, but in public, I withdrew. Alexa's voice was loud, and her laugh would echo through the stone hallways of our school. Alternatively, people often asked me to repeat myself; "A little bit louder this time," they would say.

For the summer after my seventh-grade year, my parents signed me up for Camp Deerwood, an all-boys sleepaway camp on Squam Lake in Holderness, New Hampshire. I had never been away from home for more than two consecutive nights, and the thought of spending three and a half weeks without my family in the wilderness was similar to how I now feel about skydiving: While I am terrified of heights, I figure I would be so high up in the plane that the distance would be too large to comprehend, and, therefore, almost too large to cause any premeditated panic.

My mother dropped me off on a cold, drizzly June morning. We were the first to arrive by a few hours, and a thick fog hung throughout the deserted compound. However, this was fine with me because my mother was sobbing uncontrollably and I remember feeling relieved no one was there to see us say goodbye. After she left, I carefully unpacked and refolded all of my clothes then wandered through the dark, damp woods, locating the other cabins, the mess hall and the waterfront. On the website, Camp Deerwood was described as "a place where boys have fun." As the other campers rolled in, some fist-bumping old friends and others looking excitedly to make new ones, I retreated to my bunk. I panicked. I did not have family, or friends, or anyone to talk to. In just a few hours, I decided, wholeheartedly, that this place was definitely *not* "a place where boys have fun." That afternoon, I wrote my first letter home. A few hours later, I left dinner early to write my second letter home.

Of course, my mom saved each note, and when I was with my family over winter break, we laughed as we read aloud these letters, stuffed with nonsequitors and saturated in self-pity. Here is an example, a letter I wrote to my mom when she was staying, ironically, at the Exeter Inn for the Shakespeare Institute:

6-26-02

Dear Mom,

Everywhere I look, I see something that reminds me of you, dad, Alexa, Lucinda, Olie (our dog) and Charlie (our hamster). It makes me so sad. The first few days were full of misery and sorrow. Today I had fun at camp craft and tennis and am deciding what to do in the afternoon. I can't wait to see you in July. It is way too far away. The views are amazing. I hope you are having fun. I miss you so much and love you so much.

Love,

Tyler

PS We had rain showers Monday. Tuesday was beautiful. Wednesday should be beautiful, but hot, with a chance of rain.

In each of my letters home, I'm mired in the throes of despair; I sound like Ishmael in the opening pages of *Moby-Dick*. "Whenever it is a damp, drizzly November in my soul ... then I account it high time to," in my 12-year-old mind, write home. Of course, now I am aware that in my letters I sprinkled small tales of new, exciting activities among my profound state of misery. My contradictions, lost on my 12-year-old self, are so prevalent now. I bemoaned the fact that everything I saw acted as a depressing reminder of those I missed at home, but I simultaneously found "the views ... amazing." A few of these inconsistencies must have stemmed from my Eeyore-like refusal to have fun, but at the same time, it's hard to miss the fact that I must've been so desperate to talk to someone, I wrote home about the weather forecast. My twin sister and I had been separated in classes for years, but I had not yet learned how to speak for myself, so I drifted through much of my time at Deerwood in silence.

***

Growing up, I loved birds. I pored over the *National Audubon Society Field Guide to North American Birds: Eastern Edition.* I studied the differences between a chipping sparrow and an American tree sparrow; I kept a journal of my bird sightings on my nightstand. Throughout elementary school, I dressed up as a bird for Halloween. In kindergarten and again in first grade, I was a great blue heron; in second grade, I was a bald eagle; in third grade, I was a ruby-throated hummingbird. My grandmother spent the summer months constructing and sewing each one of these elaborate outfits.

On the St. Andrew's campus, we lived next to a biology teacher and his wife, Dottie Colburn, who was an avid birder herself. Small, red hummingbird feeders dangled from the corners of her screened-in back porch; she scattered straw in her backyard for the birds to use when building their nests. Occasionally, Dottie invited me over after school, and we would sit in rocking chairs on her back porch, binoculars perched on the glass table between us, waiting for the birds to fly our way. I also accompanied her on a few of her birding expeditions. We drove along the back roads of Middletown, Delaware, past cornfields and through marshlands, stopping along the estuaries that snaked their way inland from the Delaware Bay to look for snowy egrets, common mergansers and other waterfowl. For my 12th birthday, Dottie gave me a CD collection of bird songs so I could identify different birds by the sounds of their voices. I went to Deerwood a few weeks later, and, thinking I could listen to birdcalls if I needed help falling asleep at night, I hid the album in the end pocket of my duffel bag.

About halfway through Deerwood, I signed up for the East and West Royce Mountain hiking trip. I considered myself an experienced hiker, as my family spent our summers traversing the Green Mountains, and I thought a small-group endeavor might help me make friends. The morning of the hiking trip, the counselors announced at breakfast: "Royce Mountain hikers, pack your bags for the next four nights. We leave at 2 p.m." I thought it was just a day hike. Cursing myself for failing to read the trip description, I sprinted to my cabin, jotted a panicked note home, something like "If I never make it back from this trip alive, I love you guys so much!" and packed my bag for the week.

I recollect only tiny snapshots of my first overnight hiking experience: the weight of my 70-pound pack, the yellow iodine drops swirling through the clear creek water in my Nalgene, the other campers pitching our tent on a slanted slab of rock and feeling the tent slowly slip down the boulder face over the course of the first night. I also remember that those four days represented the longest period of time I went without writing a letter home.

When my parents came to pick me up at the end of the camp, my counselor told them that on the third night of the hiking expedition, I *finally* initiated a conversation. The sun had dipped below the horizon, and as we poked our way to the final summit of the day listening to a pair of barn owls call to each other through the twilight, I asked him, "Do you like birds?" In middle school, my classmates could quote movies like *Billy Madison* or *The Big Lebowski*, movies I had never, and still haven't, seen. I suppose I knew about birds, so that is what I felt comfortable talking about.

I used to think that Alexa and I were a contradiction: twins with opposite personalities. In *Moby-Dick*, Ishmael proposes that all properties arise and thrive through contrast; he argues the coldness of his room in the Spouter Inn intensified the snugness of the bed because "truly to enjoy bodily warmth, some small part of you must be cold, for there is no quality in this world that is not what it is merely by contrast. Nothing exists in itself." My identity surfaced and congealed through my relationship with Alexa, this contrast. Looking back on my childhood, I am willing to admit that, at times, I *chose* to remain quiet. However, when peers defined me as "shy" or as "Alexa's opposite," when they asked me *why* I was quiet, I found it difficult to respond or to speak at all. I often wrestled internally with my silences and wondered how to break free of my label as "the quiet kid."

Alexa and I attended different schools for the first time in college, and when I told my college friends a few of the stories I shared earlier in this meditation, stories of when I was practically mute, they did not believe me. "Sure, you might be shy at times," they said, "but you're not *that* quiet." I do not blame Alexa for my reputation as the "silent kid" or for speaking for me; sometimes I needed the prompting.

We live in a verbal society with Facebook status updates, twitter, and texting, and we define people as either extroverted or introverted, loud or quiet, outgoing or shy. We rarely acknowledge the gradations of the social spectrum. Alexa tends to talk while I tend to listen, and that polarity magnified through our time together at school. Maybe in our approach to the world, we, like Ishmael, focus too heavily on opposites; maybe we are too rigid in understanding people or things through contrast. Why can't we be more fluid in our categorizations?

We all find our voices in different ways, whether through speaking, listening, writing, reading, music or film. When my twin sister and I were first learning to talk, Alexa called everything "ball." Her blankie was "ball;" a bush was "ball;" a drooling bulldog was "ball." I, on the other hand, stubbornly attempted to call each object what it was. My grandmother once described a moment I saw a squirrel, pointed to it, looked back to her and said, "Squ ... " my small lips folding over one another as my tongue wrestled against the roof of my mouth to form the "squ" sound followed by the rolling "r" and liquid "l." Speaking has always come more readily to my twin, but I like to think I learned to speak deliberately, savoring each syllable. For me, maybe writing those letters home from Deerwood acted as the beginning of me finding my voice, but in writing. Maybe it took being stranded on a dark New Hampshire mountainside without any way of contacting my family for me to begin to search for my speaking voice.

When I started writing this meditation, I wondered if I had found my voice. If so, when? How? Then, I wondered if anyone finds his or her voice. There were times writing this piece when words eluded me, taunted me. My voice lay hidden, and I searched everywhere for it, through letters, photo albums, personal writing prompts. Maybe I'm pessimistic, or this is just a quiet kid's problem, but I'm not sure anyone finds his or her voice permanently.

In fourth grade, my family visited my mother's parents, and we spent a day exploring the Wellesley College campus. During our picnic, we decided to play charades, a wonderful game that actually prohibits talking. It was my turn. I decided to be a deer. I signaled I was to act out an animal and then ran to a nearby grove of trees. As I was down on all fours walking as deerlike as I could manage, I ambled through a ground bees' nest. The nasty things started stinging me all over my body, flying under my shirt and inside my pants. As I sprinted out of the woods screaming, my family kept guessing which animal I was acting out. "A bear!" "A rabid flying squirrel!"

At some point between first grade when I silently peed my pants and fourth grade when I had bees trapped in my underwear, I learned how to scream; I might have been misunderstood, but I found my voice when I needed assistance. I can say now, with certainty, that my favorite color is green. What I want for breakfast changes daily, but *I* come to that conclusion. I find I am most content when I use my own voice, not my silences or somebody else's voice, to articulate my thoughts or define who I am.

When we were younger, my sisters and I loved to play hide-and-seek. The 18th-century farmhouse we grew up in provided perfect hiding spots: wooden cupboards, hidden closets, tiny nooks under the stairs. Once, my dad was the seeker and he found my twin sister and he found me, but then he forgot to look for my little sister. Fifteen minutes later while he was washing the dishes, "Where is me?" a little voice peeped from the cupboard beneath the sink.

Many of us learn to speak through our parents or siblings. We develop similar speech patterns; we acquire the accent of our geographic region. Our physical voice is created, nurtured by those who surround us. However, searching for our own individual, personal voice seems to be an ongoing process. Locating the right words to say, especially in a moment of panic or pain, is difficult. As a result, sometimes we are misinterpreted; sometimes we contradict ourselves. Finding your voice can be an exercise of trial and error, but it is a practice everyone goes through. Some loudly and others quietly; some frequently and others less so. A writer, Natalie Goldberg, once said, "I write because to form a word with your lips and tongue or think a thing and then dare to write it down so you can never take it back is the most powerful thing I know."

Sitting on the back porch of Dottie Colburn's house, we often heard a bird's call before we saw the bird itself. A chickadee sounds out his name: *chick-a-dee-dee-dee-dee*. An owl's hoot haunts the night and a blue jay's call grates the airwaves, but each bird possesses a distinct voice.

Like a bird, you might find your voice only for an instant in a burst of energy. You might use your voice to help others locate you, either physically or metaphorically in the cupboard underneath the sink. In searching for your voice, you might also discover yourself, that which is most inherent within you. Searching for our voice and searching for our individuality seem inextricably connected. Some, my twin sister included, might ponder out loud, talk as they think, but when I reach a moment of meditation, "Where is me?" I'll ask, and in the pause, I hope to find my voice, whether through listening, reading, writing or speaking, peeking through the silence.

NANCY ROCKWELL
Ark
November 5, 2014

"It is spring, moonless night in the small town, starless and bible-black, the cobble streets silent and the hunched, courters'-and-rabbits' wood limping invisible down to the sloeblack, slow, black, crowblack, fishingboatbobbing sea. The houses are blind as moles (though moles see fine to-night in the snouting, velvet dingles) or blind as Captain Cat there in the muffled middle by the pump and the town clock, the shops in mourning, the Welfare Hall in widows' weeds. And all the people of the lulled and dumbfound town are sleeping now."

— Dylan Thomas, *Under Milk Wood*

The beautiful words of Dylan Thomas are a fresh breath, in this, his hundredth birthday year. His words are rising in new editions and public readings. Also rising are the revived rumors of his hard-drinking life and dissolute death — in New York City — where he had come from Wales to

---

Nancy Rockwell lives and writes in Exeter, New Hampshire. She has earned degrees in literature at Brown and theology at Harvard where she has also been an honorary Merrill Fellow. She has studied liturgy at Canterbury Cathedral, liberation theology in Nicaragua and Mexico, Spanish in Guatemala, Spiritual Direction at Shalem, and Celtic Christianity and paganism in Scotland and Ireland. Ordained in the United Church of Christ, she has preached and taught in parishes in Massachusetts and New Hampshire for more than 30 years.

write and teach and read his works, and where he had become a legendary drinker at the White Horse Tavern on Hudson Street, and where, one night while attempting to go home, he passed out on the sidewalk in front of the pub, and was taken to the hospital, where he died.

And I have begun with his evocation of the sea at night in a small town, because something like it must have been part of that timeless legend of Noah and the Ark, which set sail on the slobeblack, slow, black, crowblack, fishingboatbobbing sea, to weather the storm of all storms, the proverbial Flood. And he did. And he saved the world. And when it was all over, he got drunk.

Life as we know it emerged from the sea. And in the legend of the great Flood, the sea was an ally, saving the life it had made, saving it from a watery death in endlessly falling rain.

And it was the animals, all the animals on Earth, who found their way to safety in the arms on the sea, aboard that bobbing boat we call the Ark, which was made by Noah's hands and God's providing.

The legend of the Flood is far older than the version we know in the Bible. Educated guesses have it first arising among the Egyptians, who called their hero Gilgamesh. The Hebrew people took it into their hearts and their Book, and kept in it the word Ark, which comes to us from the Latin word *arca*, which is a translation of the Egyptian word that was kept in Hebrew, *tebah*. *Tebah* means box — or coffin — or life preserver.

Rather different things, these. But then, in Hebrew, the word was used once again, for the basket that held Little Moses in the bulrushes, which is as unlike the Ark as it could be, reeds not wood, and only as large as a 2-year-old human. But these are the only two uses of the word. So they must be related — coffin and life preserver both seem fair meanings, given the dangers to both the Ark and Little Moses, and the hope in which both were set out upon the water. They were potential coffins. And, since both Noah's menagerie and Little Moses survived, they were both life preservers, on the crowblack sea and on the watery Nile.

Let's consider that floating menagerie: the whole creation, the full inhabitation of the Garden of Eden, is in Noah's boat, which is Noah's life-preserver, and Noah's probable coffin. Like Eden, the Ark is full of the roots from which the whole of the world can grow.

And so the story of Noah and the Ark is another creation story: water and land, animals and birds and fish and people, the garden of life contained on a boat, which is both Eden and coffin. In the first tale, Eden was saved, it is written, by putting the people out. But that turned out not to be so, for the whole of the world turned up East of Eden, where Adam and Eve went to live. The animals, the birds, the fish, the water went with them, into a world that held more than blessing.

In Noah's tale, the creation is saved again by sailing away from most of the people — except for Noah, his wife, his sons and their wives, so it says. And again, it turns out that the human race will survive, along with all the creation, and people will dwell among animals and birds, and along the shores of the teeming sea.

Saving the world is a human preoccupation. And arguments rage among us endlessly about who and what can carry us through the storms, what needs to be jettisoned, who should captain the ship.

Most *saving the world stories* involve violent conflict between Good and Evil, and there is a Hero, who defeats Evil, and that's how the World is Saved. There is no end to these tales, and no end to the devotion of people who love them.

A 5-year-old boy whom I love dressed up as Batman this year for Halloween. He hasn't seen any of the Batman movies yet, and he can only read a very few words, so he hasn't read the comic books either. But he is smitten with Batman, caught in the culture of Batman worship, and it is so widespread that his mother had to leave some of his blond curls sticking out the back of his Bat helmet, so she could spot him among all the other 5-year-old Batmen at the party he attended.

These young would-be superheroes are growing up in a spiritual world of Spider-Man and Superman and Wolverine and Iron Man and Captain Marvel and Green Goblin and Wonder Woman and the White Queen and hundreds more, modern-day versions of St George who slew dragons.

A 9-year-old girl I know told me on Sunday that she was going to be Medusa for Halloween. Medusa was a Gorgon, one of three hideous, gray-skinned sisters with writhing snakes for hair, and only one eye between the three of them, which they passed around, and if you were to look into that eye, you would turn to stone. When Medusa was finally slain, her head cut off by Perseus's sword, the winged horse Pegasus flew out of her, out of her neck. Medusa had, it seems, some powerful spiritual qualities: She was a woman intimately involved with snakes, a woman unafraid of the venom in her spirit, a woman deemed ugly but who has a stunningly beautiful animal, Pegasus, inside her. She is unafraid of the animal in her nature. She is a strange superhero, but girls don't have too many to choose from.

Noah, too, was a superhero, but he saved the world without any weapons, and without any conflict. He didn't destroy any living thing in his work of saving the world. Noah actually enlisted the world to work with him. All those animals cooperated in the journey — and we are left to imagine how life together was for them during the 40 days and 40 nights in the Ark.

Modern superheroes work mostly alone, and that's a kind of power, too. But Noah worked with the power of animals, their wisdom and knowledge added to his. He enlisted the birds to help him find a place and a time to disembark. The rest is up to us to imagine, and our ability to do that may be vital to the salvation of the world in our own time.

Noah also worked with the Sea as his ally. He — and the animals — had to trust the Sea to carry them safely into the Unknown. And Noah worked with the Sky, waiting for the rainbow sign.

No one I know has ever dressed up as Noah for Halloween. His powers are not superhuman, not thrilling. He works hard. He never gives up. He trusts the future. That's about it. In our age the superheroes are comic-book strong, and they save the world by destroying bad guys. Batman and Spider-Man have a hint of animal power about them, but not very much.

This summer Noah made a comeback, in a film called *Noah*, with Russell Crowe, Hollywood action megastar, as the Ark-builder. But the animals got almost no attention. The movie made me so angry that I've been thinking about Noah ever since. Except for coming on board. the animals didn't appear in the whole two-and-a-half-hour telling of the tale. And in the movie, Noah was a really angry man. He was not a bit angry in the Bible. His name, Noah, a Hebrew name, means Comfort. He was a caring man.

The movie asserts a lot of things that are not in the Bible—it claims that Noah is the last living descendant of Seth, the third son of Adam and Eve, their good kid, and everyone else on Earth is a descendent of their son Cain, who murdered his brother Abel. The movie Noah was determined to prevent his own children from reproducing, because they would have to mate with descendants of Cain, whose bad genetic material Noah wanted to erase from creation. The movie Noah was a man who made his whole family miserable, and almost destroyed the world with his Nazi-like devotion to genetic purity. And his foolish idea that good guys don't like, or do, violence.

None of this is in the Bible. What is it about the biblical Noah that we can't bear? Maybe the story is threatening because in it Noah, whose name means *comfort* and *rest*, chooses to be a nonviolent man. In a very violent world, he becomes God's man. He devotes his life to saving animals, and he listens to God, who tells him things like, *Take seven pairs of each bird, so there will be enough to survive.* In the Jewish scriptures, Noah also takes trees and seeds on the Ark. And after they find land, he plants a vineyard, and after the vineyard grows he makes wine, and after he makes wine he gets really drunk and passes out naked in his tent, and his sons have to cover him up and put him to bed. It isn't his finest hour. He is human. And he does save the world.

The biblical Noah leaves behind a world filled with giants and people who are half pagan, and all of them had become violent, we are told, and a lot of them are drunk, but there is nothing here that identifies them as Cain's offspring, or as genetically different from Noah. And Noah does not fight with them, nor does he encounter them in the biblical story. In the Bible, no people come near the Ark but Noah's family. Movie Noah has to fight to keep crowds of people off the Ark, and a violent stow-away does get on board, and he eats some animals, all of whom Noah has, in the movie, anesthetized with an incense of herbs. Noah does bloody battle with him, and wins, of course. Movie Noah is a modern-style action warrior, a man of sword and club, not a farmer, not a winemaker.

The biblical Noah does not anesthetize the animals — we are free to imagine how they passed their time together, and as we keep learning and dispelling our false notions of how we share this Earth together, I imagine, so did they. Noah and the animals travel to a new world to become its riches. They will not exploit the land and leave it, they will plant themselves in the land they discover and become its new creation. They aid Noah, who needs their wisdom to figure out when and how to leave the Ark. Noah could have filled the Ark with *cash cows*, with herds of sheep, goats, chickens, the clean animals that could be eaten under Jewish law. But he determined also to take the *tref* animals, the wild and forbidden creatures, who have their own agenda in this world and do not serve human uses. And the Bible tells us it is the wild animals who work with him to discover their new home.

If you think I am harping on a very small point, consider the moment in which we are living, the peril in which the world's wild animals are living. The black rhinoceros seems already to be gone, and in line to follow soon enough are the polar bear, the lion, the snow leopard, several whales, more small birds than I can name. The sea itself is sick, almost unto death, and cannot provide habitat, escape or the womb it always has. And many humans are endangered, whose moral stature is no worse nor better than any of ours, yet whose misfortune it is to be born in a place where water is scarce, also education, law and social order.

We are desperate, we the world are desperate, to answer the question: Can there still be wild animals if the human population on earth reaches the projected 10 billion by the end of this century or sooner? Will there be any wilderness? Will there be water for all? Will there be habitat, on the Earth, for creatures?

It does seem to me that our ability, or inability, to imagine heroes like Noah — to imagine cooperation between people and wild animals in shaping a future, to imagine a larger role for the sea and the Earth than to be plundered and exploited in service of humans and their cultures — may be critical to the survival of the world. For the ultimate Ark is this planet, this blue and green star on which we are all traveling through the crowblack sea of space. If conditions within the Ark become intolerable for life, what shall we do? If our imagination is too small to wonder about the spiritual powers of creatures other than ourselves, how shall we be saved? If we are always yearning to be superheroes, then when will we learn to be what we are, human animals, one with all the animals on Earth?

My hope for you, the generation now living and learning at Exeter, is that you will imagine a way forward, you will write new stories, you will explore new science. You will not be fascinated with destruction and the power of war, but with salvation and the power of life. You will care about saving the sea and the land, air, water, sky, and time as holy spaces.

I close with more words from Dylan Thomas:

> Only you can hear the houses sleeping in the streets in the slow deep salt and silent black, bandaged night. Only you can see, in the blinded bedrooms, the petticoats over the chairs, the jugs and basins, the glasses of teeth, Thou Shalt Not on the wall, and the yellowing dickybird-watching pictures of the dead. Only you can hear and see, behind the eyes of the sleepers, the movements and countries and mazes and colours and dismays and rainbows and tunes and wishes and flight and fall and despairs and big seas of their dreams.

Everything rests on your dreams. Dream Noah.

OLUTOYIN AUGUSTUS-IKWUAKOR
My Platform, My Purpose, My Testimony
November 12, 2014

Ever since I can remember, music has been a part of my life. My parents would harmonize together in the kitchen while they prepared meals or my dad would be organizing some musical performance of Nigerian culture that he would lead with my sisters and I as the ensemble trio. We always loved those performances and found ourselves trying to re-create similar performances as we grew older. My older sister, Seun, and I especially loved the 1988 Olympic album, from which we chose our favorite song, "Indestructible," which we sang passionately together, giving no thought to the possibility that one day we would be training together trying to become one of those Olympians. Giving way for each other's solos, we would carefully approach our favorite part and spin anxiously to look at each other to sing "We're Indestructible!! Indestructible." And indeed we were. In those moments we felt empowered and filled with hope. I was 8 and Seun was 9. Neither of us had started athletics, so how could I know that exactly 20 years later I would qualify to compete in the 2008 Beijing Olympics to represent my birth country? Looking back on those moments, I believe we were being prepared.

Olutoyin Augustus-Ikwuakor, known across campus as Coach Toyin, teaches in the Physical Education Department and coaches soccer and track. She lives in Langdell Hall and advises Transitions, The Exonian Encounter Committee and the Nigerian Culture Club.

With little concern for what the future might hold, we obeyed our parents, who consistently promoted excellence in academics and seldom attended track meets even as we won race after race, competition after competition, championship after championship. It was only from other zealous parents and coaches that we learned that somehow something was wrong with that picture, but for my parents this "track thing" was only a fun hobby. When my sister graduated and I was a senior, I couldn't help but feel a little disappointed that my parents didn't see me winning, but there was no doubt that my mommy and daddy loved me. I was always my mother's "Miss America" and my father was always my hero who, barefoot and fed up with his daughters being bullied in elementary school, chased down the culprits to their home one day to finally put an end to the bullying, name-calling and shouts of "Go back to your country." My parents' courage made me strong, so with a child's ignorant confidence I felt I could conquer the world. I was Indestructible!

High school state champion in three events indoors and four events outdoors; school records in more events than I can remember; and MVP of my team, I was honored as Gatorade athlete of the year for my state and competed in the national scholastic competitions. I was heavily recruited to several Southern schools, but passed them up to explore the adventure awaiting me with academic and athletic scholarships to Penn State University. Despite minor injury and some challenges in not being able to rest on talent alone anymore, I was able to rise to the occasion and become, at the time, the best female hurdler the school had ever had. I had school records both in the indoor and outdoor seasons and, 14 years later, my times in the hurdles are still in the top-five all-time fastest for Penn State. After college I was encouraged to continue my athletic pursuits, although my first inclination was to do what my peers were doing ... getting jobs. My parents left the choice to me, so I followed my heart and not my bank account.

Armed with experience in bringing sweat, hard work and tenacity to every tough situation, I felt empowered to create my own success. I was sure that the journey wouldn't be easy, but I had prepared, and clearly, if God didn't want me to do this I would find out soon enough. I held on to what I saw as promises from God and embraced the meaning of my name, Oluwatoyin, which is "the Lord deserves praise."

After college, I moved to Atlanta and joined a training group that taught me so many new skills and training methods for track. For sure, I would be faster. The seed of possibly of being an Olympian that was planted at the end of high school and nurtured through college seemed to bloom before my eyes. Wisdom would tell us that it's at these times of our lives that we should humble ourselves because where there are peaks, there are valleys. Entering my impending valley felt like I'd tripped on pride, bumped my head on poor planning, and tumbled all the way down immaturity, and landed face-down in shame. I thought the money I had saved and the credit cards I had would last me until my big break. I worked part-time doing low-wage work as a personal trainer, door-to-door salesperson and barista while trying to train full-time, pay my coach, and still have enough to eat and pay rent. I was hemorrhaging money hoping my dreams would come true and alas found myself broke, late on bills, avoiding repossession on my car and dodging eviction on my apartment. I had no money to get over to Europe to compete on the international circuit for income, and seemingly no hope left.

I remember kneeling by my bed knowing I needed to pray but feeling like I didn't deserve it. My tears felt endless, while my shame and pride wouldn't allow me to reach out for help. How could I have been so stupid? Why didn't I plan better? God, I thought You wanted me to run track. Why is this happening to me?! I thought Your promise is that You will provide all my needs? I need You now! If this isn't my purpose then what is? How can I possibly get past all of this without feeling like such a failure?! I sacrificed so much and what do I have to show for it? Why God? I found myself praying ... and singing:

> Nothing formed against me can stand,
>
> You hold the whole world in your hand
>
> I'm holding on to your promises
>
> You are faithful
>
> You are faithful
>
> (Chris Tomlin, "Whom Shall I Fear?")

I called my mother and, in a fit of tears, explained it all to her. Hardly understanding me through my hyperventilating weeps, she responded in the gentle and compassionate tone that's unique to a mother. She asked me why I hadn't said anything before and why I tried to do it all myself. She reminded me that no one is an island, that we should not try to go through life secluded. We are meant to bless each other and live in community. Her words gave me peace and she encouraged me to persevere. Although I still lost my apartment and my car, I was able to travel to Europe to compete in the international circuit, win prize money and run personal-best times.

My successful season gave me renewed hope and faith that I was still following the right path. My mistakes had made me stronger and my failures gave me new wisdom. I wasn't feeling so indestructible, but life didn't end there, so for sure I was being prepared. Equipped with a new level of resilience and determination, I knew there had to be bigger purpose for my life that I didn't know yet. I remember thinking that my success couldn't be for me alone, so perhaps it was meant to be a platform to be able to share my testimony with others. My next move was to California to enhance my training even more and continue to compete around the world, and I raced in more than 30 different countries during my career. Between 2005 and 2009 I was a three-time Nigerian National Champion, three-time African Champion, Mizuno-sponsored athlete, two-time World Championship competitor and Olympian.

"How did it feel?" People ask me all the time. Some days it felt very normal because it just became "what I do," and other days I felt overwhelmed with blessings and grace. I was somehow part of the world at large, not just my neighborhood in Southern California. I was able to experience the melodies of different languages being spoken around me, the uniqueness of culture and community among groups of people whose only recognition of yellow school buses, the Super Bowl and the World Series was what they glimpsed on TV. I am still humbled when I think back on the exhilaration of winning international competitions and being swarmed by excited fans, young and old, wanting autographs, photos, just a moment of my time. And I'll never forget the anticipation of walking into the massive Olympic Stadium in Beijing during the opening ceremonies of the 2008 Olympics. Oozing with a mixture of pride and nervous energy, I walked side by side with my countrymen and -women waving to the world and mouthing "Hey, Mom" at the enormous stadium screen, feeling hyperaware that I was in the company of the greatest athletes in the world.

I was living a dream.

And less than two years later, a nightmare.

In 2009, I received a letter from WADA (the World Anti-Doping Agency) saying that earlier that year at the World Championships in Berlin they found my urine sample to have abnormally high levels of testosterone. Since these levels were higher than their stated threshold for females, they concluded that I must have taken performance-enhancing supplements and would need further investigation.

I vividly remember the all-encompassing paralysis that took over my being when I read and reread the letter. My eyes scoured the page looking for some indication of an error. This must be someone else's letter. It must be some kind of mistake. How is this possible? Did someone try to frame me? Is this really happening right now?! My mental dialogue grew more and more aggressive ... angry ... accusing. God, how can You let this happen to me? You know I don't deserve this. You know I'm innocent. I worked so hard to get to this level, doing all the right things and playing by the rules. This is clearly unfair and a just God wouldn't let one of His children be falsely accused, sentenced and scarred, right? I tried to shake the sin of calling God a liar. I tried to "compose" myself and be a "good Christian girl" who knows how to respond like Job to the evils that befall her. Toyin, how dare you? After all, you have so much to be thankful for, right?

Scary, repulsive, chilling fear was staring me down, spitting all the negative possibilities that could result. This is going to tarnish your career. No one cares that you worked hard and made numerous sacrifices. They are going to believe what they want to believe ... that you're a cheater. People are going to judge you before they know the truth. Parents won't trust you with their children, so forget about being a coach or educator. This will effectively ruin your credibility. Maybe you *do* deserve this.

I couldn't get fear to shut up so I grasped for hope and love. In the midst of all the crying, fighting, screaming, fearing and crying again, I heard messages of love from my friends saying, "We know you would never do anything like this, Toyin. We believe you and we love you." My family stood by me looking for ways to help, offering resources and a listening ear to my inaudible sobs. "Toyin, we know this is unfair, but we love you and Jesus loves you even more." And standing by me through it all was my then-devoted boyfriend, now husband, AK, who promised to fight with me, do hours of research, talk to lawyers and anything else to help clear my name. We spent more money on doctors and testing than we could afford. The endocrinologist's results supported that the cysts they found on my ovaries correlate to inconsistent hormonal shifts, but without the money to pay a lawyer and fly to Germany to defend myself, I would not be able to clear my name. I felt I had lost my honor and there was no fixing this. I was banned.

Then and even now, when faced with fear and sadness, I take each situation one day at a time with the memory of my mother's voice beseeching me to "pray, Toyin, you need to pray. And if you try to pray and you can't think of what to say, then sing and praise God." I clutched desperately to her words like a scared child to its mother. The 23rd Psalm, The Lord Is My Shepherd, comes back to me in my native tongue:

> Oluwa ni oluso aguntan mi
>
> E mi ki yio se alaini
>
> O mun mi dubule ni papa oko tutu
>
> O ran okan mi lara
>
> O mi mu lo si ipa ona ododo
>
> Nitori Oruko re
>
> Ni tooto, bi mo ti le nrin ni arin afonifoji
>
> Oji ji iku,
>
> Emi ki yio beeru ibikan
>
> Nitori ti iwo wa pelu mi,
>
> Ogoo re, ati opa re

won ntu mi ninu

Iwo te tabili ounje sile, ni iwaaju mi

ni oju awon ota mi

Iwo da ororo si mi ni ori

Aaago mi si kun akun won sile

Nitoto, ire ati anu, yio ma tan mi lehin

Ni ojo aiye mi gbogbo, Emi yio si ma gbe ile Oluwa lai lai

Amin

And I would pray and I would sing:

'Cause I'm hopeful

Yes I am

Hopeful for today

Take this music and use it

Let it take you away

And be hopeful, hopeful

And he'll make a way

I know it ain't easy but

That's OK

Cuz we hopeful

(Twista ft. Faith Evans, "Hope")

I kept flashing back to when I fell to my knees in Atlanta reminding myself of God's promises and how He brought me through even that moment, which was nothing compared to this. Even though I had gone through all of that, I didn't feel prepared for this. How could I move on from this when being a track athlete was such a huge part of my identity? Who am I now? Even when God provided the opportunity for me to apply for a position at Phillips Exeter Academy, I was still haunted by the thought that they might find my stain and deem me unacceptable. I had to make the choice to keep hope and apply anyway. And even after being given the job, I had to relive the painful experience when people needed answers. It's never easy to talk about it, but I'm committed to not letting it define or paralyze me.

And now I'm stronger because I harnessed the supreme power of choice. One event changed the course of my life like nothing else could at the time. I wouldn't have voluntarily quit a sport that gave me so much success and validation, and I couldn't receive all that was in store for me until I was able to let it go. The ban was only for two years, but my cross-country move to PEA was a choice to give space for new adventures; growing my family to include some of the most amazing young people I have had the pleasure of knowing. You teach me so much every day and help me to discover my purpose and usefulness in this world. I pray that we continue doing life together, sharing joys and tears, and creating the kind of love that produces courage. My reminders of God's goodness despite the storm will be my living testimony proving that what Satan means for evil, God can use for good if you choose to let Him. No matter your situation, circumstance or religious beliefs, have faith, keep hope and trust love to face fear. This testimony is part of the legacy I hope to pass on not only to my Exeter family, but also to my little Haiven and her indestructible self!

MERCY CARBONELL

February 18, 2015

There is a woman who is a healer who I imagine has magic dust floating in her veins. There is a woman who is a healer who holds my head in her palms. There is a woman who is a healer who asks me where the pain is. Sometimes all we want is for someone to say, *"Tell me of your pain"* and to listen.

And so I tell her that for a few years now, I have wanted someone to take a long needle and poke it through the base of my skull and let out what I imagine to be all of the words in there. I do not tell her how I often feel like Hana, the nurse in Michael Ondaatje's *The English Patient*, how Hana *"had been immersed in the lives of others, in plots that stretched back twenty years, her body full of sentences and moments."* I do not tell her that four years ago, in October of 2010, I had a dream I had a bomb strapped to my body and all night, through sweat, I tried to diffuse it, waking drenched with the possibility that it could have happened. I do not tell her about the darker shadows of my childhood.

Instead I tell her in the abstract how there may be sentences and stories and myths and narratives and fragments of fear resting at the base of my skull, creating pressure and causing imbalance.

"That is why your shoulders are in pain," she says.

Mercy Carbonell teaches in the English Department at Exeter and co-directs The Writers' Workshop at Exeter, a summer institute for teachers.

"That is why your neck, too, is in pain.

That is why you need to heal."

Yes, I want them released, want to let them go.

Yes, I want to feel them unspool — words and letters I can perhaps *rearrange* one day.

There is a woman who is a healer and so I tell her of the painting I made three years ago, of the back of a woman's head and a small hole in the back of her skull, of the words coming out in a scrawled cursive, too curled and swerving to interpret. And I tell her how the words lay across the woman's shoulders. And I tell her how in the painting the woman is facing lines from literature I have always loved.

There is Faulkner: *"I would think how words go straight up in a thin line, quick and harmless, and how terribly doing goes along the earth, clinging to it, so that after a while the two lines are too far apart for the same person to straddle from one to the other and that sin and love and fear are just sounds that people who have never sinned nor loved nor feared have for what they never had and cannot have until they forget the words ... like the cries of the geese out of the wild darkness ... "* (*As I Lay Dying*)

There is Morrison: *"'When I was a little girl the heads of my paper dolls came off, and it was a long time before I discovered that my own head would not fall off if I bent my neck. I used to walk around holding it very stiff because I thought a strong wind or a heavy push would snap my neck ... I got my mind. And what goes on in it. Which is to say, I got me.' 'Lonely, ain't it?' 'Yes. But my lonely is mine.'"* (*Sula*)

There is Woolf: *"When life sank down for a moment, the range of experience seemed limitless ... Beneath it is all dark, it is all spreading, it is unfathomably deep; but now and again we rise to the surface and that is what you see us by. Her horizon seemed to her limitless. There were all the places she had not seen ... There was freedom, there was peace, there was, most welcome of all, a summoning together, a resting on a platform of stability ... Often she found herself sitting and looking, sitting and looking, with her work in her hands until she became the thing she looked at — that light, for example. And it would lift up on it some little phrase or other which had been lying in her mind like that — "Children don't forget, children don't forget" — which she would repeat and begin adding to it, It will end, it will end, she said. It will come, it will come ... " (To the Lighthouse)*

***

Now the woman who is a healer leads me through a guided visualization one evening. And so I lie on my back and she places her hands beneath my head at the base of my skull and she holds the very weight of all I carry in her palms. And she tells me to imagine I am very small. And that I have a lot of tools: whatever I want. I picture myself tiny. I picture myself with sandpaper, a rake, a broom and moleskin. She asks me to describe what is in there, in my neck. And so I go in. *And I tell her what I see is in there and I see what I tell her is there.*

At first, they look like peas, like the bumps of peas in a pod, perhaps; or tamarind seeds, like the ones the children knocked with rocks from trees in Malawi last summer. Or maybe more like stones washed wet with ocean water. They are smooth. *Yet.* There are cobwebs between each stone. And she asks me to remove the cobwebs. *So I try.* And I see the stones have some small places where they are bruised, soft, hollowing. And so I don't want to puncture them. Her voice is steady. She says to remove the cobwebs.

And so I try.

And yet, I am distracted by words: a jumble of steel letters, a nest, like the design my mother sent me from the flower show in Philadelphia last March. And they are that color, too — moss green sage green deep green. *What if I place my foot through a slanted Q and get my leg stuck in that space between an S and a J? What if I get caught on the angle of a W? What if I fall through an L and end up in my heart?* I try to scour down the steel letters, tangled. And then, I tell her, I will have to carry them out of my mind. They will be heavy. I can rearrange them perhaps. *One Day*. And I am conscious of something hovering, something present I cannot quite name. And I can hear Elizabeth Bishop's voice:

It is like what we imagine knowledge to be:

dark, salt, clear, moving, utterly free,

drawn from the cold hard mouth

of the world, derived from the rocky breasts

forever, flowing and drawn, and since

our knowledge is historical, flowing, and flown.

She tells me to stay present. *And so I try.* I am very small again and I am here. I have the tools I can carry. I am standing on the edge between vertebrae. I am standing between the stones of the ocean I am made of. And I think of Adrienne Rich's poem, "Diving into the Wreck":

This is the place.

And I am here,

the mermaid whose dark hair

streams black,

the merman in his armored body.

We circle silently

about the wreck

we dive into the hold.

We are, I am, you are

by cowardice or courage

the one who find our way

back to this scene

carrying a knife, a camera

a book of myths

in which

our names do not appear.

And then, unexpectedly, without warning, I begin to cry and I am slightly self-conscious and yet I feel I am in good hands. Like Dubus in his essay on "Breathing": "*I surrender myself. I slow my breathing and try to remain absolutely in the present.*"

And suddenly I realize what it is —

There are people I wish I could bring back into my life, *into* my head. People I wish were still with me, with us all. Voices I miss so very much. And I am crying because it is *not* necessarily a nest of words I want released. It is that I miss the gifts of those gone now. I miss Sam Aaronian and Preeya Sheth, students I loved who are no longer in our lives. I miss the way Peter would call and say "*Merc*" and tell me about a trip he and Dale were taking. Or the way Nina would laugh so hard and tilt her head and speak to me in French. Or the way Gramps called me "*Sweetheart*" and asked me about my life. Or the way Bill would tell me a story with his voice and his long hands. And I can hear Caravaggio say to Kip at the end of *The English Patient*, "*I am going to have to learn how to miss you.*"

***

There is a woman who is a healer "*in whose hands I could trust the world.*" And I can hear my dear friend, my priest friend, Jamie, saying, "*You are on a spiritual journey. You have been for a while now.*" So, I am here to excavate. I am here to dust. I am here to brush off the cobwebs I discover. I am here to place my foot gently along one of the vertebrae. Because there are places where I could step through. There are soft spots, like snow. There are places I am afraid I might fall into.

Step lightly, the woman who is a healer tells me.

Dust off what is covering, she advises.

And so I do.

And once dusted and sanded and raked and brushed gently, once I can see the crevices in my vertebrae, once I know where I can stand, I am here to wade between the stones. I am here to find the spaces where the people I love are missing.

I am here. And I am crying —

Because Sam passed away in his sleep en route coming home for healing.

Because this summer Preeya took her life

Because Gramps was old and his heart finally fell.

Because last December, we lost Peter.

Because 12 years ago, Nina's ashes became the dust bones I float with in the ocean.

Because this September, Bill died of cancer.

Because sometimes all I want is a full moon to stand beneath.

Because I seek that natural guardianship.

Because I do not know how to carve the concrete from what I feel now.

Because I do not know where the ghost and the soul of someone I loved as a child rest now.

Because I sometimes cannot sleep easily within the absence of this knowledge.

Because it is as Woolf writes:

"'Children don't forget, children don't forget'

which she would repeat and begin adding to it,

It will end, it will end, she said. It will come, it will come ... "

***

"Never again," John Berger reminds us, *"will a single story be told as if it is the only one."* And so I am falling into Adrienne Rich's poems, I am *"Diving into the Wreck"* and I am *"Waking in the Dark ... "*

"The thing that arrests me"

is often a shadow, a shadow that can still me in time. We are walking along Fairville Road, a mile now from my parents' house, a mile past the

Archers' old farm, where Rebecca's death stole our childhoods from us in a single breath and night. It is along this road where I have run miles alone, witnessing certain seasons in Pennsylvania light, resettling myself through heat or rain or the heavy hang of the branches that grow along here that form a canopy when it snows. When I run, I watch the trees and listen for birds. When I run, I look for the dollhouse by Ann Wyeth's pond and think of the miniature world she created in there. Today, Julia is with me — oldest friend, closest confidant, the one who has seen me grow into myself and sometimes break from my own contours. Back at the house, her husband, Matthew, sleeps beside their new daughter, Christine reads, my brother is taking his young son on a tractor ride, my sister swims, and my parents harbor themselves in the folds of old habits and routines. Now, Julia and I are walking and letting each other back into our lives. It is July, the sun is high and she is telling me about what it feels like to be a mother, what it feels like to live in D.C., what it feels like to be a wife, what it feels like to be a woman on the edge of 40 who may or may not have a novel waiting in her. I am telling her about teaching, about what it feels like to come home to a family I continue to hope for. We laugh together at the summer when we worked at her father's law firm, at the night when we snuck away into the barn, at the games we used to invent with imaginary horses, at the years we have moved far from but still hold close.

When we near the Archers' house, I feel her step slow, feel my own slow in pace with hers.

"*I wonder about Honor,*" she says, and we both remember, without saying it out loud, that night in our sixth-grade year when Honor and her brother, Henry, came home to find their mother raped and dead on her bedroom floor. There is a new wing built on the old 18th-century structure, the window to Rebecca's room no longer visible from the road — a relief in a way because a new shape can shield some of the pain of that night. But the fence is the same, the driveway still the arc it has always been, the white shutters thatched to hold out the summer heat. Later that evening, after dinner, after the children are in bed, we will sit on my parents' porch with my sister and brother and his wife, with Matthew and Christine and another childhood friend, Bill. And Julia will tell us about Honor's tattoos on her body, how she was studying to be an art therapist. *"Her way of healing,"* Julia tells us. There is a long silence, some of us taking in imagined shapes and colors along the body of a girl we grew up with. The crickets click and the stars secure the horizon line and for a moment I am reminded of how childhood never really lets us loose.

"Sometimes every aperture of my body leaks blood"

when I imagine what it must have been like for Honor and Henry to find their mother on that late-September afternoon. Seventy-two stab wounds, the paper said the next day. *"George Smith"* written in Rebecca's blood across the wall after he raped her and stabbed her. I have lived for so long with this image, have tried through verse to dim the pain even as I keep it reeling. And still it comes back to me. For a long time, I wondered how she had the strength to rise in her dying to name him. For a long time, I thought only of the old woman who lived on the hill above the Archers' farmhouse, the woman who said she heard the screams but did not register that they were real. I used to imagine that woman standing at her kitchen window, opened enough to let in new autumn air. I used to see her eating a pear, washing a cup, rinsing her hands, listening to Rebecca's final voice. For a long time, I pictured Rebecca alone before George Smith came in, the last call made to my mother: *What did they talk about? What did she sound like hours before she was stolen from us?* For a long time, I could not sleep and imagined my own body losing its life, the blood seeping out of me. *"We be of one blood, thou and I,"* Kipling writes. *"We be of one blood."* Because she was my mother's closest friend. Because she taught me how to cut roses. Because I rolled down the hill in their yard, tumbling into hay through laughter. Because memory, too, is an artery.

"*It is strange to be so many women,*"

to be my mother the night she stormed out of the house in a fury screaming, "*I should have been killed. Not Rebecca,*" her first words of this so many years after her friend was killed. To be Honor, whose pain I have invented and tried to sift through a fictional dream, for I no longer know her. To be Rebecca in a navy kilt the last afternoon I ever saw her. To be George Smith's daughter, who works now at the Sunoco station on Route 1 near the Brandywine River Museum. To be the other girls he had once molested before he came to work for the Archers that summer: girls perhaps grown into women; girls swollen with pain and girls healing.

"*I dive back to discover*"

what else I keep with me. And yet the same images keep coming through, resurrected without chronology, fragmented, some quiet, some loud:

Chandler Collison at the water fountain at school,

whispering to Zeke Sieglaff about Rebecca's death

within earshot.

My grandparents' house late that night and the spiral staircase with

a banister that felt smooth beneath my touch.

All of the children being taken to play miniature golf,

to keep us occupied.

Gathering in the Boardmans' house

after the police came,

after the ambulance came.

My father rushing down the road to our car

to tell my mother, *"Rebecca has been killed,"*

my mother doubling over, the car still in motion,

my father reaching through the window to grab the emergency break.

Cleaning the Archers' house a month later

and finding a note in the cabinet where

they kept their markers and crayons and pads of paper,

a note that said in a child's scrawl, *"I am lucky to have two parents who love me."*

"Here in the matrix of need and anger"

My sister tells me 10 years ago something I did not know, something she learned years later when she asked my mother. They were planning on moving to Cambridge to open a food co-op, planning on re-envisioning their lives. My sister is angry, resentful. *"How could she even have thought of this?"* she asks me through tears. *"How? Would she have come back for us? Would she?"* My own anger feels far away; I do not share her resentment. Rather, I study this fact for clues with an objectivity that surprises me. It is, I know now, a distance that allows me to see a new story: a woman who would not have been raped and killed, perhaps; two women remaking their lives, doing something they care about. I do not think of the husbands, Paul Archer or my father. I do not even think of the children, of whom I am one. This new narrative arcs toward something I believe is bound by necessity, arcs toward something I want to call freedom. And although I have lived long enough to know that this story, too, might have bled, I want to choose to listen to other voices, other fragments, other stories. For now I am beginning to trust that,

"The words are purposes. The words are maps"

And so I dive back again and I wake in the dark again and I think of all the years I lived in fear, in a deep fear too loud to name, a paralyzing fear at times. And I think of the summer I began to move out of that fear, the winter I knew I had to speak to my father about all he had witnessed. And so I call him and ask him to meet me in NYC. He does not ask why and he comes. We meet at the corner of Bryant Park, a snowstorm just having fallen all around us, slowed now enough for us to walk. We go to lunch at Columbus Circle, to Bouchon Bakery, and I begin to ask him to speak, to name his experience of that night when Rebecca was found murdered, to break what I find out is his 30-year silence. The restaurant looks out over the beginning edge of Central Park, and from where I sit I can see the trees Christo once wrapped in orange, the shapes between the branches, the negative space of so much life. He looks down at his octopus salad, takes a sip of his Brooklyn Lager and tells me that he had had nightmares, that he felt as if it was his fault. If only he had called the police when he saw the car parked on our road that September morning. If only he had done something. Rebecca might have lived. He tells me that Paul Archer had asked him, because my father is an architect, if he could watch over the house while the forensics team came to take out the wall where she wrote her murderer's name in blood. He tells me that he could not sleep for months because of all he saw.

I look at his face, see the hollows in his eyes, catch the glimmer of kindness I always feel is there and tell him it is not his fault. *"I know,"* he says. And yet I can tell he still does not believe this. And so I ask him to keep speaking, and he tells me he wishes he and my mother had found us a grief therapist or a counselor to talk to. *"I am so sorry,"* he says, and I feel the depth of his apology and I take his hand across the table and tell him, in that space where reassurance lives beyond tenses, *"It is OK. It will all be OK."*

Later, my father takes my hand in his and holds it steady, and later we walk out into the snow and cold and I lead him to Penn Station to catch the train. On the platform, I thank him and hold him and allow myself to be held and I remember Maxine Greene's beautiful lines, *"There is a need for wild patience. And when freedom is the question, there is always a time to begin."* And I remember the evening with poet Kristin Fogdall after a writing workshop she gave one summer, how we sat with wine on my porch late into the night and she said, like Brodsky, that she believes that *"language can save our souls."* And when the train moves along, I watch my father through the window; he has chosen a seat that is moving backward.

"Thank you," I offer in silence.

"Thank you," I wave to him as the train pulls out of the station.

"Thank you," I remind myself years later.

***

For years, I have lived with my father's silence, felt my mother's stoic despair. I have wondered about Honor, the girl with all the healing tattoos who went to RISD, whom I saw one afternoon in Providence. I have talked with my oldest friend, Julia, on the anniversary of Rebecca's death each year. I have listened to the stories of women and men across the globe begin to speak. And I have felt the pressure at the base of my skull growing.

Because for too long my parents lived in silence.

Because for too long I lived in fear and wanted George Smith to die in the electric chair.

Because one year I read Dubus' essay, "About Kathryn," about his sister raped on her lawn two nights after Christmas, how "she prays so she can forgive him," how her "anger and hatred will burn to white ash."

Because there are too many women raped.

Because there is a Femicide in the Congo.

Because there are women killed for being women.

Because men, too, are raped.

Because — paying witness, listening matters.

Now, there is a woman who is a healer who I imagine has magic dust floating in her veins. Now, there is a woman who holds my head in her palms. And so I tell her I want to know where Rebecca's soul has gone.

"What do you believe in?" she asks me.

And I can hear Jamie saying,

"You are on a spiritual journey. You have been for a long time."

Often, I can feel those I have loved and those who have died still present in certain places. Often, I believe they rest where they wanted to be, where they imagined themselves, where they felt at peace. I imagine Peter in a field somewhere, in a wind, along the coastline, still seeking the call of birds. I imagine Nina and Bill are so close, their ashes tossed into the Atlantic at Little Boar's Head here in New Hampshire so that when I swim, I know I am with them. I imagine where Gramps is and my Grandmother Bloom, too; they are dancing in what they believed to be Heaven. I know where Rich and Peg have placed some of Sam's ashes and there is a space by the river here in Exeter where he rises up at times. It is a place where he and I used to walk. I feel the transcending spirit of my Grandmother and Grandfather Carbonell in a marsh field along I-95 en route from Boston. And I know Preeya rests at times in her friend's poetry, in what Rachel Baxter writes: "*The stars are so beautiful in the dark/and pain is a song too.*"

And yet — there is a vacancy, an ethereal pause, an absence with Rebecca, the woman who taught me to cut roses and held my mother's heart, the woman whose children have now grown up to create beautiful lives. I wonder where she rests, I wonder where her soul travels. And I know, in some ways, *this* is the peace I am seeking.

* * *

What do I believe in? I am just beginning to know.

"*You are on a spiritual journey,*" I can hear Jamie reminding me.

"*This is the place & I am here.*"

Somewhere over the world, beyond my vision, I am starting to believe there are angels watching. I imagine them wondering about whom they want to save.

"*How could we not save this one?*" one angel says to the other.

"*We cannot save her,*" another angel says.

"Shouldn't we even try?"

"How do we save someone who does not know herself?" one asks.

"This," the other angel says, *"I do not know."*

"Does she even act like she wants to be saved?"

"I don't think we have to wait for that, do we?"

They are sunbathing briefly, taking off their wings to feel the sun hold them steady. Somewhere someone is playing music. *On earth as it is in heaven.* And somewhere someone is asking to make love. *On earth as it is in heaven.* And somehow, somewhere within the beginning of belief, I rise up out of my chair and lean against the window frame in my house. I am facing the hemlocks and remembering how a small bird came to me again and again the September I felt my fear floating off.

"This is the place. And I am here."

I am here and I rise and lean and remember three years ago when my friend Lenny Willis left me a note on my porch. *"Let's Meditate."* At first Lenny was a bird in the window where the hemlocks hang. At this time of year, they are beautifully weighed down with snow. In the wind, they sway and brush up against the windowpanes. Squirrels chase one another on their branches. Birds settle here. The fall I met Lenny, there was a bird who came to visit me. Peter Greer told me later that bird was a harbinger of something, perhaps the beginning of Hope. Later, Lenny and I sat on the hill by my house in the autumn grass, September still holding summer's heat, and he spoke me through the process of recognizing what is in my mind and then ushering it out. Allowing it to be present. Letting it go. Releasing it. That day, I sat cross-legged and felt the wind and felt the cool grass and listened to his calming voice and allowed and let go and released.

"This is the place & I am here."

And so I lean and look out the window and think of Jamie and her two beautiful daughters, Lizzie and Cahaley. And that drive with Lizzy out to Dublin, New Hampshire, to see Jamie preach a last sermon at Emmanuel Church. That drive when I was teaching Lizzie how to change lanes on Route 101, how to track the middle of the car with the dividing lines and move slowly over, how Lizzy knew my sadness that night was real and put on music and began to sing as if offering a lullaby. I remember our conversation on that car ride: about forgiveness and how it works, what releases it, does there need to be anyone there to receive it? I remember Lizzy's intuition, her curiosity and her wonder. And in the morning over coffee, Jamie saying,

"One morning you will wake and you will know. You will feel it."

And so I rise and lean and I can see the concrete of the observatory between the branches and I know beyond that are the fields and the turf and the trails and the bridge and the swings beyond the children's school. I rise and lean toward the windows and for a moment, I am falling down the hills into hay at the Archers' house with Honor and Henry. For a moment, I am wishing back time. For a moment, I am that small girl again.

And there is that echo:

"'Children don't forget, children don't forget'

which she would repeat and begin adding to it,

It will end, it will end, she said. It will come, it will come ... "

This is the place & I am here.

"And it will end, it will end," she said.

Because there is a woman who is a healer whom I imagine has magic dust floating in her veins. And I am small. Because I am standing in the ocean I am. Because I am untangling the steel letters. And I am rearranging the words in my mind. Because I am letting the people I miss back in. I am hearing their voices.

And what of Rebecca's soul?

Last night, in a beautiful and unexpected convergence, my oldest friend, Julia, calls. She is on a train. She has just gone through a tunnel. We speak of our lives and I tell her that tomorrow, now today, I am speaking of Rebecca's rape and murder and I am wondering where her soul rests. Julia says, *"I have never been there. To her grave. You have."* Yet I have no memory of this. *"You have, it is on the way into town from your house,"* she tells me. And yet all I can see is the fields where we grew up: the rolling hills; the valley; the way frost covers the fields in November; the stacks of hay; the Archers' old house; a blank wall now in a room where once a woman-mother-friend was stolen from us.

And I think again of Arundhati Roy's passage in *The God of Small Things*: *"Perhaps it's true that things can change in a day. That a few dozen hours can affect the outcomes of whole lifetimes. And that when they do, those few dozen hours, like the salvaged remains of a burned house — the charred clock, the singed photograph, the scorched furniture — must be resurrected from the ruins and examined. Preserved. Accounted for. Little events. Ordinary things, smashed and reconstituted. Imbued with new meaning. They become the bleached bones of a story."*

And after Julia and I hang up, I think to myself, *"We will go there."*

***

"Children don't forget. Children don't forget."

This fall I discover Honor Archer on Instagram. She is 43 years old now and working as an art therapist in South Carolina, working for Social Services and in prisons, working for people who have experienced heinous crimes against them. This September 17, 2014, she posts a photograph of her and her mother, Rebecca.

"1974 mom and I, safe and happy,

probably looking off in the distance at some animals we can go

and pet donkeys, sheep, goats.

Fast forward to 1980, to the rape and murder of my mother.

No more safety in petting animals.

No more safety in reading Goodnight Moon, goodnight stars, goodnight porridge.

But to the goodnight killer hiding under my bed,

goodnight killer hiding behind the bathroom door,

goodnight killer who has already slaughtered the rest of my family.

I guess I need to dream a way out of this one."

***

"It will end. It will end," she said.

"This is the place & I am here."

At their home in Chadds Ford, Pennsylvania, in the Brandywine Valley where I grew up, in the room I always pass through, on a wooden chest, my parents have a photograph: of Rebecca Archer in a field on a hill where we used to play. She is wearing a light skirt and she is barefoot.

She is with her children, small & chubby & floating in what seems the arc of summer. And on the back of this photograph, Mr. Archer has offered William Wordsworth:

What though the radiance, which was once so bright

be now forever taken from my sight.

Though nothing can bring back the hour,

of splendor in the grass,

of glory in the flower.

We will grieve not, rather find, strength in what remains behind.

***

"It will come, it will come."

And I hear Jamie whispering: "*And one morning you will wake & you will know and you will feel it.*"

I hear Wordsworth:

In the soothing thoughts that spring

Out of human suffering;

In the faith that looks through death,

In years that bring the philosophic mind.

Thanks to the human heart by which we live,

Thanks to its tenderness, its joys, and fears,

To me the meanest flower that blows can give

Thoughts that do often lie too deep for tears.

I hear Nanci Griffith singing *"Let the angels teach us. Only Love Remains."*

Because Maxine Greene reminds us, *"There is a need for wild patience. And, when freedom is the question, there is always a time to begin."*

Because *"This is the place & I am here."*

And for now there is Robert Hass, from his poem, "Cuttings":

Small song.

Two beat:

The robin on the lawn

Hops from Sun

Into Shadow.

Shadow into Sun.

EIMER PAGE

November 18, 2015

"I have walked through many lives,

Some of them my own,

And I am not who I was,

Though some principle of being

Abides, from which I struggle

Not to stray."

— Stanley Kunitz, "The Layers"

I came across this kid recently. She's a teenager. You'd probably recognize her in some of the students walking the pathways outside. She's rather lazy but she works hard in sporadic bursts and does fine in exams, even when she shouldn't. Teachers tend to think well of her, and she twists that to her advantage. I wonder how she'd cope as a student here, where learning is so cumulative and absences need to be excused. She's definitely a risk-taker, but the adults in her life are fairly clueless about it.

Eimer Page has been teaching English at the Academy since 2004, after moving here from her native Ireland. She lives in Exeter with her husband, John, and sons, Oscair and Cormac.

She's also a total drama queen in her communications with me. She seems to believe that she's the first human to have had feelings of angst and joy. At one point after a messy breakup, she actually said, "I wish I was dead and rotting underground in a quiet cool grave with a granite slab at my head. Maybe in years to come, someone would look and ask themselves, 'What was it like for her? The only answer is 'agony'!" Um, yeah. I want to shake her and remind her of all that she has in her corner — a supportive family, good school, great friends and a whole wide world before her.

If I were her adviser, I'd be dispensing advice when she reveals that "it's 12:55 a.m. and I don't have my French, chemistry, physics or math finished. I've spent all evening on art." I might have a thing or two to offer to her perspective on the talented musician who has just turned 30 and is casting glances in her direction, or even the black-haired college dropout who comes up to her house on his motorbike and gives her his leather jacket to wear. But, of course, she would never take advice from a married mother of two. How could I possibly relate to her experiences, or she to mine?

***

As Salman Rushdie tells us in *Midnight's Children*, "Memory has its own special kind. It selects, eliminates, alters, exaggerates, minimizes, glorifies, and vilifies also; but in the end it creates its own reality, its heterogeneous but usually coherent version of events; and no sane human being ever trusts someone else's version more than his own."

My parents recently moved. John's parents also moved this summer, causing both of us to lose our childhood phone numbers in the same week! Odd feeling to know that dialing the familiar pattern won't lead to my dad's deep 'hello', or my mum's delighted greeting when she sees the international number come up. I don't even know their new number, since who actually memorizes phone numbers anymore!

Moving requires much casting off of the old. I flew to Ireland for a few days in August to help my parents with the final push in their old house before they handed off the keys to the new owners. They had already taken care of the big stuff. Their furniture had been moved to their new apartment and the house had been staged for selling with more contemporary pieces. The stuff that remained was really hard to deal with. A kitchen full of heavy baking sheets that have been used so often that they've created their own nonstick permanent coating; china tea cups that had been cradled in the hands of four generations; Le Creuset casserole dishes given as wedding gifts for the staples of the '60s and '70s — beef bourguignon and Irish stew — and had later been adapted to serve dishes my parents encountered on their travels in Turkey: lamb dishes fragrant with cinnamon and cumin, aubergine, fish in saffron; decorative trivets and trinkets acquired during my father's time working in Zimbabwe. None of this stuff is easy to categorize, and certainly none of it can be discarded without a profound sense of loss. Molly, a dear friend here on campus, introduced me, tongue-in-cheek, to "the life-changing magic of tidying up: the Japanese art of decluttering and organizing," and I tried bringing with me the book's philosophy of keeping only those items that spark joy.

I entered my parents' house with a grim determination to avoid sentimentality and be as productive as possible. My mother's response soon knocked that out of me. It might have been the sight of me hurling my wedding dress over the upstairs balcony bannister onto the tiled floor of the hallway, or maybe our indecision about what to do with her mother's leather gloves, or maybe the speed with which I wrapped the red-and-white earthenware dinner service in newspaper to bring it to the St. Vincent de Paul thrift store, but something tipped her into mourning. The dinner service had graced everyday meals throughout my childhood. I don't remember the purchase. For me, it was always part of our home, and the instruction to set the table always involved placing five heavy white plates with their pattern of red poppies in the warming oven. We had a matching tea set, and it didn't take me long to wrap it, either. When I entered the living room, I found my mum sitting in a chair, with tears welling in her eyes. "It feels like I'm giving away my children," she heaved. I could have pouted about her mistaking a dinner service for one of her beloved offspring, but it didn't seem the time. I told her: "I know it hurts. It's OK to feel it. This is a genuinely big deal."

My family tends to be "doers." We don't acknowledge feelings; we find solutions or make each other look on the bright side. My father's response to anyone's tears in my childhood was to whip out his hankie, dance it in front of us between swipes at the streaming eyes and nose, and to sing "Happiness, happiness, that's the thing that I possess. Happiness, happiness, more than my share of happiness." I love him for it, and I know and recognize the place it comes from, but it has led all of us to avoid giving more than token time to tears and wallowing, and has encouraged us to pick ourselves up and get on with fixing the Problem. Becoming part of John's family in my early 20s brought me into close contact for the first time with people who could simply say, "This is hard and it hurts." If I had followed my own family's modus operandi, I would have tried to cheer my mum by reminding her how beautiful the view of the mountains and the bay is from their new living room, how easy it is going to be to turn the key and go on a vacation without having to stress about the garden, what a lovely opportunity it is for some other young woman to have the chance to pick up my silk wedding dress for a song … but what she needed most was for me to acknowledge that this had been her literal dream home — she had designed it with my dad from the foundations up, and that crying at its loss was appropriate. Memory creates meaning from our experiences, and I wanted her to be able to make meaning of this significant departure by acknowledging all that she was leaving behind in this home. Her memories are allowed to be poignant and tinged with sadness about the change she has volunteered to make in downsizing.

***

Neil Gaiman says, "Memory is the great deceiver. Perhaps there are some individuals whose memories act like tape recordings, daily records of their lives complete in every detail, but I am not one of them. My memory is a patchwork of occurrences ... the parts I remember, I remember precisely, whilst other sections seem to have vanished completely." (*Smoke and Mirrors*)

Along with all of the practical items that my mother and I wrapped, boxed and brought to the thrift store, I found a plastic bag full of old diaries where I recorded every day of my life between the ages of 13 and 21. It won't surprise you, I'm sure, to learn that the anguished teen I introduced you to in the opening did make it through school, college and grad school, despite her fears about her French and chem homework. She avoided the snares of biker boy and the older musician, and ended up in the English Department at Exeter, dispensing advice to girls in her care who are much more mature than she was at their age. I find myself looking through her, my, diaries and being shocked by how much I have changed. I barely recognize myself. Some of the moments I describe are as clear to me now as they were when I wrote about them a quarter-century ago, but many others have just gone and that is troubling to me:

"Peter, Sean, Paula, Paul, Siobhan and Susan came up to my house and we didn't go to bed. We watched the sun come up." May 26, 1991. Of that list, I remember Paula best. She died in a car crash one week after getting her driving license in October of that same year. Susan is clear in my mind, too, but I don't even know who Sean and Paul are. How odd. We were close enough to pull an all-nighter, and I don't remember them at all.

I've been fascinated all my life by people who record their days. There was an exhibit in the art gallery from September to October 2013 which some of you may remember. The artist was Melanie Mowinski, and she has recorded her daily life for the past 20 years in a visual calendar. One can see a whole year of her life on a single sheet. In an act of enormous generosity, I recall that she even let Exeter display her current, incomplete calendar and she would come along periodically and fill in the blank spaces. I loved seeing the intricate order of her journaling, with a tiny computer scribbled on the day taxes were due, or a picture of a throbbing head revealing a migraine, and I found that seeing a record of 20 years of this woman's life felt like an intimate invitation from the artist to the viewer. It seems to me that this form of journaling, with mixed images and words, is my ideal response to a deep-held desire to chronicle my world. I don't want to let experiences slip into the black hole of memory loss that I saw affect my grandmothers and now see in my mother-in-law. Dasha Kiper, in a recent article for *The Guardian* on "The Deviousness of Dementia," describes memory as "responsible for creating continuity, meaning, and coherence both for ourselves and for those around us. Its integration into every function of life, from speaking and learning to the forming of relationships, actually makes its loss all the more difficult to comprehend, since the visible repercussions ... distract us from the deeper, more intangible privation." Kiper goes on to reveal the sobering statistic that 5.3 million Americans experience dementia and that the number is set to triple by 2050. What do we make of a fickle brain that alters each memory in the remembering process? And what happens to our memories when the synaptic connections begin to fade, when plaques form and when the first symptoms of dementia appear?

***

Toni Morrison tells us: "Some things go. Pass on. Some things just stay. ... Someday you be walking down the road and you hear something or see something going on. So clear. And you think it's you thinking it up. A thought picture. But no. It's when you bump into a rememory that belongs to someone else." (*Beloved*)

I grew up in a unique time in my country's history. That's a truism for all of us, but it struck me as a revelation when John asked me whether I ever think about the fact that ours is the only generation in my homeland that knew nothing of childhood outside conflict. I had never considered that my parents had known a childhood of peace and that my nephews and nieces have the same. Northern Ireland is a young country. It was established in 1921 with the partition of the island, and endured decades of cold hostility between its populations. Violence fueled a flame in the late 1960s, and I was born in the following decade into a conflagration of car bombings, knee cappings, rubber bullets, mortar attacks and internment without trial. My first serious boyfriend watched from under the table as a child when his father, a human rights lawyer in Belfast, was shot 14 times in front of him and his younger siblings over family dinner. That act shocked the world when an Amnesty International inquiry revealed that loyalist terrorists had acted in collusion with the British intelligence service MI5 to silence him. Uncertain ceasefires were declared by the two main paramilitary groups in the 1990s, beginning two years after I left the country to study in Dublin. Sporadic violence broke out over the next few years, but the Good Friday Agreement of 1998 marked the end of the Troubles with a capital T, and the beginning of a new era of relative cohesion.

What did I write and record of those anxious days when I was growing up? Nothing. Not a mention. Any political events that reached the pages of my journals tended to be about events in England, America or the Middle East. Why on earth not? Is it because, as the saying goes, a fish knows nothing about the water in which he swims? I don't think that was it. I knew that other places were different. I spent childhood vacations in the calmer climes of France, Spain, America, Yugoslavia (the irony there won't be lost on some). As I began to reread the old diaries I had uncovered, I found myself wishing that I had been more attentive to events, and wishing for a different kind of recording of that time. I had spent so much of my time recording my emotions that I hadn't captured many of the experiences those emotions were attached to. While I was wallowing in adolescent self-pity and calling for a cool grave, real events were happening and slipping through my memory's sands. In trying to articulate why, I think I believed that I would never be touched, never personally affected by what was happening around me. My parents' optimism and the happiness hanky created a sort of force field that couldn't be penetrated. Even my direct personal experience of bomb blasts didn't pierce the mantle. I was shaken, but not injured. Maybe it's for the best that I didn't capture the confusion and fear that I kept at arm's length as a child, but little remains of that time in my memory. If I were to try to capture the remaining snapshots, here's what I have:

Driving on a country road with high, dark hedges, returning home from a visit to my grandmother on the other side of the small country. I'm sitting in the back, in the middle, while my brothers are on either side. I complain about the seat, but I'm the smallest and that's the way it goes. It also gives me a great view of the dark road ahead through the front seats. I'm hypnotized by the rain flying toward the windscreen. A small red light moves in circles up ahead at the side of the road and my father slows the car. For a moment, none of us know whether the flashlight that has called us to a halt to question our name, our address, our reason for travel is in the hands of a British soldier, or a paramilitary vigilante.

Looking out my bedroom window at the neat house of our neighbor. I'm 6? Seven, maybe. Mr. Kerr comes out of his front door, gets down on his hands and knees, and peers under the back of his car. Then he moves around to the front and has to lie on his back and shimmy under the hood to examine the underside. A few weeks later he and his family post a For Sale sign in the front garden and then they move away. The last Protestant family on our once-mixed avenue has now left. How many years before I understand what he was looking for, and why it would have been necessary for him, a police officer, to do that check before turning his key in the ignition?

Lying in bed after watching the evening news. I'm 10, and 38 IRA prisoners have escaped the maximum security prison known as the Maze. Some have been recaptured, but many are on the run. The reporter revealed on the 6 o'clock news that some of the prisoners had been found hiding under floorboards in an isolated home, and encouraged farmers and people with outbuildings to exercise caution in case they surprised any of these desperate men, many of them wounded. I press myself into the mattress, holding my breath to listen for sounds coming from the floorboards that might indicate the presence of an escapee. Thinking it through, my room was on the third floor of our house, so the whole floorboard phobia was somewhat misplaced, but the thumping heart was very real.

Walking home from school up the narrow lane in my school uniform. Usually I walk with Patricia, my neighbor who moved in after Allison and Barbara Kerr left, but I had to stay late for orchestra. My viola case bumps against my legs and I put it down for a moment to adjust my grip. I spot a dark gun barrel sticking out from the shrubbery at the side of the lane, and a flood of realization shows me the line of young soldiers, spread out at intervals the full length of the lane and camouflaged in the undergrowth, all pointing their weapons at me. The soldiers I've passed and those ahead squint through their sights, a trick I came to learn they used on girls to get a closer look. I pick up my instrument and trudge awkwardly on, feeling like I've forgotten my natural gait under the glare of their weapons and their silent gaze. Looking back on this, I may have been 13 and some of them may have been only 17 or 18, but a gun gives one an unearned authority.

Standing in the dining room of my boyfriend's house on Christmas night. His mother and siblings have gone to bed, and I'm switching off the lights on the Christmas tree. I don't even know where he is in the house, probably indicative of the future of that doomed relationship, and I'm transfixed by the sight of the thick security beams that lock into place once the door is closed. I know this is the room where his father was murdered, that those beams were installed to increase security for his family, who chose to remain in that home, and I feel as if the scene is replaying in front of me and that I'm powerless to look away. I hear the events unfold in my head, and I don't have the words to put them to paper. Am I a victim of indigestion after a heavy meal, or does a rememory live in that room with its barricaded doors?

I'm not even sure why I want to remember these moments, or whether desire has nothing to do with their permanence in my brain. I know that I see them as more honest and raw than the words I wrote at the time, but who knows how much is accurate to the time in which all of this happened. Maybe there were only two or three soldiers in the lane, although I know they tended to move in packs for protection. Maybe I imagined seeing my neighbor check for car bombs later, and in fact Allison's soccer ball had just rolled under the wheel.

**

I've changed the way I record my experiences over time. I no longer journal every day, and no longer write about my feelings in a place. Instead, I take my own advice as a teacher of writing and try to record only sensory snapshots that place me back inside my own body in the moment. In India last March, I wrote fragments of sensation: "cool smooth marble under my feet. Disoriented by the sensation of walking barefoot in the street ... Taj is rose colored in the dusk, and it is now cool and breezy ... Smell of charcoal and rice popping in a blackened pan over an open fire ... Flaming marigolds bobbing and floating on the surface of the Ganges ... Stepping on cow shit, again and again. It squelches under my shoes ... Smell of burning bodies. Sizzle of human fat rendering in the cremation process." I don't need to say how I felt, because the synapses fire strongly and surely when I reread these words. I remember. I remember.

For me, my parents' recently sold house was never my own home. They had designed and moved into it after I went to college. My childhood home was the house on Windsor Avenue and not this one. For my children, however, Nanny and Pops' house was the constant in their relationship with Ireland. Both of them went through the phase of thinking that Ireland was the house's name. "Are we going back to Ireland now?" a tired wee voice would pipe up from the back seat after a day at the Titanic Quarter in Belfast, or a raucous visit with cousins. When I find myself thinking of the house, two mental Vines replay in my mind. The first was when Oscair was about two and went through a temporary terror about bath time. Maybe water had splashed him unexpectedly, or the gurgling of the emptying bathtub made him think a monster inhabited the drain? Whatever it was, he didn't want to get clean. My dad came back from a trip downtown with a paddle pond in the shape of a whale, and he half-filled it with the garden hose. He let it lie in the late-afternoon sun, warming as much as one can expect at 54° latitude, and he settled in to do some weeding of the raised flowerbed beside it, while his solemn-eyed grandson watched the water warily. I can see my dad digging out weeds beside the beautiful blushing peonies that my grandmother had given him as slips, the ones she called "bowls of cream." I step inside to help my mother with dinner, probably slipping those same plates with the red poppies into the oven, and then I hear my son's delighted squeal as he splashes his grandfather. Next thing, he has stepped fully clothed into the paddle pool, and he's scooping water onto his beloved Pops, who tips his head back and laughs. That night, he enters the tub without a protest, and he has been a water baby ever since.

The other Vine is more recent. June 2014. My folks have bought official soccer balls for both boys, and night after night Cormac begs to play World Cup after dinner. For him, the matches he plays with his brother, his dad and his grandfather are more real than the games being played in Brazil. June brings magic nights that far north, and the sun doesn't fully set until close to 11 p.m. I can see the four most important men in my world, sliding tackles on the grassy lawn, golden light embracing them, balls disappearing into our neighbors' yards and being retrieved by my sons, who are gathering twigs in their hair, grass stains on their clothes and memories in their hearts. This place that we call home in Ireland is what I will miss, but if I just let myself think about it I can replay it. It's still there in my world, and I can rub up against it when I choose. And if my mother's memories fade, or my own in time, will my sons recall those times? And when their lives draw down, will there be some ghost of a child forever laughing on that lawn?

PETER ANDERSON

Home, Land, Security: The View from Vulture Gulch

December 9, 2015

Home. Land. Security. These three words evoke the strongest of human yearnings: for home — a shelter, the place that calls us back, the center from which we experience the world; for land — the ground that sustains us; for security — safety, relationships in which we care and are cared for, freedom from high doses of anxiety and danger.

Home. Land. Security. In Genesis 2, after forming "every animal of the field and every bird of the air," the Creator brought them before the first human to see how they might be named. Naming the world, this creation story tells us, was the part of the human vocation that initiated our primeval sense of place. Out walking with my daughter Rosalea, I give her the names of things — chickadees and prickly pear; juncos and rabbit brush; rosehips and chipping sparrows. Halfway through her second year in this world, she knows gray jay squawk and chickadee serenade. She can tell the difference between the blue grama and the Indian rice

Peter Anderson was the 2015-16 George Bennett Fellow at the Academy. His books include *Going Down Grand: Poems from the Canyon*, an anthology of Grand Canyon poems, and *First Church of the Higher Elevations*. He teaches writing at Adams State University in Alamosa, Colorado, and lives with his family on the western slope of the Sangre de Cristo Range. This meditation is adapted from *First Church of the Higher Elevations* (Conundrum Press, 2015).

grasses that grow out behind our house. She can identify the sprigs of pinyon (*pin-yone*, as she pronounces it) and juniper (*june-ah*-purr) I give her to hold in her hand. She knows the leaves of scrub oaks and aspens. She lights up whenever we walk through patches of the spiky yucca, knowing that their pods — dry, hard and full of seeds — make wonderful rattles. By the time she is 2, she knows more about her place than I knew about my new home in the West after my first year of college.

One day, Rosalea and I are following a sandy two-track that runs through a stand of ponderosa pine. Recently, she has managed to link her first few steps and she is now eager to walk on her own. I scan the ground ahead for cactus, yucca and other possible hazards. Seeing none, I turn her loose. She takes a half dozen steps, bends over, promptly gathers up a handful of dirt and pine needles and stuffs it all in her mouth. Naming one's place is just the beginning.

Home. Land. Security. On the way to the North Crestone Creek Trailhead, we hear the news on the radio. The World Trade Towers are on fire. The Pentagon has been hit. We walk the trail up past the old gold diggings, past deep eddied pools below big rocks and falling water, through a yellowed grove of aspen only now beginning to let go of those first few leaves. Rosalea rides quietly in the pack, looking over my shoulder at the trail ahead of us. In that moment, I want nothing more for my daughter than this "true blue dream" of mountain sky.

"*Huh-tail, huh-tail,*" she says as we pass a patch of horsetails, a tubular green plant that turns up in low shady spots where moisture gathers.

"Horsetail," I say.

"*Huh-tail,*" she says again. For her, our usual routine hasn't changed. For that I am grateful.

Farther along, Grace and I wonder aloud who was behind the attack and what their motives were. Gradually, our words trail off. We keep on walking, rising up over the creek as we follow the switchbacks, looping slope. Soon we break through the last of the aspens, walk out onto open ground, and see the big walls of granite to our east. Once known as the spine of the earth to the Jicarilla Apache, it is the Spanish name for this range — Sangre de Cristo — that we have inherited. Blood of Christ. It is a name that has its own resonance on this day of human suffering. And it is a name that always seems right at the end of the day when peaks like the one at the head of this canyon gather in the last light.

What has happened in Manhattan, on the far edge of this big country, seems so far away. But fewer than a hundred miles to our north and east, sequestered inside of the great granitic core of Cheyenne Mountain near Colorado Springs, the heart of North American Aerospace Defense Command (NORAD), all eyes are scanning the radar screens for anything out of the ordinary. A few hours to our south is Los Alamos and the national lab where the atom bomb was developed, surely one of the military hubs now identified as a vulnerable target.

Down off the mountain later that morning, we drive past a group of college kids in a creek-side campground. Some are crying. Some look puzzled, numb or despondent as they sit on rocks and logs around the van whose radio we hear as we drive by.

Back home, we bring sandwiches out behind the house and settle in beside a big pinyon tree, catching the latest news reports on KRZA, the community radio station for our region and our primary link to the rest of the world. I am grateful that I can't see those horrific images replaying again and again on the television news. That Rosalea is still young enough to be spared our shock and sadness is some consolation.

Then again, we wonder what she has picked up from our eyes, from our voices and from the words she hears on the radio report. A reporter's commentator thanks him for his on-the-scene report. "Goodbye, people," Rosalea says, while an ethereal piano plays in between news segments. "Maybe that's enough for now," Grace says, as she walks over to shut off the radio.

Home. Land. Security. December. First snows and fresh tracks. Rosalea peers out over my shoulder, as we follow a rabbit's trail down the Forest Service road toward town. "Where does the rabbit live?" she asks.

"Rabbits like little holes in the ground," I say. I am reminded of the president's words for the terrorists on the radio earlier that morning: "We're gonna do whatever it takes to find 'em and we're gonna smoke 'em out of their holes." That metaphor doesn't work for me. The phenomenon of terrorism seems more akin to an invasion of thistles, many of which have already gone to seed. You can hack down the thistles all you want, but you only spread the seed and invite more thistles. Let's bring the criminals to justice, sure, but let's also find out how we can reseed the damaged ground on which they thrive.

"Where do the bears live?" Rosalea asks, as we continue down the road toward town. I am glad for the diversion.

"They like dark places," I say. "Sometimes they dig holes. Sometimes they sleep in caves or old mine shafts." I am thinking of previous walks past all the caves, all the old glory holes and all the bear trees up nearby Burnt Gulch. There I had shown Rosalea all the bear claw markings left behind by younger bears that had climbed up the aspens. "*Ohhhhhh,*" she said, running her fingers across the scarred bark.

"Yeeeha," she whoops now, as we come around the bend and town appears, a half-mile or so down the road, nestled in the cottonwoods along Crestone Creek.

"Yeeeha," I answer, as is our custom on this final descent into town. With several hundred residents, the town of Crestone includes the Crestone Mart or C-mart (where you can buy a quart of milk, rent a video, pick up a bag of nails and some two-by fours), the post office (town hub), and the 21st Amendment liquor store. There's a motel, a Laundromat and a small log chapel that is open all the time. At Black Bear Video, you can rent a foreign film. At Curt's store, you can pick up some fresh produce, some locally grown beef, maybe a pint of Ben & Jerry's. Or you can gas up for the occasional run into bigger towns like Alamosa or Salida, both of which are about an hour away.

In a place as remote as Crestone, it is possible to live into an illusion that urban areas or foreign countries have little to do with one's own home, land or security. Similarly, in this country, bounded as we are on both sides by the great oceans, it is possible for us to imagine we can maintain a level of homeland security beyond the capability of other countries. America as gated community. But homeland security is only real when it is just as real for Afghanis, Iraqis, Palestinians, Israelis, Syrians and the rest of our global neighborhood.

On this morning, we find little traffic downtown — only Dogman dragging a muffler as he drives his station wagon over to his usual parking space across from Curt's store. We leave the pavement, and walk the dirt road down past the cemetery ("Burial Permit Required: Please check in before you check out," the sign says). As usual, Rosalea notices the brightly colored whirligig that someone has planted, in lieu of flowers, next to a headstone. A few coyote yip somewhere out in the edge-land forest, which soon gives way to the cactus, rabbit brush, yucca and grasses that cover the valley floor.

"I want to go hug the coyote," Rosalea says.

"They're a long ways off, Honey," I say.

"I want to hug the coyote," she insists.

"Coyotes don't like to be hugged," I say.

"I want to hug the coyote," she continues, her insistence morphing into the tears that tell me she will soon be nodding off. A few hundred feet down the road, passing through a gate in the fence, and farther out into this high-altitude savannah known as the San Luis Valley, Rosalea gives me her mittens, places a thumb in her mouth, wraps her other hand around a lock of my hair, and lays her head down at the base of my neck.

Home. Land. Security. Since our town is at the end of an obscure county road, since we live a mile or so south of town, and since we are the last house on this street where our backyard morphs into thousands of acres of greenbelt and wild federal land, I tell friends that our neighborhood is one of the most remote subdivisions in the Lower 48.

Once, while we were gone, a black bear broke in through a backdoor window and emptied the refrigerator, departing the same way he had come. We found his telltale claw marks on the window screen that he had ripped to shreds. Nearby tracks suggested a younger bear, one that we figured to be a transient since we were familiar with an older, bigger and less outgoing bear whose tracks we often saw nearby and whom I had once seen from a distance. Breaking-and-entering bears are an increasingly common occurrence along the edge of the Sangres (and elsewhere around the state), even in some cases for those who have, as we had, taken many of the usual precautions: removing bird feeders, stowing away backyard grills, sequestering trash, etc.

We live in an odd interface of residential neighborhood and back of beyond. If this is the "stupid zone" as *Denver Post* columnist Ed Quillen liked to say of those places that are more prone to fire and other upcountry hazards, it is one that we came to knowingly, willing to throw the dice, as it were, in exchange for the kind of backyard wildness that only public lands can provide those for whom the privilege of large land holdings is not an option.

Our home is a house in a neighborhood, as was my childhood home. We like to imagine Rosalea riding her bike over to a friend's house someday or maybe down to Curt's store, something Grace had never been able to do growing up on a mountain 7 miles east of Mancos, Colorado. When Rosalea is old enough, she may also choose to head out in the other direction, gaining a few thousand feet into wild mountain country, much as Grace might have done growing up in the La Plata Range.

Maybe every parent wants their kid to have something they have not had. I want to help create for Rosalea a home that may later be thought of as sanctuary or refuge. I want her to know this place — its rocks and trees, its birds and flowers — in ways that I never really knew my own home. That kind of familiarity is the beginning of a bonding to place that has given Grace a sure-footed way of moving out into the world. When my parents chose to sell our childhood home, I wasn't unhappy. Our bonds with that suburban home had never grown strong. But Grace still has that material link with her home place and therefore with her own beginnings. She dreams often of her childhood home, and she can go there in real time as well. I want that for Rosalea.

And yet, I also know that images of home are far from static. Rosalea's vantage point and therefore her experience of this place have already changed. She has moved on from riding in the sling — close enough to my chest to hear my heartbeat — to riding in the pack on my back. The first day she rode behind me as we walked is one of many thresholds she will cross between this time, this place, this home and the inevitable urge she will have for leaving it. It was the first step, I imagined, on that path toward a driver's license and the road headed west out of town.

A few months after her transition to the pack, I push her in a stroller around the road that loops down through our neighborhood. The moon is out. Its light flickers across ice crystals in the snow. "I can reach the moon," Rosalea says, stretching out one of her arms.

Her imagination, as much as any other factor, will transform her orientation to this place, this home and this world over time. Inward worlds of the imagination and the objective world "out there" are both a part of her life's (of any life's) collaborative unfolding.

Looking out from our perch on the flanks of the Sangre de Cristos as I wheel her down our street, I can see the San Juan Mountains, some 50 miles or so off in the distance across the San Luis Valley. Given the width of our valley — 80 miles across in places — the nighttime optics are such that lights scattered here and there out toward the San Juans seem to line up as if on a distant coast, not unlike the views I once saw as a kid looking out across Long Island Sound toward Connecticut. Sometimes coming home to the edge of this valley is like sailing a small boat into a safe harbor.

Home. Land. Security. Too much security can stifle the soul. At least, that's what the Buddha seemed to think, having abandoned privilege and palace for a better look at the world. Jesus and his disciples, who had exchanged their homes and their vocations for the road and for "the way," also seemed to be moving away from any security they had known.

"For religions, home in its deepest sense ultimately means mystery," writes theologian John Haught. "Religions require for the sake of religious authenticity that our lives not be embedded too comfortably in any domain short of the inexhaustible mystery that is the ultimate goal and horizon of our existence."

"What about the here and now?" I wonder. "What about home and place?"

Haught asks similar questions: "Can we interpret religious homelessness in such a way as to foster a sense of being at home in the natural world?" Having posed the question, he goes on to seek out an answer. And he finds a way to respond to his query from the perspectives of cosmology and evolution.

The universe itself is restless, he reasons. As near as we can tell, it is still expanding. And we can see that life seems to be moving, here on our little piece of the rock, anyway, in the direction, biologically speaking, of more and more complexity. If we think of ourselves and our religious stories as yet another expression of that evolutionary and cosmological pilgrimage, he wonders, might we not be more at home in a world that is fundamentally on the move?

My story, your story, stories read in the Bible and the ecological story in which human lives are embedded, are all part of the Big Story moving forward. It is an adventure that is fundamentally wild, which is to say that it is an adventure into the unknown.

"The restlessness that launched matter on its pilgrimage toward complexity 20 billion years ago has apparently not been quieted," he writes. "It continues now in our questioning minds and our spirit of exploration."

In thinking about the relationship between the longing for home and that inward restlessness that encourages movement toward a spiritual center, I am reminded of the dust and the breath in Genesis 2. In that story, the human soul is made from the dust of the ground, which is then infused with God's breath. The dust of the ground and the breath of life aren't understood as separate parts. They are as intertwined as the strands of a DNA molecule. Rather than seeing the dust of the ground and the breath of life as being in relationship, we have come to regard them as separate, maybe even opposed to each other.

The same can be said of our relationship with place: We have come to see ground and Spirit (from the Latin *spirer* — to breathe) as separate entities. That which might be gleaned from Genesis 2, from cosmology and evolution, and from a little girl's sense of wonder on the flanks of the Sangre de Cristos, questions that view. What if we understood place and Spirit as akin, respectively, to the dust and the breath? What if the need for home (dust) and that restless spirit (breath), which leads one further into the Great Mystery, were both understood as elemental and interrelated on the human pilgrimage?

Home. Land. Security. Around our house, some of the biggest pinyon and juniper trees I've ever seen offer us a little shelter from the wind and weather that often blows in hard from the southwest. Nearby, a little to our south, a line of aspens that follows Crestone Creek down the mountain adds to our sense of enclosure and harbors warblers and Western tanagers during the warmer months, as well as a colony of turkey vultures.

In the mornings, the vultures leave their nearby roost, drifting down along the line of aspens then cottonwoods that follow the mountain drainages out onto the valley floor, scanning county roads with eye and nose for the latest roadkill. In the evenings, we watch them come home to our perch on the flanks of the Sangres, circling by overhead and spiraling down to their roost in the aspens along Crestone Creek, about a quarter of a mile to our south. The arroyo they often seem to follow to and from their roost runs by our house. In their honor, we call it Vulture Gulch.

One morning, I entice Rosalea into the pack with the prospect of a visit to the vulture roost down the road. It is early enough in the morning that few of them have left. As we follow the trail along the creek into a little clearing, we see them overhead, at least 20 vultures, several of them facing toward the sun, their wings outspread and gathering sunlight.

"Don't disturb them, Papa," Rosalea says, after a minute or two of looking up at them in that clearing. We keep walking. Down the trail, several vultures fly overhead.

"Where do you think they're going?" I ask Rosalea.

"They're going to school church," she says.

"Where's that?"

"It's way out there," she says, pointing out over the valley. "And it's where your dreams go when you close your eyes."

SARAH ANDERSON

February 3, 2016

He opens his mouth, squints his eyes. His hands reach always in the air — someone's shirt button, the sky. Older brothers, in other family portraits, pick up their little sisters and put them on their shoulders. His wheelchair, his laughter, loud, unhinged. The screen door slammed those summer nights until my mother fixed it. We flinched, our eyes and ears expecting a sudden door the way she expected his special school to call, daily. She waited until it came. Pneumonia. An immune system — fire forehead — fever-soaked — not built for this. We waited for his life to unspin itself from the swing set chain, twisting. That rush, sneakers scuffing a sandy oval until I sat steady, eyes adjusting. Oak tree, complete gold.

I knew my brother Adam in the silences.

Flecks of silver mica peeling from stone. A lake at night, an empty bed. I remember the first Christmas my mother did not hang his stocking — five years gone. I watched her pull it from light-and-ornament tangle in a dented cardboard box, shake it, fold it in half and put it back.

***

Voice, which clings to identity, runs through us from the moment we say our first words until we die. It is in us even if for some reason we cannot

Sarah Anderson is a former English instructor, a faculty adviser to *The Exonian*, and an assistant girls varsity soccer coach.

speak. By voice, I mean both a physical one and an inner and, sometimes, poetic one. All versions shift throughout our lives. We are here living and breathing and finding our own voices, hearing them, aloud and in our minds, then hearing them change, fade out, reappear.

Writing instructors say, "Find your voice" or "I think you have found your voice here," and we may wonder what that even means or how long it takes. What *does* it mean to have a voice in a situation? A conversation? In your own life? Some say voice is what makes your writing sound like you. It's not tone or style, but rather the way you look at the world. In my 13 years of teaching high school students, I have seen some abandon their natural voices, replacing them with academic ones. Then they work to return to the authentic. I have had students who doubt the voice of their writing and the way it has shifted. I say question it, but don't doubt it so much that you freeze. I tell them to be open to the changes. When asked, "What is the most valuable advice you received as a young writer?" author Bruce DeSilva said his teacher taught him that people think they read with their eyes, but they really read with their ears. He writes, "They hear the writer speak to them from the page. If the writer's voice is appealing, it will draw readers into and all the way through a story about something they didn't know they were interested in."

***

I wasn't trying to hide him. I wasn't trying to feel ashamed. In my adolescent years, I wanted to be strong and make it seem like everything was going to be OK and that my brother didn't really have anything wrong with him. I am not proud of this covering up, this acting, but sometimes it was easier to answer people when they asked with a simple, "Yes, it's just my twin sister and me."

My mother, a photographer by profession, who adored my brother completely, confessed to some of that dishonesty herself. She told me that at one point when he was still living, she realized that she printed only the images of my brother Adam in which he looked handsome. All the others on her contact sheet, the images she didn't print, might have shown him distorting his face, rolling up his lip, not looking well. "I had been editing him," she tells me. "Literally editing the photographs and printing only the ones where you couldn't see his handicaps." She described a necessary journey she had to take through herself to say, "No, I had to hang up a picture of what he really looked like ... and see it. And it was hard to see in those later years."

Today, when someone asks me about my family, I say, "Yes, I have a twin sister, and I had a brother who died when I was 16. He was 24." He was only supposed to live to be 15, according to doctors. Those extra nine years were a sparkling bonus. They were just enough in number, those years, to trick me into thinking he would always be here, into thinking he was a miracle, would be an uncle one day to my children — a loud, laughing, severely handicapped uncle. I pictured him sitting in his wheelchair, as he did from age 13 onward due to a virulent form of muscular dystrophy that had been diagnosed in him. He would wave his hands in the air at my children, shout and make them laugh. That's why when people ask me about him now, I say, "My brother could not talk or walk but he could laugh." That's why I say, "You would not believe how much he could laugh."

My mother learned later, through genetic testing, that she was the carrier of the muscular dystrophy gene, but that this genetic defect could only be passed to her sons. I felt guilt when I learned this, about being a daughter. I felt all of this, but I told myself to be open to the reality, and to the changes.

***

I am still a husky-voiced little girl. I am the voice of a 20-year-old studying abroad in Ireland, and I am the voice of a married, almost-40-year-old with children. Last year, due to developing a vocal cord problem, I lost my voice almost completely. I saw a vocal specialist for months, I spoke into a microphone so that she could record pitch and endurance. Some days I could see progress on the computer screen where the lines indicated steadiness or breaks in my voice; other days I felt like crying because only every other word came out. I knew it was not a health threat. I knew I did not have what my brother had. I felt silly for feeling so anxious about this setback, but I really was losing my voice. I was told I could do irreversible damage if I stopped voice therapy prematurely or if I didn't drink enough water throughout the day. I asked myself: What will happen if I can't talk? How will I be able to teach? How will I be able to say anything to my own children? I cannot even call to them.

Daily, I practiced exercises, like singing gently with a tissue dangling in front of my face to see how much breath and sound I was emitting, or reciting over and over a passage about a pot of gold at the end of a rainbow, because vowel sounds put more strain on the vocal chords. I was told to speak in a "confidential tone" and to lean in when talking to people, but never whisper and never yell. I trained both of my children no longer to call to me, but rather to come right up close, so that I didn't have to strain my voice. People commented on the scratchy sound. My children were unsettled by it. I am sure my students were unsettled by it.

In time, after several months, and much vocal practice, my real voice began to return.

**

My mother and my brother are two of several people featured in a book called *An Exposure of the Heart*, advertised as, "The moving chronicle of a year the author spent with the profoundly disabled," by Rebecca Busselle.

About my mother, Busselle writes: "At twilight Jennifer and I stood in a doorway between a friend's kitchen and screen porch, where a small breeze cooled us. In the kitchen, other friends made pesto from fresh basil." "I want to tell you about the Christmas party where I met Adam and what he did for me," Busselle says to my mother. In this chapter, she describes that my brother was 14, autistic and probably dying. "I had only seen Jennifer once since," she writes, "at a time when we could not talk; I wanted her to have every scrap of meaning from Adam's life."

Then, she describes the arrival of my family: "Jennifer walked in, each of her healthy twin daughters holding one of her hands. There were kisses and greetings from the many that knew them, then a lull. A minute later Adam appeared, well bundled against cold, carried in his step-father's arms. Our host followed with a folding wheelchair." She describes that looking at Adam was difficult. "I was afraid of his visible, physical misery and preferred my own, psychic and less substantial."

A scene of guests singing carols unfolded. Above the singing, Busselle heard Adam's screeches and wild movements as he responded to the chorus of voices. She writes, "At first Jennifer tried to quiet his noisy delight, holding him and putting his head on her shoulder." But Adam was too excited and his voice would not be stifled. Then, to my mother, she says, "There was something about his presence in that room that made things whole — for all of us, I think."

***

Because of the impact autism had on him, my brother never learned to speak. I have tried to answer why I write poetry — and perhaps it is simply to give voice to so much. It has become clear to me that I have used writing as a way to explain the world to myself, as a way to try to understand what I may never understand, and as a way to express both my voice and my brother's. Maybe my poetry is what I couldn't say then.

Maybe it's a place to navigate whatever guilt or sadness I felt; maybe it's a place to put the hope that must also exist. A place to acknowledge how truly gorgeous it is to be alive.

A poet and teacher I admire, Tony Hoagland, once wrote: "So much of what I love about poetry lies in the vast possibilities of voice, the spectacular range of idiosyncratic flavors that can be embedded in a particular human voice reporting from the field. One beautiful axis of voice is the one that runs between vulnerability and detachment, between 'It hurts to be alive' and 'I can see a million miles from here.' A good poetic voice can do both at once."

***

She would get lost every time — driving the hour to and from my brother's group home. We would have visited him on a Sunday, arriving early and leaving at sundown. I would have held him in my gaze, always knowing it could be the last time. My sister and I would have watched her laugh, cry and hold the frail frame of her grown-up baby boy, and then every time, every single week, we'd climb into the car and get lost. We would fall asleep, waking up to find my mother pulled over on the side of the road, squinting at a map beneath the small interior car light. "Go back to sleep, girls. It's fine. I'll get us home." She did not want to face the hurt or leave the hurt. I think about the image of our brake lights, the only brightness on a side street in some small Connecticut town between Hartford and home — and I want to be a stranger to that scene. Yet a few blocks away a caregiver was turning off Adam's bedside lamp for him, putting some vinyl on the record player because my brother requested good music before sleep, saying goodnight. There is no way to know when that last night will be.

***

At Adam's memorial service, after the ceremony at a gathering on the church lawn, a man I had never seen before shook my hand. "You should know that your brother was my best friend." I stood there wondering what that meant, to be the best friend of someone who never spoke to him. "I saw him every day," he said. I learned that this man, telling me with an urgency about his friend, was the custodian at my brother's school. I walked away from that encounter on the lawn, and questions, like an old slide projector, clicked their way through my mind:

What is it like to never hear your best friend speak? Who took my brother's place when that man went back to work the next day? If he is living still, does he think about my brother? Does he remember his voice?

I have always found it fascinating that an able-bodied and able-minded person often feels sympathy for someone like my brother, assuming that an awareness of joy was something he lacked. I am confident that while he lacked many natural abilities, one thing he was not missing was an awareness of joy. When I think about the people I have met in my life, he takes the number one spot of those able to express joy unabashedly.

I wonder if perhaps the sympathy should be reversed. Perhaps the able-bodied and able-minded, like me, are always searching for something, always thinking too much — seeking to improve ourselves, to keep worry at bay, to find and hold onto fulfillment, to try to express joy in an uninhibited fashion.

In Aimee Bender's short story "The Rememberer," the narrator's partner, a man experiencing reverse evolution — transforming from a man into an ape into a turtle and finally into a salamander — complains about a basic challenge of being human. "We're all getting too smart," he says. "Our brains are bigger and bigger and the world dries up and dies when there's too much thought and not enough heart."

My brother's beautiful blue eyes expressed his uninhibited joy. I will never know how aware he was of his situation, of the differences that made him glow against a deep-blue sky. I will never know if he knew his timing was out of sync with the rest of us in his family. When one person was talking, this did not stop him from bursting out a sound or banging his fist rhythmically against the cushioned part of the arm of his wheelchair. When I think of my brother, I think of tilting my head to the side so that our eyes could meet straight on. He looked at me, his face mirroring my mother's, and his expression said, "I'm so excited to see you, little sister, and I'm about to scream or flap my arms. For now, I'm just looking at you."

***

Once, I knew gestural sign language and used it every day, but my hands have lost their language. In fact, I have forgotten every gesture except one that involves turning a knuckle against a cheekbone, which I believe means "I'm hungry" or "I want an apple."

Having the ability to give voice to something, to speak our minds, whether out loud or on the page, is a sparkling part about our humanity.

When each of my children first spoke, a knot formed in my throat. I had to unspin the swing set chain, unravel the guilt I felt. I had to embrace these two new voices, my son's and my daughter's, and I listened to them form words out of sounds over time.

You don't know if your child will speak until he does. I waited nervously. Despite genetic testing that confirmed I was not a carrier of the autism or muscular dystrophy gene, I still worried until both of my children spoke. I remember my mother admitting that she used to dream about a child who could speak to her, and then she had two.

I remember my now-9-year-old son, Aengus, when he was 2, saying, "No, Mama, no."

I remember my now-5-year-old daughter, Ari, when she was also 2: "Look, Dada! Look!"

My own voice has still not returned to normal. And I tell myself to be open to the changes.

I believe my desire to tell stories, write poems, to be around songwriters and singers — to be with people who express themselves in these various ways — began with knowing Adam.

Perhaps the reason I write poems and the reason my twin sister writes songs is it's our way of honoring our brother.

What started as guilt perhaps has turned into a gift I have given my mother. She lost a son. She gained a grandson who adores her. He does not take my brother's place, but in my son's blue eyes, we all see and feel Adam.

Our voice is a gift. It can be elusive. It can dart off. But it's always a gift.

I am still finding my voice, as a writer and a mother. I am learning to welcome the changes, to recognize that the antonym of "elusive" is "definite." That life is both elusive and definite, and we have this time now, and only this time, to speak or write what we must.

Giving voice to my brother's life in some way keeps him here. Then I turn toward my son.

When He Turns to Me

Not yet three, my son scales

a rock the shape of a mountain.

Its summit is wide where water pools

before the tide recedes. A small climber

without ropes or clips,

he searches blindly for foot holds,

hand holds, his reach instinctual. His naked body glows

against green-black seaweed tumbling,

pouring down stone in beadlike strands.

I inch forward. He's steady. I stop. He slips.

Reach forward. Stop. I stand behind him, my arms ready.

I imagine holding my arms this way

for the rest of my life, as if the space I create

with my limbs will endure him turning to go,

as if I will ever endure his turning to go.

At two in the morning, when he wakes up

and gently asks for water, I listen to him gulp

and breathe, like a runner mid-race.

I kiss his tousled hair, his hot red cheek.

I hold him, boy, not baby,

all arms and legs around me,

and my questions simmer: When he's not yet twenty ... ?

When he turns to me leaving ... ?